JOHN HENRY NEWMAN

IN HIS TIME

FAMILY PUBLICATIONS

OXFORD

JOHN HENRY NEWMAN

In his Time

Edited by Philippe Lefebvre
& Colin Mason

Images courtesy of the Fathers of the Oratory, Birmingham

ISBN 978-1-871217-69-8

FAMILY PUBLICATIONS

6A KING STREET
OXFORD
OX2 6DF

www.familypublications.co.uk

PRINTED IN MALTA

FOREWORD

Men live after their death – or still more they live not in their writings or their chronicled history, but in that ἀγραφος μνημη exhibited in a school of pupils who trace their moral parentage to them. As moral truth is discovered not by reasoning, but by habituation, so it is recommended not by books, but by oral instruction.[1]

Shortly before he left the tutorship at Oriel College, John Henry Newman shared with a friend this wish, to have no other posterity than that of Socrates – the posterity of an 'unwritten memory' living on in the minds of pupils formed in his school and heirs to his thought. Did the Fellow of Oriel anticipate that this memory that he left behind would be as much the memory of his written works as of his life? His life's work is written down in his books and these books cannot be dissociated from Newman the man. The particular insights which drive his thinking in his works cannot be separated from the human and spiritual experience which underlies it. Yet, even if he admitted that he had never written unless forced by circumstances, did he ever imagine that his youthful wish would be denied by our libraries, whose shelves are full of translations of, and commentaries on, his works, which are still relevant to our moral and religious reflection today?

The exceptional influence of the life and thought of John Henry Newman, which has shone through the past century and extended over many continents, is now seen in the publication of this anthology, the initiative of Family Publications. Continuing the rich tradition of Newman studies, a new generation of young scholars also seeks to bear witness, for today's world, to the perennial value of the Oratorian and the inspiring character of his example and message. By renewing

---

[1] *Letters & Diaries*, vol. II, p. 255. Letter to S. Rickards, 20th July 1830. The Greek words mean 'unwritten memory'.

our knowledge of the cultural and ecclesial environment in which he lived, and our understanding of the great insights that made his genius, this fresh exploration is bound to stimulate a revived interest in Newman as a key figure in the future of our culture and spirituality.

The editors have thought that the various approaches to the life and thought of Newman were too vast and too teeming with multiple aspects not to demand two separate volumes of studies. One of them is devoted to the life and personality of the convert. The second one is more thematic and outlines the principal ideas developed in the major works. Personally, I am delighted to present this first book which attempts to reveal the character of the Oxford 'master' and to situate him in the places and times along his religious journey.

Jean Cardinal Honoré

2nd May 2007

CONTENTS

John Henry Newman

INTRODUCTION

by Keith Beaumont

These are exciting times for Newman scholars. The recent recognition by the Archdiocese of Boston of a miraculous cure, attributed to Newman's intervention, of one of its permanent deacons, and the expectation of a rapid decision on the part of the Congregation for the Causes of Saints, open up the perspective of his forthcoming beatification, to which Pope Benedict XVI is known to be favourable, and eventually to his canonisation – a prelude, in the eyes of many, including myself, to his being one day declared a Doctor of the Church. This is the context which has led Family Publications, in the persons of Colin Mason and Philippe Lefebvre, to publish this, the first of two volumes designed to broaden knowledge of the great Cardinal's life and work. For if Newman is universally known, throughout and often beyond the English-speaking Catholic world, as the figure *par excellence* of the 'convert', the details of his thought and writings are, it must be admitted, somewhat less well-known.

This first volume aims, then, to present Newman in relation to his age and in connection with various places, and to illustrate different aspects of his life and work. The second volume will explore more deeply major aspects of his thought, in order to point up his continuing – indeed, increasing – relevance for today.

Whilst I am flattered, as one whose efforts are chiefly focussed on extending knowledge and understanding of Newman in the French-speaking world, by the invitation of the editors to introduce the present volume, I must confess that it is not an easy task to write an introduction to a work which one has neither conceived nor planned! Perhaps I can most usefully emphasize the points made by each contributor which have most struck me personally, adding here and there a few observations of my own.

The first five chapters study the relationship between Newman and those places with which his name is chiefly associated. At first glance it might appear a little surprising to find only two chapters devoted wholly to his Anglican years (which account for almost half of his long life), but later chapters (Newman and Rome, Newman the Preacher) return in fact, at least in large part, to this period.

In the first of these two chapters, Peter Nockles examines both the influence of the University of Oxford upon Newman, and the impact which he and the 'Oxford' or 'Tractarian Movement', of which he rapidly became the undisputed leader, had in turn upon the town and its university. Of particular interest is his exploration of the concept of *ethos* (Oxford having retained, in Newman's eyes, its Catholic 'ethos' which Cambridge had long since lost) – a concept which will figure prominently among the reasons for Newman's conversion in 1845 and in his *Essay on Development*. Nockles offers also some suggestive comments concerning the primarily Aristotelian theory of knowledge which underlay Tractarian thinking (despite its protagonists' alleged 'Platonic' leanings). More importantly, he stresses the impact of Newman and the Oxford Movement not only on the Church of England but also on the University of Oxford, the fruit of their ardent desire to "restore the moral and spiritual dimension of collegiate education."

In the following chapter, Mary Dechant writes on 'Newman and Littlemore', rightly stressing the remarkable pastoral zeal and activity displayed by Newman in this small rural community which was attached to his Oxford parish of St Mary's of which he became vicar in 1828, together with the progressive realisation of his dream of creating a 'monastic house' in Littlemore – the first of its type since the suppression of all the English monasteries by Henry VIII three centuries earlier. Finally she recounts certain of the circumstances, particularly associated with Littlemore, of his conversion of 1845.

In a long chapter on 'Newman and Rome', Brigitte Hoegemann then studies Newman's four visits to Rome in the course of his life, highlighting in particular the striking contrast between his first, troubled visit in 1833 and his rediscovery of the Eternal City during his sojourn of 1846-7, whilst a student of theology at the college for the Propagation of the Faith and during his brief Oratorian noviciate at Santa Croce. Particularly interesting is her account of the complex of contrasting emotions felt by Newman in 1833. Imperial Rome was for him both an object of fascination, on account of its grandeur, and repulsion, for its paganism and hostility to Christianity. Even more complex was his attitude towards the Church of Rome: we see him torn between, on the one hand, his extreme Protestant-inspired aversion for the mediaeval and post-Tridentine Church and, on the other, his admiration for the Church of the patristic period during which Rome appeared as a beacon of the faith, shining out amidst the surrounding darkness. We see also signs of a perplexed if grudging admiration for the Roman clergy and for traits of behaviour which he observed among contemporary Catholics. His second visit and sojourn were marked by the search for his own 'vocation' – finally found in the Oratory of St Philip Neri – and by his delight in further discovering the concrete reality of Catholic worship (a "real religion" in his eyes), in particular the Eucharistic presence in every single church and chapel.

Paul Chavasse, Provost of Newman's Birmingham Oratory (and postulator for the cause of his canonisation), gives us a vivid portrait of the complex relationship between Newman and the city in which he lived for the last forty-one years of his life. Although Oxford remained "nearest to [his] heart", Birmingham – a city with which he had seemingly at first little in common – came eventually to take the place of Oxford, however inadequately. Though his involvement in the broader civic affairs of his adopted city remained slight – with the notable exception of its musical life – Newman, through his humble ministry of preaching, instructing and confessing (his stinging reminder to Mgr Talbot that "Birmingham people have souls" is eloquent in this respect), and through his discreet assistance to the city's poor, succeeded in winning the love and respect of his fellow-citizens, as was shown by the estimated fifteen to twenty thousand people who lined the streets on the occasion of his funeral.

A chapter on 'Newman and Dublin' concludes this first section of the book. In it Angelo Bottone gives us a clear and precise account of Newman's role in the establishment and running of the Catholic University of Ireland and of his various discourses and writings on university education. He suggests also something of the difficult relationship which existed between Newman and the Irish bishops, in particular the Archbishop of Dublin, Mgr Cullen, which recent research has shown to have been even more complex than scholars had previously imagined.

The second part of the volume is devoted to major aspects of Newman's multifarious activities. In 'Newman the Preacher', Paul Chavasse gives us a masterly study of both the major themes and the manner of Newman's preaching. He shows the continuity, but also the subtle changes in manner, between his Anglican and his Catholic preaching. He emphasizes the preacher's extraordinary ability to enter into the minds and hearts of his listeners and readers, and abundantly illustrates the remarkable impact which both his reading of Scripture and his preaching had on his listeners. Above all, Chavasse stresses the underlying *aim* of all Newman's preaching, which he illustrates by a formula applied to the latter by Fr Henry Tristram, that of "Father of Souls": for Newman, preaching must constitute an incentive not only to "living better" but also to "praying better". However stern a moralist he may appear to be at times, he never indulges in mere moralising, any more than he simply expounds doctrine for its own sake: both are, on the contrary, placed in the service of helping listeners and readers to progressively deepen a lived relationship with God. Thus his rediscovery – through his reading of the Fathers – of the central role of baptismal regeneration, and especially of the doctrines of the Incarnation, the Resurrection and the Trinity, leads him to explore the implications for the Christian of the doctrine of the "indwelling" of the Holy Spirit and to suggest that the "true Christian" may "almost be defined" as one "who has a ruling sense of God's presence within him."[1] It is above all, in fact, in this exploration of the intricate relationship between dogma, ethics, psychological insight and spirituality that Newman's true greatness as a preacher lies.

Newman's work as an educator, in the broadest sense of the term, spans seventy-five years of his life and covers almost every age group. In 'Newman the Educator', Paul Shrimpton provides an excellent account, at once narrative and analytical, and grounded in a thorough knowledge of the historical context, of the former's work and ideas as Oriel College tutor, creator of a parish school, founder and rector of the Catholic University of Ireland, and creator of the first Catholic public school in England. The story is well-known, but the author brings to bear a number of fresh and interesting insights – into, for example, Newman's continuing and growing influence on the Oxford tutorial system *after* the cessation of his own tutorial activity, and his ideas concerning the respective roles of lecturers and tutors and, later, those of teachers and parents. He concludes with a balanced evaluation of Newman's contribution to education. One may only regret that, though the subject is dealt with clearly and precisely, lack

---

[1] *Parochial and Plain Sermons*, Longmans edition, V, n° 16, p. 225.

of space does not allow for a fuller analysis of Newman's insistence upon the importance of what he calls "philosophy" or the acquisition of a "connected view of things", as well as his exploration of the relationship between theology and other branches of learning and that existing between religion and morality – areas in which his ideas remain as relevant today as they were a hundred and fifty years ago.

'Newman the Oratorian', by fellow-Oratorian Daniel Seward, recounts Newman's gradual discovery while in Rome in 1846-7 of the Oratory of St Philip Neri and his lifelong devotion to the figure of St Philip. Despite the historical and cultural gap which separates the two men, Newman felt a deep resonance within his own inner being with the gentle Christian humanism of Philip, his playfulness and joyfulness, the importance he accorded to what the former liked to call "personal influence", and above all his openness to the work of the Holy Spirit within him. Not only did St Philip provide a constant source of inspiration to him for over forty years, but he sought also to explore and to promote the Oratorian "idea". So successful was he in this that, after St Philip, Newman stands as the most important figure in Oratorian history, to whose influence can be traced, directly or indirectly, almost all of the Oratorian foundations of the last one hundred and fifty years.

In an age of eminent letter-writers Newman stands out as one of the greatest, on account of the sheer volume of his correspondence, the scope and variety of subjects dealt with, his huge network of personal relations, and the insight which his letters provide into his own thought and development. None is better equipped than Joyce Sugg to present for us 'Newman the Letter Writer'. Rather than the man of ideas, she chooses to reveal his rich and multi-facetted personality: her subject comes vividly and wonderfully alive as she illustrates in turn his playfulness, his sharp wit, his powers of observation, his keen sensibility, the value for him of friendship, his capacity for biting irony, his deep and tender humanity. She reminds us also of Newman's firm belief that "a man's life lies in his letters," and of the immense debt which all Newman's biographers owe to Fr Stephen Dessain and his successors, who have ensured the systematic publication of his correspondence. Finally, she reminds us that letter-writing was not only for Newman a means of self-expression and of communication, but was also a form of apostolate; indeed we can even study throughout the many years of his letter-writing his practice of the art of spiritual guidance or direction.

In the next chapter, Michel Durand, a specialist in the field of the Victorian novel and translator into French of several works of Newman, offers us a scholarly discussion of 'Newman the Novelist'. He reminds us that the "astonishing variety of literary genres" to which the latter turned his hand must not blind us to the underlying unity of all his work and thought: his novels are not mere diversions or sidelines but form an integral part of his overall vision. While *Loss and Gain* can in no way be described as autobiographical, alongside its brilliantly satirical portrait of Oxford it contains a good deal of Newman's own experience of, and reflection upon, conversion. *Callista* offers an even richer source of insight in this domain. Michel Durand examines Newman's skills (and occasional weaknesses) as a novelist, the (relative) value of his historical tableau – since history here is in the end, and despite the huge amount of research undertaken by the author, ultimately subordinated to the expression of his own ideas – and, most importantly, the autobiographical interest and the religious dimension of the novel. An apologetic intention can be clearly detected in Newman's emphasis upon the authority of the Church, the importance of the priesthood, the central place in Christian life of the Eucharist, the role of penance, the importance of the liturgy, the place of angels, of the Virgin and of saints, the question of relics, the place of miracles, the nature of evil and sin, and the significance of martyrdom (of which – in contrast to certain contemporaries – he gives us a very restrained and balanced portrayal). But the most important by far of the novel's autobiographical and didactic elements is to be found in the theme of conversion to Christianity: in a masterly analysis we are shown how, through the person of Callista, Newman expresses much of his own experience of and his teaching concerning both conversion and the role played therein by conscience.

Joseph Salvatore Pizza contributes next a chapter on 'Newman the Poet'. He offers us a study not only of his poetry in the conventional sense of the term (i.e. verse) but also of what we might call Newman's poetic sensibility together with that of other leading figures of the Oxford Movement. In the *Apologia* Newman himself acknowledges the influence of Coleridge, one of the chief exponents of English Romanticism, on the men who created the Movement and stresses the role of John Keble's volume of poems *The Christian Year* in preparing the ground for it. The author underlines what he sees as "the essentially poetic character of the Oxford Movement," which he sees as manifested in two ideas in particular: that of "analogy", which Newman found essentially in Butler and which led in turn to the discovery of the "sacramental principle", and the principle of "reserve", which he learned from the Alexandrian Fathers and which in religious terms found expression in a profound sense of the Mystery of God. There follows an interesting analysis of Newman's actual verse in terms of these underlying principles. Finally, the author examines Newman's Roman Catholic poetry as represented by the *Dream of Gerontius*, in which he sees both a degree of retreat from these key principles of his Anglican years, and an underlying continuity and development which would prepare the way for later Catholic poets like Gerard Manley Hopkins and Francis Thompson. Indeed, in his eyes, this work "marks the end of one poetic tradition and the beginning of another."

In 'Father Newman at Confession', John Kirwan deals in fact with two subjects. The first is Newman's progressive discovery as an Anglican, and then his practice as both an Anglican and a Catholic priest, of sacramental confession. Here the author offers us an informed and penetrating analysis. He sets the question clearly in the broader context of the Tractarian rediscovery of the sacraments, and uses a parallel study of the evolving thought of Pusey and Newman – contrasting the individualism of the former with the profoundly ecclesiological approach of Newman, for whom the would-be confessor *must* have received an official mandate – to show the role that sacramental confession most probably played in Newman's decision to join the Roman Catholic Church. He shows also the probable role of St Philip Neri's practice of confession and spiritual direction in Newman's choice of the Oratory. The remainder of the chapter deals with a second, rather different subject, being an attempt to elicit a hidden 'self-confession' from Newman himself, through an analysis of the *Apologia* and of *Callista*.

In 'Newman's Spirituality in Relation to his Conversion Experiences', Robert Christie traces the way in which a series of close "interpersonal relationships" were instrumental, one after the other, in directing Newman's mind to God and his steps towards the Roman Catholic Church. Each of these relationships is examined in turn to show nine separate but related "stages" in a continuing process (though it might be argued, on the basis of the author's own evidence, that Newman's discovery – probably through his close epistolary relationship with Dr Charles Russell of St Patrick's College, Maynooth – of St Ignatius of Loyola's *Spiritual Exercises* was of such importance as to constitute effectively a tenth "stage"). Indeed, as this last example itself implies, one should not overlook also the role of prayer and direct spiritual experience: does not the beginning of the process, which will lead ultimately to the embrace of Roman Catholicism in 1845, lie in the experience of 1816, Newman's first, and in many ways most determinative, "conversion" centred on his discovery – to quote his own celebrated formula – of "myself and my Creator"?

Finally, in a long but brilliantly argued and exceedingly well-documented concluding chapter Drew Morgan poses the question of Newman's eventual proclamation as a "Doctor of the Church". He sets out to answer systematically the three questions of "what it means to be a Doctor of the Church", "what authority does a Doctor's teaching possess", and lastly (doubtless with a nod in the direction of Newman's own suggested "tests" or "notes" of a true "development", in his *Essay on Development*) "what is the process of discernment which the Church utilizes to include someone in that select school of saints". He then traces the history of the term and of the practice in the Western and Eastern Church. Quoting from popes, historians and theologians, he emphasises the importance in Catholic tradition of such selection criteria as "shedding new light", bringing about a "deeper understanding", "originality", "profound influence" and – most importantly – constituting a "reliable guide". Particular attention is then accorded to the six *Norms and Criteria* proposed by the Congregation for the Doctrine of the Faith in connection with the doctorate of St Thérèse of Lisieux. Newman is then assessed in relation to these various criteria. Fr Morgan argues persuasively that Newman's thought and influence has produced "one of the major watershed moments in the history of Catholic thought," comparable to that brought about by Augustine and Aquinas, not simply in the realm of ideas but in that of "theological method" – Newman's major contribution being his conception of the development of Christian doctrine and his teaching on conscience. Indeed, just as, for example, St Thomas Aquinas has received the title of "Angelic Doctor" or St Thérèse that of "Doctor of Confidence and Missionaries", so Newman is already prophetically recognized as the "Doctor of Conscience". Fr Morgan brings together in fact such an impressive panoply of papal pronouncements, made by John Paul II and (both as Cardinal Ratzinger and Benedict XVI) the present Pope, that it is tempting to think that the ground is already well laid for the proclamation of Newman's doctorate, and that there remains little further work –

apart from finding the necessary miracle – to do! (The chapter closes with two valuable appendices, a list of all the existing Doctors of the Church, and the text of the CDF's *Norms and Criteria*.)

As with any collective work, this one may appear somewhat uneven; the general level nevertheless remains remarkably high, and some chapters are truly outstanding. The volume presents us overall with an informative, enlightening and very well-rounded portrait of the life and work of John Henry Cardinal Newman – whom we would all love one day to be able to invoke as "Blessed John Henry Newman", pending the day when we shall be able to address ourselves to "Saint John Henry Newman, Doctor of the Church".

PART I

TOWER & SPIRE OF SAINT MARY'S CHURCH.

St Mary's church, the University parish church in Oxford, where Newman served as a vicar between 1828 and 1843.

Chapter 1

———————

NEWMAN AND OXFORD

by Peter Nockles

From June 1817, when he first went into residence at Trinity College as an undergraduate, until 1845 when, on the eve of his submission to the Catholic Church he resigned his Oriel College Fellowship, to which he had been elected in 1822, having already resigned as Vicar of the University church of St Mary the Virgin in September 1843, Oxford and its ancient University were the centre and focus of Newman's life, hopes, and energies. The salient facts are that he was active as a college tutor only for a few years in the 1820s before notoriously being relieved of his tutorial role by the Provost of Oriel, Edward Hawkins, after a dispute about tutorial methods. It was a dispute which was to have profound consequences on the course of the future 'Oxford Movement'. For thereafter, Newman became free to extend his influence within the University by other means, not least religious and intellectual leadership as he masterminded the so-called Oxford Movement (whose birth is usually dated from John Keble's 'Assize Sermon' on 'National Apostasy' delivered from the pulpit of the University church on 14 July 1833).

It is impossible to understand the formative religious influences on Newman and the evolution of his spiritual and intellectual destiny without seeking to understand the character and nature of Oxford University and of its ancient traditions to which he owed so much. One needs to appreciate the remarkable influence and impact which Newman himself through his preaching and personal magnetism had on those around him in Oxford. He was both moulded by the Oxford of his day (especially the intellectual influences he found within Oriel Common Room) and, in turn, helped remould it. It is a testimony to the extent of his influence that to write a history of Oxford in the period 1833-45 is to write of the history of the Oxford Movement, of which Newman was to become the acknowledged leader. One could add that to write the history of the Oxford Movement in these years is almost to write a history of Oriel College and of its famous Common Room (which was reputed to have 'stunk of logic'), perhaps the Movement's real *genius loci*.

The spell and sheer beauty of Oxford was well captured by several contemporary and later commentators. One of the most famous panegyrics on Oxford was that composed by Matthew Arnold in the mid-1860s:

> Beautiful city! So venerable, so lovely, so unravaged by the fierce intellectual life of our century, so serene ... spreading her gardens to the moonlight, and whispering from her towers the last enchantments of the Middle Age ... home of lost causes, and forsaken beliefs, and unpopular names and impossible loyalties.[1]

Others were no less lyrical. Writing of the 1830s, William Tuckwell recalled in his *Reminiscences of Oxford* (1900):

> It was said in those days that the approach to Oxford by the Henley road was the most beautiful in the world. Soon after passing Littlemore, you came in sight of, and did not lose again, the sweet city with its dreaming spires ...[2]

Newman was susceptible to the architectural and ancient historical associations of the University of Oxford. The atmosphere, *ethos*, and *genius loci* of Oxford and its colleges, with its monastic, Cavalier, Jacobite, Tory, and high church heritage, exerted a potent spell on a rising generation already infused with the historical Romanticism exemplified in the novels of Sir Walter Scott, and poetry of Wordsworth, Southey and Coleridge. Newman's own vivid imagination and Romantic sensibility rendered him particularly open to Oxford's spell. The almost apocalyptic mood of resistance to change which he embraced in 1829 when rallying against the University's MP, Sir Robert Peel, on account of his bringing in Catholic Emancipation, was fuelled by potent images of historic Oxford as a "place set apart" to "witness to the nation." Newman recalled that as he walked along the "old road" from Oxford to visit his mother and sister at Horsepath in the autumn of 1829 at the time of the Peel election crisis, "King Charles and his Bishop [Laud] seemed to rise before him."[3] He was

---

[1] M. Arnold, preface to *Essays in Criticism* (London, 1865).

[2] W. Tuckwell, *Reminiscences of Oxford* (London, 1900), p. 3.

[3] J.H. Newman to J.W. Bowden, 16 January 1830, T. Gornall & I. Ker, *Letters & Diaries of John Henry Newman*, vol. ii (Oxford, 1979), p. 189.

infused with an urgent sense of special vocation to be best fulfilled simply by remaining at one's 'post' in the university. It was an attitude which could even induce a certain disdain for 'outsiders' or intruders upon the university. In discussing the invasion of journalists into Oxford in the same year to report on the impending Peel election, Newman was provoked into remarking upon, "their littleness ... amid the buildings of old Oxford, yet wishing to strut with all the bad taste and banausic of republicanism – they understood us about as they would Sophocles or Pindar."[4] The same mindset helped determine Newman's ambivalent, if not slightly condescending, view of his erstwhile friend and ally in the early years of the Movement, William Palmer of Worcester College (commonly thus designated to distinguish him from his namesake of Magdalen College). Palmer of Worcester was a graduate of Trinity College Dublin, and in 1828 was incorporated into the University of Oxford. However, for all Newman's recognition, generously expressed in the *Apologia,* of his friend's massive learning, it was still counted as a point against him that "he never had really grown into an Oxford man."[5] The same disdain for non-Oxonians was reflected in the somewhat superior attitude which Newman, along with other Oxford Tractarians, adopted towards the sister University of Cambridge and his view that Oxford alone was qualified to lead a reaction to the forces of liberalism and secularism. Indeed, it is arguable that had Newman gone to Cambridge, he would ever have emerged as a leader of a religious movement of the character of that which he formed and led at Oxford. Why was this?

Something far more than aesthetics and a mere nostalgic longing for 'the olden times' determined the loyalty to Oxford which inspired Newman and many of his followers. What then was the secret of Oxford's enchantment and power for someone like the young Newman? To understand this is to discern the key to Newman's early intellectual formation. Why was the University regarded with such awe and as so special? Beauty and historical association were only part of the allure, pointing to something deeper and more intrinsic. The key to Oxford's enduring power for Newman and his later Tractarian followers lay in the notion of *ethos.* It was Oxford's 'catholic' *ethos* which infused and grounded the characteristic course of educational studies pursued there, and it was the concept of *ethos* itself, signifying an intertwined combination of sound belief and right

---

[4] J.H. Newman to J. Newman, 17 March 1829, ibid., p. 132.
[5] J.H. Newman, *Apologia pro Vita Sua* (London, 1864), p. 108.

conduct, which for Newman was to lie at the root and heart of the Oxford Movement of which he emerged as the acknowledged leader. Judged by the criteria of this uniquely 'catholic' *ethos,* Cambridge could not compare to Oxford. Cambridge (despite its Laudian phase in the 1630s) historically had a different dominant theological temper and tradition, intellectual character and interests, and *ethos.* For Oxford Tractarians, Keble as much as Newman, a catholic *ethos* symbolized reserve, self-restraint, reverence. By admitting Dissenters without taking degrees (since 1772-3), Cambridge was deemed to have breached these cardinal markers of a correct religious *ethos.* As George Moberly, a Fellow and Tutor of Balliol College put it in 1834 at the time of a failed government-supported attempt to get Oxford to admit Dissenters:

> How different is their religious system from ours. In our colleges a Roman Catholic, or Socinian, would feel their doctrines denied more or less directly every day of their lives. In the regular course of our religious reading, every form of Dissent would in turn be exposed and refuted. We have instituted, and we wish to perfect, a higher system of religious education than is there possible.[6]

In short, from an Oxonian Tractarian perspective, Cambridge had already fatally compromised with the forces of latitudinarianism.[7] She was in no position to take a vanguard position in the academic as well as religious counter-revolution against the forces of liberalism and secularism which Newman was convinced that Oxford alone was destined to lead. As he put it: "let Cambridge wish us well, and cheer us to our work. We have at present the post of danger and honour; it may be hers another day."[8]

How far did the University of Oxford as an institution in its concrete intellectual and curricular character, rather than merely historical spirit, lend itself to Newman's Tractarian vision? Many later historians as well as contemporary liberal critics have argued that the Oxford Movement stifled intellectual enquiry and speculation, that it distracted from the real purpose of a university. Thus, for Mark Pattison, disillusioned and one-time acolyte of Newman, who came to embrace an overtly secular viewpoint, the Movement in retrospect represented a fatal and damaging diversion from "the true business of

---

[6] G. Moberly, *A Few Thoughts on the Proposed Admission of Dissenters into the University of Oxford* (Oxford, 1834), p. 14.

[7] An approach that allows a wide freedom of interpretation in religion.

[8] J.H. Newman to H.J. Rose, 17 March 1834. T. Gornall & I. Ker (eds), *Letters and Diaries of John Henry Newman,* vol. iv (Oxford, 1980), p. 209.

the place."[9] The point was most forcefully made by one contemporary liberal critic, who wrote of the so-called 'Oxford theology', that:

> It never would have been produced in a place where scientific thought or historical criticism had flourished. Had Oxford minds understood the laws of evidence, or had they been imbued with the principles of mathematical proof, Newman and his disciples would have laboured in the fire. Had even logic flourished as a science, Puseyism must have been strangled at birth.[10]

Yet the younger Pattison, who had come under Newman's spell, must have seen things very differently at the time. He himself was a product of the Oriel intellectual renaissance of which the Oxford Movement was to become one of the most striking manifestations.

It would be wrong to overlook the real extent to which lively intellectual debate, enquiry and argument played in the rise of Tractarianism at Oxford under Newman's leadership. For the firmament of Oriel Fellows in the 1820s known as the *Noetics*, a group which included Edward Copleston, Edward Hawkins, John Davison, Richard Whately, Renn Dickson Hampden, Joseph Blanco White, and others, helped forge the very climate in which the Oxford Movement was forged. As an acute observer looking back noted in 1852:

> It is our object, to appeal to anyone who was acquainted with the inner life of the Oxford religious world twenty and five-and-twenty years ago, whether two very opposite, and now very prominent, parties in the English Church [Tractarian and Liberal], are not the development of private discussions and every-day conversations within the walls of Oriel common-room.[11]

Tractarianism probably could not so readily have taken root in Oxford without the free-ranging intellectual atmosphere of the 1820s in which ideas and influences, such as those of Whately and Hawkins in their different ways brought to bear on the young and impressionable Newman. As Tuckwell put it, the *Noetics* provoked "by their political and ecclesiastical liberalism the great revolt of the Newmania."[12] The Tractarian counter-revolution also owed much to the earlier academic reforms of Eveleigh and Copleston at Oriel, Parsons at Balliol and Cyril Jackson at Christ Church. In particular, the Oriel emphasis on

---

[9] M. Pattison, *Memoirs* (London, 1885), pp. 236-7. However, elsewhere even the later Pattison recognized that the Newmanite and Tractarian ideal promoted academic learning. See H.S. Jones, *Intellect and Character in Victorian England: Mark Pattison and the Invention of the Don* (Cambridge, 2007), p. 152.

[10] *Tait's Edinburgh Magazine*, New Ser. xvi (August, 1849), p. 530.

[11] *Christian Remembrancer*, xxiii, 'Memoir of Bishop Copleston' (January 1852), p. 18.

[12] Tuckwell, *Reminiscences*, p. 17.

the value of intellectual debate and mental activity for its own sake as something more important than a narrowly technical commitment to 'the drudgery of the Schools' (notwithstanding Oriel's academic successes in the wake of examination and curriculum reforms) also left its mark on the rising Tractarian generation.

It was the particular character of Oxford's mental training that helped play a key role in fostering the appeal of Tractarian ideas among the rising generation of undergraduates and young Fellows. Bishop Butler's moral philosophy, rooted in Aristotelianism, was held in higher esteem than at Cambridge, and permeated Oxford's system of education. It was to leave an indelible mark notoriously on Gladstone as well as Newman, Froude, and Keble. Many years later, Frederick Oakeley pointed out the tendency of Oxford's prevailing Aristotelianism to make men's minds more receptive to Tractarianism:

> The Aristotelian ethics, with the Christian philosophy of Bishop Butler as their commentary and supplement, entered into the academical education of all the more cultivated minds of Oxford, and contributed, in a pre-eminent degree, to form their character and regulate their tone ... No one can read Mr Froude's 'Remains', for instance without seeing, that with him, and with those whom he corresponded, the ethical system of Oxford had exercised no small influence in the formation of mental habits ... constantly he used to appeal to this great moral teacher of antiquity ('Old Stole', as he used playfully to call him), against the shallow principles of the day. Thus, then, it was that the philosophical studies of Oxford tended to form certain great minds on a semi-Catholic type.[13]

As it was with Froude, so it was with Newman, who, as is well known, came under the lasting moral and spiritual influence of the former (Newman's and Keble's publication of his posthumous *Remains,* 1838-9, being very much an act of homage).

One of the insights which the Tractarians drew from Aristotle's teaching (especially from the *Nicomachean Ethics*), was that mere 'head-knowledge' alone was not enough, that 'heart-knowledge' was a pre-requisite for the cultivation of a truly catholic *ethos*. It is true that sometimes Tractarian theology, infused as it was with poetical and Romantic sensibilities, assumed a Platonic temper: Newman attentively studies the Alexandrian Platonists, and his thinking was

---

[13] F. Oakeley, *Historical Notes on the Tractarian Movement* (London, 1865), p. 180; F. Oakeley, *Remarks on the Study of Aristotelian and Platonic Ethics, as a branch of the Oxford system of Education* (Oxford, 1837), pp. 26-9.

deeply influenced and infused by them. Nonetheless, the understanding of knowledge in Tractarian thought was primarily Aristotelian in emphasis. Newman and many of his Tractarian followers might have been 'born' Platonists, as David Newsome memorably observed, but they became Aristotelians through their Oxford education and formation.[14]

In the stand which they made against plans for university reform in the 1830s (which I have discussed elsewhere), Newman and the Tractarians took issue not with the principle itself but with the ideological premises on which it was advocated both in Parliament and by a minority of advanced liberals within the University itself. The Tractarians defined education in terms quite different from that of 'secularising' liberal reformers. The Tractarian Henry Woodgate succinctly summed up the difference – "they think Education consists in knowledge; we do not."[15] A Tractarian sympathiser, William Sewell, Fellow of Exeter College and White's Professor of Moral Philosophy, was still more uncompromising in refutation of the utilitarian ideal of education promulgated by critics of the Oxford system such as Sir William Hamilton (one-time Snell exhibitioner at Balliol College and the eminent Scottish philosopher and author of strictures on Oxford education in a series of articles in the *Edinburgh Review* between 1831 and 1835). Sewell insisted that:

> We ... do not consider the communication of knowledge as the chief design of our post, or the grand end of education ... We are ... entrusted with the care of the young ... and our consideration is to form and fashion and bring them to that model of human nature, which in our conscience we think is perfection.
>
> This model ... we do not find, and therefore we will not place in the intellect of man. And this is the grand point in which we differ, wholly and irreconcilably differ, from the maxims of the present day.[16]

Hamilton's criticisms were easily rebutted and could be portrayed as outdated. Of course, the intellectual ferment in the Oxford of the 1820s with its concomitant college rivalries for honours and prizes represented a welcome advance over the apparent (if exaggerated) sloth and lethargy of the preceding century. However, the Tractarians

---

[14] D. Newsome, *Two Classes of Men: Platonism and English Romantic Thought* (London, 1972), pp. 62-72. See also F.M. Turner, *The Greek Heritage in Victorian Britain* (New Haven, Conn., 1981), pp. 333-6.

[15] H.A. Woodgate, *The Study of Morals Vindicated and Recommended in a Sermon preached before the University of Oxford* (Oxford, 1837).

[16] W. Sewell, *Thoughts on the Admission of Dissenters to the University of Oxford, and on the establishment of a State Religion* (Oxford, 1834), p. 7.

were concerned to prevent the university from degenerating into an education 'factory' on the lines of what Oxford men most despised, 'some Prussian or French academy', lacking in collegiate or corporate identity and *ethos*, with students living in outlying lodgings and lacking personal contact with remote and over-proud professors. William Sewell, in the Tory *Quarterly Review* in 1840, again well expressed this viewpoint when he roundly asserted:

> Colleges were not mere educating machines; and this is a fact to be stated the more openly, and the more carefully borne in mind, as the narrow utilitarianism of the day has frequently availed to contract the view taken, even in Oxford itself, of their privileges and duties.[17]

The theory behind Oxford's tutorial system appeared to support Newman's and the Tractarian view of university education. The conviction that religion came first, 'head-knowledge' second, permeated Newman's philosophy as a public tutor at Oriel College from January 1826 until he finished tutoring the last pupils assigned to him in June 1832 (the Provost having closed his supply of new pupils from June 1830 onwards). Academic standards needed to be raised but alongside religious and moral ones. Both elements provided the ballast for Newman's well-known stand against Provost Hawkins over the character of Oriel tuition from 1828 until 1830, and his determination to reduce the numbers and influence of the sometimes profligate Gentlemen-Commoners for whom Oxford sometimes was no more than a 'finishing school' of pleasure and for whom a degree did not often matter. In Newman's view, the role of a college tutor, while it was certainly that of raising academic standards, should at the same time involve far more than the mere imparting of knowledge or preparation for examinations. For Newman, the tutorial office possessed an inherent moral, spiritual and pastoral dimension. As he reiterated many years later:

> When I was a Public Tutor of my college at Oxford, I maintained, even fiercely, that my employment was distinctly pastoral. I considered that, by the Statutes of the University, a Tutor's profession was of a religious nature. I never would allow that, in teaching the classics, I was absolved from carrying on, by means of them, in the minds of my pupils, an ethical training; I considered a College Tutor to have the care of souls.[18]

---

[17] *Quarterly Review*, lxvi (June, 1840), p. 165.
[18] W.P. Neville (ed.), *Addresses to Cardinal Newman, with his replies, 1879-81* (London, 1905), p. 184.

He also described in detail his model for relationships with undergraduates and pupils at Oriel, a model which he claimed went against that then pertaining in the college:

> With such youths he cultivated relations, not only of intimacy, but of friendship, and almost of equality, putting off, as much as might be, the martinet manner then in fashion with College Tutors, and seeking their society in outdoor exercises, on evenings, and in Vacation. And, when he became Vicar of St Mary's in 1828 the hold he had acquired over them led to their following him on to sacred ground, and receiving directly religious instruction from his sermons; but from the first, independently of St Mary's he had set before himself in the Tutorial work the aim of gaining souls to God.[19]

It is clear that Newman's preaching at St Mary's consolidated, complemented and widened the initial hold over young Oxford minds which he first established among a narrower circle through the tutorial medium at Oriel. There are many testimonies to the power of his preaching, and such was its influence that by the late-1830s during the high noon of the Oxford Movement, it had begun to attract the suspicion of the University authorities as a consequence.[20]

Although critics of Newman and the Tractarian educational vision, such as the later embittered Mark Pattison, complained that he and they were intent on reducing the University to the level of a mere school of divinity or theological seminary, Newman was well aware of the important distinction between the two, though historically the University of Oxford had a role as a training ground for candidates for holy orders as well as in educating laymen. In fact, Newman's pastoral concept of the tutorial office, while it had fallen to some extent into disuse or misuse, can be regarded as integral to the system of education which had evolved in Oxford University over many centuries. Newman was right to claim countenance and support from the Laudian Statutes (1636), in particular, for his view that a college tutor "was not a mere academical Policeman, or Constable,

---

[19] *John Henry Newman: Autobiographical Writings. Edited, with an introduction by Henry Tristram of the Oratory* (London, 1956), p. 90.

[20] For an evocative impression of Newman's preaching, see C.J. Shairp, John Keble (London, 1866), p. 17. Significantly, by 1839 the University's Vice-Chancellor, Ashurst Turner Gilbert, Principal of Brasenose, was complaining to the University's Chancellor, the Duke of Wellington: "that Mr Newman has availed himself of the opportunity for making his parish pulpit much more an organ for propagating his views among those who are educating for the church, than the plain instruction of an ordinary congregation." A.T. Gilbert to Duke of Wellington, 26 December 1839, Wellington MSS 2/250/65, Southampton University Archives.

but a moral and religious guardian of the youths committed to him."[21] Moreover, Newman had good grounds for fearing that this higher view of the vocation implied in the tutorial office was in danger of being lost sight of, even as the academical reforms of the 1800s from which Oriel gained its ascendancy took hold. That it had come to represent by no means the norm on the eve of the Oxford Movement is clear from the rapid growth of private tutors (of whom Newman himself was one) or 'crammers' whose role often became a purely technical one of getting their pupils through the Schools. However, this development was in itself an essentially short-term response to the marked academic improvements that had been instituted within Oxford since 1800, as the demands of the new examinations placed a strain on the old system.

It is possible to determine the extent to which Newman put his educational principles into practice in his time as Oriel tutor and to measure some bench marks of the religious, pastoral and academic successes of his tutorship. In a recent scholarly study of Newman's time as tutor at Oriel (private and public) from 1821-31, Philippe Lefebvre has demonstrated that there was a decline among the student population in the number of men of family and fortune (the Gentlemen-Commoners), a decrease in the number of students who did not graduate (with fewer Gentlemen-Commoners among them), an increase in the number of undergraduates sitting for honours, and an increase in the number of future clergy among his pupils.[22] Lefebvre shows (from evidence in Newman's *Autobiographical Memoirs* and Newman's published correspondence) that Newman had a clear conception of what he identified as evils in the then existing system, one of which was the over-preponderance of the aristocratic Gentlemen-Commoners,[23] a body whom Edward Copleston as Provost and James Endell Tyler as Vice-Provost had tended to favour and protect. Thomas Mozley wrote of Tyler that it was commonly held that he "had cared for gold tufts and silk gowns more than for the college generally" and that his "especial fondness was reserved for the Gentlemen Commoners."[24] In a letter to his friend and former

---

[21] Ibid., p. 91. Pattison himself, for all his loss of religious faith, retained this ideal as a tutor at Lincoln College. Jones, *Mark Pattison*, p. 152.

[22] P. Lefebvre, 'The student population at Oriel College and Newman's pupils (1821-1833)', Annexe 1.A, 'John Henry Newman tuteur: Tradition, rupture, développement (1826-1831)' (unpublished dissertation, Université de Paris III, 2004), pp. 105-115.

[23] J.H. Newman to S. Rickards, 6 February 1829, *Letters and Diaries*, vol. ii. p. 117.

[24] T. Mozley, *Reminiscences Chiefly of Oriel College and the Oxford Movement*, 2 vols (London, 1882),

Oriel Fellow, Samuel Rickards, in February 1829, Newman outlined the 'innovations' which he had introduced into the college over the preceding year, among which he included the marked diminution (by over half) of the Gentlemen Commoners, the rejection of unprepared candidates and the refusal of testimonials to unworthy candidates.[25]

Newman as tutor had his 'failures', and perhaps not surprisingly it was some of the Gentlemen-Commoners who remained immune to his influence and charm. Thus, James Fitzharris, third Earl of Malmesbury (matriculated 1825), one-time Foreign Secretary and Lord Privy Seal, left on record a highly critical account of Newman's tutorial methods in his *Memoirs of an Ex-Minister*. Malmesbury, writing in 1884, charged Newman with cowardice as an Oriel tutor in 1826-7, in suffering his students to advance a table on him in his lectures until he was jammed in a corner, and in passively enduring a shouted rebuke from Copleston in Oriel Hall for mutilating at table a fine haunch of venison. Copleston's bellowed rebuke entered Oriel College folklore and was overheard by many but there seems to have been poor foundation for Malmesbury's first charge (Frederic Rogers, Lord Blachford, asserting that the incident involved another Oriel tutor, William James). Newman, however, delivered an impressive snub to Malmesbury, alleging the table incident to be entirely fictitious.[26]

It can be said that Newman as a tutor at Oriel was to be partly a victim of his own success. Newman admired Hawkins and had preferred him over Keble at the election of a new Provost in 1828. Hurrell Froude had urged Keble's claims, arguing that he "would bring in with him a new world, that donnishness and humbug would be no more in the College, nor the pride of talent, nor an ignoble secular ambition."

The implication was that Copleston had encouraged these things, but Newman at the time was unmoved, backing Hawkins as "the more practical man," and famously declaring, "that if an Angel's place was vacant, he should look towards Keble, but that they were only electing a Provost."[27] Newman himself conceded that Hawkins at first backed up his Tutors "in their measures of enforcement of discipline and the

---

i, p. 82. Newman privately accused Tyler of 'tuft and silk courting'. J.H. Newman to S. Rickards, 19 March 1827, *Letters and Diaries*, vol. ii, p. 8.

[25] Newman to Rickards, 6 February 1829, *Letters and Diaries*, vol. ii, p. 117.

[26] S. Gilley, *Newman and his Age* (London, 1990), p. 414; D.W. Rannie, *Oriel College* (London, 1903), p. 223.

[27] *Autobiographical Writings*, p. 91.

purification of the College."[28] The quarrel, when it came, involved (because Hawkins had taken Peel's part in 1829) ecclesiastical as well as practical academic differences over the organisation of the college lecture system.[29] The conflict came to a head in 1830 when Newman, along with two other tutors (who were also former pupils), Hurrell Froude and Robert Wilberforce, sought to exercise greater control in the choice of undergraduate students. Hawkins obstructed them and all three resigned as tutors. Newman represented the view among college tutors (which would gradually grow into a constitutional crisis in the University and give added edge to the theological controversies of the 1830s and 1840s) that the Heads of Houses had, in Newman's words,

> usurped, or at least injuriously engrossed power in University matters, and that those who did the work, the resident fellows, not those who had no work to do, should have the power.[30]

Copleston stiffened Hawkins's resolve in countering this view. He insisted that the examination reforms themselves of the turn of the century had necessarily changed the academic balance of power in the University by increasing the educational responsibility of the Heads and thus making the action of the Oriel tutors the more dangerous.[31]

Whatever the merits of the opposing views, Newman felt let down by Hawkins who "when a member of the Common Room, had ever used the language of a Tribune of the people." It was soon felt to be otherwise when Hawkins assumed the Provostship and declared "that all was as it ought to be." Newman described the change in attitude towards the new Provost among the Oriel Fellows, clearly including himself:

> They accused him also in their talk with each other, of assuming state and pomp, and of separating himself from his Fellows, as if his membership in the Hebdomadal Board was a closer tie than his membership with his College, and moreover, of courting the society and countenance of men of rank and fortune, whether in the world, or in the state, or the Church. They smiled, when instead of speaking of the Provost's 'lodgings', he talked about 'my house'.[32]

---

[28] Ibid., p. 92.

[29] See K.C. Turpin, 'The Ascendancy of Oriel', *The History of the University of Oxford*. vol. vi. *Nineteenth-Century Oxford, Part I. Edited by M.G. Brock and M.C. Curthoys* (Oxford, 1997), p. 189.

[30] *Autobiographical Writings*, p. 96.

[31] D.W. Rannie, *Oriel College* (London, 1903), p. 201.

[32] Ibid., p. 97.

According to Thomas Mozley, however, Newman's most intimate friends could not remember a single word of self-accusation when it became clear that Hawkins had disappointed him as Provost. As Mozley explained, it "was his wont to accept his own acts as Providentially overruled to purposes beyond his own ken." Consequently, Newman was dismayed and embarrassed when he read in a sermon preached by Pusey at the consecration of Keble College chapel many years later, that he "had lived to regret the part he had taken in Hawkins' election to the Oriel Provostship."[33]

Hawkins was accused of sacrificing college interests on the altar of Westminster political allegiances and non-Oxonian influences, but for Newman deep religious principles were at stake. He was adamant in regarding his educational engagements as a fulfillment of his ordination vow, but conceded that he was "not always respectful" in the "manner and style in the conversations and correspondence which ensued" with the Provost and that he "might have acted more generously to a man to whom he owed much."[34] Newman later recalled that the Provost could not understand the intensity of his feelings and could only impute Newman's conduct to irritation or wounded pride, ostentatiously for ever inquiring "how he felt today?"[35]

Even prior to the formal era of the Oxford Movement itself, it was the nature and extent of Newman's personal religious influence as college tutor that gave Provost Hawkins misgivings and which underlay the dispute between the two which culminated in Newman's relinquishing of his public tutorial role. Copleston, by then Bishop of Llandaff, disliked the tone of Newman's letters to Hawkins which he was shown. Copleston fully shared Hawkins's incipient theological misgivings, as he made clear in response to a letter from the new Provost on the subject:

> From what you say of Newman's religious views, I fear he is impractical. His notion of dangers to church and state I cannot understand. For even under the system we wish to continue religious instruction is part of the class lectures, and in private it is part of each tutor's business with his own pupils.[36]

Copleston himself had first developed the tutorial idea that there should be a greater potential for intercourse between tutor and pupil with more exclusive attention focused on the individual needs of the

[33] Mozley, *Reminiscences*, i, p. 39.
[34] *Autobiographical Writings*, p. 101.
[35] Ibid., p.103.
[36] Quoted in Rannie, *Oriel College*, p. 202.

latter. This whole development in turn owed much to Oriel's system of Open Fellowships which Provost Eveleigh (died 1814) had instigated. In short, it is impossible to represent Hawkins and Copleston (though by then removed from Oxford) as part of any secularizing trend. It was not so much that the two sides differed over the importance of the religious dimension of the tutorial office but over its application and direction. As D. W. Rannie, historian of Oriel College argued:

> The religious revival which was coming to the English Church was the real cause of the tutorial quarrel at Oriel in 1830. The tutors had the new wine of it in their veins; they were the subjects of an enthusiasm which they were compelled to communicate, and which was intolerant of restraint; whilst the Provost was, and was to remain, outside the range of the new ideas. In such a situation compromise was impracticable.[37]

Yet while the theological rupture between the *Noetic* and Tractarian schools of thought in the 1830s (which I have analysed elsewhere[38]) coloured and exacerbated what were initially minor differences of academic emphasis, the evidence of Lefebvre's study shows that academic achievement as well as religious orthodoxy and cultivation of good moral habits was always a high priority for Newman as tutor. The care which he took over his pupils as individuals whom he took into his close confidence is clear from the fascinating evidence to be gleaned from the manuscript memorandum books on his pupils which he kept and the originals of which are in the archives of the Birmingham Oratory. A sample entry, dated 'Easter 1826', for a particular favourite, his future brother-in-law Thomas Mozley, is revealing: "very promising – clear & elegant mind – hopeful in religion; a good scholar."[39] In fact, Newman's very successes with his pupils may have attracted jealousy. One reason for this may have been because, as Lefebvre suggests, he regarded his tutorial office as a way of preparing some of his pupils for the ongoing task of defending the church and the cause of catholic truth in certain future trials and battles which he evidently envisaged.[40] Certainly, the names of many of his pupils (several of whom in turn became Fellows of Oriel,

---

[37] Ibid., pp. 202-3.

[38] P.B. Nockles, 'An Academic Counter-Revolution: Newman and Tractarian Oxford's Idea of a University', *History of Universities*, x. (1991), pp. 137-97.

[39] [J.H. Newman], 'Memorandum Book about [Oriel] College Pupils', Ms. A6.15, Newman Archives, Birmingham Oratory. I am grateful to Monsieur Lefebvre for allowing me to consult his photocopies from a microfilm version in Yale University Library.

[40] Lefebvre, 'Student population at Oriel College'.

reads like a roll-call of his intimate Tractarian followers and disciples in the 1830s: Robert Wilberforce, Thomas Mozley, Charles Marriott, Samuel Francis Wood, Frederic Rogers, Sir George Prevost, George Dudley Ryder, James Bowring Mozley, Charles Page Eden, and many others. It was as if he was training them up for an expected national and ecclesiastical crisis. When that crisis came in 1833, many of his pupils were indeed at their posts and ready to enter into the fray. The refrain, 'Credo in Newmanum', inspired a generation.

Newman's hopes for Oriel College extended far beyond what he could achieve under his remit as college tutor. At a time when government-inspired liberal reformers were seeking to revise Oxford's college statutes and urging the University to 'put its house in order', Newman at Oriel advocated a return to the spirit of its fourteenth-century founder, Adam de Brome, with the Provost and Fellows living together in spiritual brotherhood, sharing a common table, all devoted to a life of study and using their learning in the service of God. In particular, Newman explicitly wished to restore, that portion of the ancient college which had faded away, namely the idea of a resident body of Fellows engaged not in teaching but in advanced theological study.[41]

Comparing the college statutes with current practice, Newman found

> only two things which are not in substance … observed; the Provost living with the Fellows, and the Fellows residing. This excepts of course the great deviation common to all the Catholic Foundations; the cessation, i.e. of Prayers for the Founders.[42]

Prayers for the dead being one of the practices of the primitive church which the Tractarians wished to restore, Newman made a special point of praying for Oriel's founders and benefactors. Newman also wished to highlight the criteria of "good character, good capacity, and poverty," as criteria in elections to fellowships. He wished to encourage Fellows to reside, living frugally, and not be lured off to secure livings or get married. His aim was a rekindling of a sense of spiritual and scholarly brotherhood among all members of collegiate society, regardless of academic status. His educational vision found at least limited expression in a private initiative which he and Pusey inaugurated in 1836-7 involving his younger followers working with him in collaboration on the 'Library of the Fathers'. In 1837, Newman

---

[41] A.D. Culler, *The Imperial Intellect: a Study of Newman's Educational Ideal* (London, 1955), p. 90.

[42] J.T. Coleridge, *Memoir of the Rev John Keble M.A.* (London, 1869), p. 248.

took a house in St Aldate's, with the object of "occupying it with a sufficient number of men without Fellowships, but who wish to stay up regularly in the University." It was to be "a reading and collating establishment," carrying out the spade-work for the 'Library of the Fathers' in an atmosphere of prayer, piety and frugality.[43]

Of course, intellectual 'jousting' had its place. Newman and the Tractarians in general did not carry a reaction against the absolute supremacy of intellectual attainment so far as to make them ever lose sympathy with the basic Coplestonian ideal of a 'liberal education' – the notion "that the purpose of the curriculum was simply to provide abstract training or mental discipline." Newman emphasized the independence of mind and antipathy to 'low utilitarianism' of those pre-Tractarian defenders and reformers of Oxford's educational system such as Copleston.[44] The Oriel tradition that Copleston had won an outright victory in 1810 in his controversy with the *Edinburgh Review* (over criticisms of Oxford therein which long predated Hamilton's later attacks) remained strong. Newman appreciated that the genesis of the Oxford Movement itself owed much to the enormous boost to Oxford's self-confidence provided by Copleston's brilliant defence. Copleston was an intellectual giant in his day. He was described as "substantial, majestic, richly coloured," though "a man not without asperities of mind and manner,"[45] while the "richness and melody of Copleston's voice surpassed any instrument."[46] So strong was the impression that Copleston's defence of Oxford's educational system made on the young Newman, that as a Roman Catholic in the 1850s he strove relentlessly to persuade an Irish Catholic audience that the true doctrine of a university lay in that protestant source.

After their mutual parting of the ways in the early-1830s, the Tractarians increasingly came to fault the *Noetics* for a certain over-intellectualism and relative neglect of the moral and religious dimension of university education. Even Copleston did not escape later Tractarian criticism in this respect. Although his academic reforms had represented a break with the apparently more easy-going ways of the eighteenth-century University (though these have been exaggerated),[47] Copleston was himself criticized for having done too

[43] A. Mozley, (ed.), *Letters of J. B. Mozley* (London, 1885); Pattison, *Memoirs*, pp. 180-1; H.P. Liddon, *Life and Letters of Edward Bouverie Pusey*, 4 vols (4th edn, London, 1894-7) i, pp. 338-9.

[44] J.H. Newman, *The Idea of a University* [1854], I. Ker (ed.), (New edn, London, 1976), p. 138.

[45] Tuckwell, *Reminiscences*, p. 16.

[46] Mozley, *Reminiscences*, i, p. 384.

[47] It was claimed Copleston "filled his College with Fellows strangely alien to the port and

little to effect a moral reformation to match the undoubted intellectual reformation which he had inspired in the Oxford and Oriel of the 1810s and 1820s. As a later Tractarian writer complained, Copleston

> had left a certain high moral tone out of his system at the first start of life, and was never able, and even became physically incapacitated, to nerve up his resolution to be the advocate of that severity of manners and disinterested self-devotion which graced the teaching of his successors in academic life.

Copleston was accused of cultivating men of fashion, and of making "the gentlemanly character too primary and single a consideration."[48] Clearly, when viewed against the burning sense of religious mission along with a conscious cultivation of familiarity that infused the teaching methods of the rising generation of Tractarian tutors, Copleston's somewhat lordly and urbane style appeared to belong to a different world.

Hawkins as Provost remained in close correspondence with Copleston after Copleston's elevation to the see of Llandaff, and the letters between them chart their growing bewilderment and disapproval of the direction of Newman's theological course, especially as religious controversy appeared to widen divisions within the University as well as college. Hawkins sensed a growing Tractarian challenge to the *status quo* in the academic polity of both University and college. On the issue of statute reform and college fellowships, Hawkins was convinced that Newman had misconstrued the intentions of Oriel's founders. He insisted that college fellowships had not, as Newman and others seemed to imply, been intended by the founders for monastic clergy and not for "merely learned academic clergy," but rather, for "a learned clergy qualified to teach the people by their life and doctrine." In fact, Hawkins's line represented a traditionalist or conservative Anglican position, and was also directed against radical secular reformers in Oriel and elsewhere such as Henry Halford Vaughan who was demanding that fellowships be applied solely to the needs of secular learning. Hawkins used it now against the Tractarians, whom he felt were making a false appeal to a spurious medieval ideal.[49]

---

prejudices, the clubbable whist-playing somnolence, which Gibson, then Sydney Smith, found characteristic of Oxford society." Tuckwell, *Reminiscences*, p. 17.

[48] *Christian Remembrancer*, 'Memoir of Bishop Copleston', p. 5.

[49] E.G.W. Bill, *University Reform in Nineteenth-Century Oxford: a Study of Henry Halford Vaughan, 1811-1885* (London, 1973), p. 57. Hawkins strongly insisted that the Charter of the Foundation of Oriel College and the original statutes laid down that the character of the college "was to be Ecclesiastical: a School of Divinity; not for Education generally, but especially for Theology,

For their part, Newman and the Tractarians convinced themselves that Hawkins's prosaic, legalistic mind quite failed to understand the underlying 'medieval spirit' which they read into the original college statutes.[50]

The following of disciples which Newman had built up, if not consciously cultivated, among pupils and former pupils, paved the way seamlessly for the following of acolytes which characterized his leadership of the Oxford Movement from 1833. This is not the place to retrace the familiar ground of the history of that Movement and notably the *Tracts for the Times*, the publication series from which the 'Tractarians' first acquired their name. However, it was a primarily University movement until at least 1845 and Newman's vision for Oxford lay at the heart of this, its classic phase. To restore the moral and spiritual dimension of collegiate education to more of a living reality remained as much a central aim of the Movement *qua* the University, as the propagation of high sacramental teaching and the call to 'apostolicity' defined its aim *qua* the Church of England as a whole. A robust defence of the terms and nature of undergraduate subscription at Oxford formed an early aspect of this campaign. Controversy was triggered by the challenge of a proposed liberal reform of the terms of subscription and an attempt to admit Dissenters, albeit under strict conditions, in 1834-5. The controversy exacerbated embryonic theological differences within Oriel between the *Noetic* and Tractarian camps. The impetus for reform may have come from the University's parliamentary critics such as Lord Radnor, but to the dismay of Newman and his followers, the proposals had modified and limited support from former Oriel *Noetics* such as Hawkins and more wholeheartedly from Hampden.[51] Newman and his supporters such as Henry Wilberforce were less than fair in lumping advocates of very limited change such as Hawkins with radical, secular reformers

---

and the training up of Christian Ministers." Burgon, *Lives of Twelve Good Men,* 2 vols, 'Edward Hawkins: the Great Provost', i, (4th edn, London, 1889), p. 454.

[50] Hawkins had an almost eighteenth-century horror of 'enthusiasm', but Burgon maintained, "his practice was so very much better than his theory." Ibid., p. 433. William Tuckwell who had been an undergraduate at Oriel in the late-1840s, referred to "fussy, jealous, meddlesome Hawkins." Tuckwell, *Reminiscences,* p. 193. Tuckwell's verdict on Hawkins, however, was strongly criticized in contemporary reviews of his *Reminiscences.* See Ms. Top Oxon b. 164, Bodleian Library.

[51] For a more detailed account of this controversy, see P.B. Nockles, "'Lost Causes and … Impossible Loyalties": The Oxford Movement and the University', *History of the University of Oxford,* vi, esp. pp. 216-22.

from outside, as assailants of the 'foundations of faith' in Oxford.[52] In reality, *Noetics* such as Hawkins and even Hampden, never questioned the essentially religious character of the University and did not accept the principle of religious pluralism being countenanced at Oxford. Hampden supported a continued hegemony of 'Church of England' principles at Oxford, while advocating the admission of Dissenters. However, even more than in 1829, Newman and his friends became convinced that Oxford liberals and their former *Noetic* friends were in league with external parliamentary forces and thus acting as a sinister political 'fifth column'.

In face of the internal liberal and external Whig challenge to Oxford's existing arrangements for undergraduate admission and subscription in the mid–1830s, Newman and his followers went on the offensive in articulating more clearly their counter religious vision of the University and its collegiate character. In contrast to the secular model of a university propounded in the *Edinburgh Review* and by Oxford's liberal reforming critics, Newman and his followers regarded the University "in the light of a corporate minister of religion." It was the solemn duty of all her members

> to regard her as the sacred ark wherein the truth has been preserved … not as skeptical disputants, who would investigate for themselves a new road to the shrine of truth; but as humble and teachable disciples, labouring to ascertain what has been the church's faith and practice.[53]

For this reason, Newman invested the University ordinance of 1581 which first prescribed the test of subscription to the Thirty-Nine Articles at matriculation with particular significance as a symbol of church as well as academic authority. It is notorious that Newman, as Tract 90 was to exemplify, was no great friend to the actual theological content of the Articles themselves. As early as 1835 he privately expressed the wish that the Creeds might be substituted for them. However, what mattered to Newman was that subscription to the Articles on matriculation impressed

> upon the minds of young men the teachable and subdued temper expected of them. They are not to reason, but to obey; and this quite independently of the degree of accuracy, the wisdom etc. of the Articles themselves.[54]

---

[52] See [H.W. Wilberforce], *The Foundations of the Faith Assailed in Oxford* (Oxford, 1835).

[53] Ibid., p. 6; F. Oakeley, *A Letter to his Grace, the Duke of Wellington* (Oxford, 1835), pp. 15–16.

[54] J.H. Newman to A.P. Perceval, 11 January 1836, T. Gornall, ed. *Letters and Diaries*, vol. v (Oxford, 1981), p. 197.

To tamper with this system of subscription, as Hampden and others threatened to do, was to strike at the cornerstone of Newman's then understanding of the religious character of university education. Therefore, Newman's disciples such as Henry Wilberforce bitterly criticized even Hawkins's modest compromise proposals in 1835 in favour of another binding substitute for subscription. The arguments of Hawkins and Edward Denison that such a substitute might actually prove more exclusive and effective as a confessional test of membership were deemed to be irrelevant, because ultimately for Newman and his followers this was not the paramount concern.

The next challenge which forced Newman on the offensive in defence of his vision of the University came with the Whig Government's appointment of that suspect Oriel *Noetic*, Renn Dickson Hampden to the Regius Chair of Divinity in February 1836. This controversial appointment was perceived as one more in a series of liberal and Whig threats to the University. The Hampden controversy has been widely discussed elsewhere (including by the present author),[55] but Newman's part in the attack on Hampden is relevant to our broader theme. The outcry against Hampden's appointment (sharpened by the knowledge that Whately and Copleston had assured Lord Melbourne of his orthodoxy and the external and intrusive affront to Tractarian Oxford's sense of its own theological purity), owed much to an ostensible objection to the supposed rationalism of Hampden's Bampton Lectures in 1832. As has been well argued, however, those Lectures were not widely known or read at the time of delivery and only took on a retrospective reputation for unorthodoxy in the context of Hampden's own controversial intervention in favour of admitting Dissenters to the University in 1834. The campaign against Hampden, culminating in a formal censure in Convocation and ratification of a new statute depriving the Regius Professor of certain limited powers, was driven by the so-called 'Corpus Committee' (an assorted body of Oxford MAs who rallied against Hampden in the Common Room of Corpus Christi College). This body encompassed protestant high churchmen and Evangelicals as well as Tractarians, but the latter made the most noise and went furthest in denunciation. Newman distinguished himself by the publication of a controversial work entitled *Elucidations of Dr Hampden's Theological Statements* (1836). Hampden's supporters

---

[55] For a fuller discussion of this episode, see Nockles, 'The Oxford Movement and the University', pp. 222-31.

accused the author, along with Pusey (author of *Dr Hampden's Past and Present Statements Compared*) of selectivity and misrepresentation by listing certain propositions for anathema which they denied were in the text of the original Lectures.[56] Hampden's Oriel friends such as Nassau Senior amused themselves with mocking accounts of the "recent *auto-da-fe* at Oxford."[57] However, the Tractarians were deadly serious. Whereas Hampden's many Evangelical opponents focused on Hampden's anti-dogmatic misuse or rationalizing away of scripture and denial of 'prevenient' and 'co-operating grace', Newman's friends objected to the self-willed exaltation of private judgment and speculation involved, reasserting the obligations of reverence and 'teachableness' in the face of church authority.[58]

Other theological controversies in Oxford came and went in the later-1830s, notably that over a proposal for a Martyrs Memorial in Oxford to which Newman refused to subscribe, and Newman's devastating published riposte to the Lady Margaret Professor of Divinity, Godfrey Faussett's blundering attack in a sermon, entitled *The Revival of Popery* from the pulpit of St Mary's in May 1838. However, it was Newman's publication of the last (No. 90) in the series of *Tracts for the Times* in February 1841 which cemented the breach and called forth a crescendo of opposition from older liberals, protestant high churchmen and Evangelicals alike. As is well known, in Tract 90 Newman set out to demonstrate that, though drafted "in an un-catholic age," the Thirty-Nine Articles were "patient" of a "catholic" rather than merely protestant sense.[59] As Newman made clear in his *Apologia*, responding to the pressures from his followers increasingly disenchanted with the protestant *status quo* in the Church of England, it had become to him "a matter of life and death" to demonstrate this.[60] Whereas six years earlier Newman had only been concerned

---

[56] *The Propositions attributed to Dr Hampden by Professor Pusey Compared with the Text of the Bampton Lectures, in a Series of Parallels* (Oxford, 1836), pp. ii–iv. Newman was castigated for his part in the Hampden affair by his brother Francis late in life. See F.W. Newman, *Contributions Chiefly to the Early History of Cardinal Newman* (London, 1891), pp. 89–92.

[57] For Nassau Senior's account of the Oxford *'auto-da-fe'*, see H. Hampden (ed.), *Some Memorials of R.D. Hampden* (London, 1871), pp. 66–8; *The Oxford Persecution of 1836* (Oxford, 1836). In his *Apologia* (p. 53), Newman playfully rebutted any such Inquisitorial leanings: "Not even when I was fiercest could I have cut off a Puritan's ears, and I think the sight of a Spanish *auto-da-fe* would have been the death of me."

[58] Nockles, 'The Oxford Movement and the University', pp. 230–1.

[59] [J.H. Newman], *Remarks on Certain Passages in the Thirty-Nine Articles* (*Tracts for the Times*, No. 90, 1841), pp. 4, 82–3.

[60] Newman, *Apologia*, p. 231.

with the principle of the act of subscription itself (one of submission), theological developments had prompted him to question and attempt to refine its terms and content.

Among Oxford's Heads of Houses, Edward Cardwell's response was typical:

> The object of the Tract appears to be to introduce such an interpretation of the 39 Articles as would make them consistent with the real system of the Church of Rome, and exclusive only of its local and grosser corruptions.[61]

Philip Wynter, President of St John's and Vice-Chancellor of the University from 1840-44, pointed out another danger: "The Tract suggested a mode of interpreting those passages which if adopted would render subscription to the Articles themselves a mere mockery."[62] Prompted by the famous Letter of the Four Tutors, A.C. Tait of Balliol, H.B. Wilson of St John's, T.T. Churton of Brasenose and J. Griffiths of Wadham, the Hebdomadal Board (the University's governing body comprising the Heads of Houses) was moved to denounce Tract 90, with only two dissentients, Routh of Magdalen and Richards of Exeter.[63]

Newman was later to be portrayed as having been the object of a cruel campaign of obloquy and persecution by the Heads of Houses, Hawkins of Oriel included. Dean Church described the Board's action as "an ungenerous and stupid blunder" and that the Heads had not so much condemned Newman "as insulted him."[64] There was now a distinctly constitutional as well as theological basis to Tractarian resentment, a resentment which would manifest itself in opposition to the nomination of a new Vice-Chancellor, Benjamin Symons, in 1844 by the Chancellor of Oxford University, the Duke of Wellington[65] (opposition, voiced by C.P. Eden of Oriel, resurfaced in 1845). As noted, the seeds of this constitutional disaffection and sense of grievance, at least in Newman's case, stemmed back at last to 1829 but was now enhanced by the *odium theologicum* characterizing subsequent controversies and the apparently high-handed way in which the Heads were deemed increasingly to be exerting their

---

[61] E. Cardwell to Duke of Wellington, 10 March 1841, Wellington MSS. 2/251/21, SUA.

[62] P. Wynter to Duke of Wellington, 15 March 1841, Wellington MSS. 2/251/27, SUA.

[63] Oxford University Archives WP/7/8/24 (5), fol. 237, Hebdomadal Board Minutes, 12 March 1841.

[64] R.W. Church, *The Oxford Movement. Twelve Years* (London, 1891), p. 292; Newman, *Apologia*, p. 242.

[65] Nockles, 'Oxford Movement and the University', p. 257.

disputed powers. In a *volte face* from their earlier standpoint, Newman and his followers, now being at the receiving end of the judgment of the University authorities, questioned the very entitlement of the Heads to act as theological arbitrators or censors in the University. In contrast to what happened in 1836, when the censure of Hampden was eagerly demanded from the Heads by Newman and his followers, the Heads were now deemed to have overstepped their powers. Newman's brother-in-law James Mozley articulated this view:

> It is generally thought that the Heads of Houses have gone out of their sphere in deciding on the theology of a work; they are merely a committee for practical business; besides that, some of them are laymen.[66]

Keble now denied that the Heads' censure had any theological validity, regarding it as "not an act of the University ... merely the opinion of the majority of individual members of the Board."[67] The Tractarian spirit of submission to established authority was proving to be a selective one; the University's Convocation was now the only authority which Newman and Keble were able to acknowledge. Ironically, the varied opponents of Tract 90 could at least claim to be the more faithful in upholding the traditional religious powers invested in the governing authorities of the University and which Newman and his followers had earlier championed. Robert Scott, Fellow of Balliol, thus assured his Balliol colleague A.C. Tait of his support for the Letter of the Four Grounds against Newman's Tract 90 on precisely these grounds:

> There was undoubtedly a cause why the University, which exists on the condition of teaching – i.e. affixing a sense to – these Articles, should protest against their having a no-sense-at-all peremptorily fixed upon them ... this publication struck a blow at the very mission of the University, and therefore the interference could never at another time have been so well timed.[68]

Scott accepted the Tractarian constitutional point that the Hebdomadal Board of Heads had confounded itself with the University and agreed that such a decree as that which the Board finally issued against Tract 90 would have been better coming from Convocation. Nonetheless, he insisted that the Heads were wise in their action, since an endless split

---

[66] J. Mozley to T. Mozley, 5 April 1841, Mozley, *Letters*, p. 116.

[67] J. Keble, *The Case of Catholic Subscription to the Thirty-Nine Articles Considered with especial Reference to the Duties and Difficulties of English Catholics in the Present Crisis, in a Letter to the Hon. Mr Justice Coleridge* (privately printed, 1841), p. 8.

[68] R. Scott to A.C. Tait, April 1841, Tait Papers, vol. lxxvii, fo. 34, Lambeth Palace Library.

would otherwise have resulted. If it was the duty of tutors to instruct undergraduates in the Articles – and this, all the pamphlets (not least Tractarian ones inspired by Newman) in defence of Oxford's system of subscription at matriculation in 1834-5 had taken for granted – then it could not be a matter of indifference to the Board in what sense those Articles were subscribed and their meaning conveyed. Such was the perception of ambiguity that had been introduced into the act of university subscription at various levels that some college Heads, notably Provost Hawkins at Oriel, now insisted upon as an additional condition of election to college fellowships a repudiation of the interpretation of the Articles advocated in Tract 90. Richard Church's refusal thus to disavow Tract 90 prompted Hawkins to remove him from his Oriel tutorship, and the granting of a testimonial to another Oriel luminary, Charles Page Eden (Newman's successor at the University church), was delayed on similar grounds.[69]

The wheel had indeed turned full circle. In a striking reversal of roles, liberals now appeared as conservative defenders of the Articles, while Newman and the Tractarians, who had defended the Articles to the hilt in 1836, in the words of one critic, "now tell us that they are a bondage which, as they cannot get rid of, must be evaded to the utmost of our power."[70] Hampden settled a few scores by seizing his moment and preaching a conservative defence of the Articles against Tractarian 'innovation', insisting, in sharp contrast to the ambiguous language on this subject in his earlier works, on a literal interpretation of the Articles in a dogmatic sense.[71] As is well known, the condemnation of Tract 90 by the Oxford authorities and, subsequently, most of the episcopal bench, was one of the hammer blows which shook Newman's Anglican allegiance and paved the way for his protracted Anglican 'death bed' in self-imposed retreat at Littlemore from 1842.[72]

---

[69] R.W. Church to G. Moberly, 26 June 1842, *The Life and Letters of Dean Church. Edited by his daughter Mary C. Church* (London, 1895), pp. 36-7; E. Hawkins to C.P. Eden, 30 October 1843, Hawkins Letterbooks, no. 83, Oriel College Library. According to Thomas Mozley, Hawkins came to feel himself "like the Captain of a crew on the verge of mutiny." Mozley, *Reminiscences*, i, p. 236.

[70] P.N. Shuttleworth to unnamed correspondent, 31 May 1841, Bodl. Ms. Eng. Hist. c. 1033, fo. 226, Bodleian Library.

[71] R.D. Hampden, *The Thirty-Nine Articles of the Church of England: the eleventh of the public course of lectures, in Trinity Term, and before the University, in the Divinity School, Oxford, June 1, 1842* (Oxford, 1842), pp. 40-1.

[72] See P.B. Nockles, 'Oxford, Tract 90 and the Bishops', *John Henry Newman. Reason, Rhetoric and Romanticism*. Edited by David Nicholls and Fergus Kerr (Bristol, 1991), pp. 228-87.

Oxford would continue to be plagued for three or four more years by Tractarian-related theological controversy and drama, with Newman's main tormentor, C.P. Golightly (a former curate of Newman's at Littlemore who appeared to bear a grudge), keeping the pot boiling.[73] These controversies included the Oxford Poetry Professorship contest in late 1841, the suspension of Pusey from preaching from the University pulpit in 1843 after a controversial sermon on the Eucharist and his condemnation by a committee of six Doctors of Divinity (presided over and directed by Provost Hawkins), and the Tractarian challenge to the candidate for Vice-Chancellor in 1844; but Newman's direct involvement and even interest in internal university affairs steadily waned so that they are not strictly germane to our discussion.[74] Battles continued to be fought by his disciples in his name and on his behalf but his heart and sympathies were now elsewhere.

There was sadness and bitterness as Newman felt himself growing apart from his beloved Oxford. Thus, he wrote from Littlemore in February 1842:

> For some years, as is natural, I have felt I am out of place at Oxford, as customs are. Everyone about is my junior … I have long given up all intention, if it were in my opinion, of being Provost myself.[75]

The despondent tone had deepened by August 1844 when he noted:

> I do fancy I am getting changed. I go into Oxford, and find myself out of place. Everything seems to say to me, 'This is not your home.' The college seems strange to me, and even the college servants seem to look as if I were getting strange to them.[76]

---

[73] For Golightly, and also the Martyrs Memorial controversy, see a forthcoming study by Andrew Atherstone, *Oxford's Protestant Spy: The Controversial Career of Charles Golightly*, to be published by Paternoster Press. Golightly was given many undignified nicknames and was butt of Tractarian humour. He was regarded by some as harbouring a grudge against Newman. He seems to have had time on his hands to organise anti-Tractarian protests in the University. He had been for the previous six years, as he solemnly put it in 1842: "a constant resident in the University, without tutorial, I might almost say without parochial responsibilities, to divert my attention from this very painful subject." [C.P. Golightly], *Correspondence illustrative of the actual state of Oxford with reference to Tractarianism, and of the attempts of Mr Newman and his party to unprotestantise the national church* (Oxford, 1842), p. 14.

[74] See Nockles, 'Oxford Movement and the University', pp. 246–58. For a sense of Newman's detachment from the Vice-Chancellorship contest and similar controversies, see J.H. Newman to J.B. Mozley, 25 August 1844, F.J. McGrath (ed.) *Letters and Diaries*, vol. x, (Oxford, 2006), pp. 321–3.

[75] J.H. Newman to Mrs J. Mozley, 15 February 1842, G. Tracey (ed.) *Letters and Diaries*, vol. viii (Oxford, 1999), p. 463.

[76] J.H. Newman to Mrs J. Mozley, 13 August 1844, *Letters and Diaries*, vol. x, p. 312.

Nonetheless, as C.S. Emden has demonstrated by a close examination of the Oriel College Buttery Books and other sources, Newman's physical withdrawal from Oriel was much more gradual than has been supposed, even if his spiritual moves towards Rome can at the same time be dated somewhat earlier than has sometimes been suggested.[77] Newman may have been on unhappy terms with Provost Hawkins, with his plans for the college thwarted, but the continued frequency of his visits to the college suggest that they were not merely for the purpose of doing duty at St Mary's and continued well after he had resigned as Vicar in autumn 1843. Emden suggests that his visits were to close friends among the Oriel Fellows such as Richard Church and Charles Marriott and that he hoped to vote for Marriott as a candidate for Provost should Hawkins (like Copleston) have been elevated to the episcopal bench.[78] Newman's withdrawal to Littlemore did not then mark a complete severance from Oxford. On the contrary, Newman's Oriel ties were the very last to be broken and may even have delayed his final departure from the Church of England. He only finally resigned his Fellowship a mere six days before joining the Church of Rome on 9 October 1845.

Newman may have been out of the limelight after 1842, but Newman's spirit in Oxford was not easily dislodged. One of the last acts in the drama of Newman's increasingly troubled relationship with the University was finally played out in his absence in the Sheldonian Theatre on 13 February 1845. The Heads had proposed three propositions for vote in a stormy scene of the University's Convocation on that memorable day. The first two, a condemnation of certain objectionable passages in the *Ideal of a Christian Church* (1844) by W.G. Ward, Fellow of Balliol, and the deprivation of Ward's degrees, were passed, but the third, a proposal to condemn Tract 90 was defeated by the dramatic intervention of the two Tractarian proctors, Guillemard and Richard Church, with the resounding cry of *'non-placet'*.[79] The Sheldonian erupted and the Vice-Chancellor was unceremoniously snowballed by jubilant undergraduates in the Sheldonian quadrangle. The Oxford Heads had won only a pyrrhic victory.

---

[77] Emden, *Oriel Papers*, (Oxford, 1948), pp. 169-75.

[78] Ibid, p.173.

[79] There are numerous accounts of this dramatic *dénouement*. For examples, see Church, *Oxford Movement*, esp. pp 377-84; W. Ward, *William George Ward and the Oxford Movement* (London, 1889), p. 350.

Chapter 2

NEWMAN AND LITTLEMORE

by Mary-Birgit Dechant

Littlemore was of great importance in Newman's life. This place was crucial in the spiritual pilgrimage of a man who in the words of Pope Paul VI "guided solely by love of the truth and fidelity to Christ, traced an itinerary, the most toilsome, but also the greatest, the most meaningful, the most conclusive, that human thought ever travelled during the last century, indeed one might say during the modern era, to arrive at the fullness of wisdom and of peace."[1]

Newman himself expressed what Littlemore meant for him in the following words: "And there it has been, that I have both been taught my way and received an answer to my prayers."[2] Much has been written already about Newman's connection to Littlemore.[3] Some new insights in this essay derive from Volumes IX and X of his *Letters and Diaries.*[4] Every reader of these lines is invited to research in greater detail than can be shown here how Newman arrived "at the fullness of wisdom and peace."

Newman as Vicar of Littlemore

Littlemore became part of Newman's life when he was appointed Vicar of St Mary the Virgin in 1828. Oriel College, whose original name is 'The House of the Blessed Virgin in Oxford', has had for centuries the task of providing one of their own fellows as Vicar of St Mary the Virgin.

---

[1] From the Homily of Pope Paul VI at the Beatification of Blessed Dominic Barberi, 23 October 1963, in: *Acta Apostolicae Sedis* LV (1963), p. 1021.
[2] To William Copeland, 10 March 1846 (LD XI, 132f.).
[3] The most important study remains Bernard Basset, *Newman at Littlemore*, published by the Friends of Newman, s.d., s.l., p. 52.
[4] LD IX and LD X were both published in 2006.

As Littlemore was an outlying part of the parish of St Mary's, Newman became Vicar of this small hamlet, too. Newman was interested in the historical link between Oxford and Littlemore. He mentions in his book *Historical Sketches:* "What was its original connexion with Oxford does not appear; but for some reason or other, the church which Alfred is said to have built on the site of the present University Church, and which is spoken of as 'St. Mary's', in the Doomsday survey, is known to have been dedicated to 'our Lady of Littlemore'."[5] Newman became aware that there had existed at Littlemore in Saxon Times a Benedictine convent, which had been rebuilt after the Norman Conquest. Although small, the convent had influence and was endowed with several pieces of land in Oxford. The chapel of the convent had been dedicated to Our Lady and St Nicholas. The convent was dissolved in 1525 and the building transformed into a farm which retained the name, Mynchery Farm (derived from the Old English 'myncen' meaning nun), and still existed in Newman's time.[6]

On Friday 28 March 1828 Newman went with the Provost of Oriel, Edward Hawkins to see Littlemore for the first time.[7] "Littlemore is a straggling street between two and three miles from Oxford extending from Cowley Church across the Henley Road down to the river near Sandford."[8] This is the description Newman himself gives, writing to his bishop in 1830. There was no church, not even a village school. If people wanted to go to church on Sunday, they either had to walk three miles to St Mary the Virgin in town or they went to one of the neighbouring parishes (Iffley, Sandford or Cowley).

Newman took his duties as Vicar very seriously. He was true to the insight he had received after his ordination to the diaconate in 1824: "I have the responsibility of souls on me to the day of my death."[9] He started to visit his parish two to three times a week. The distance between Oxford and Littlemore he managed first on horseback, later he preferred to walk or took a horse carriage, called a fly. On his way

---

[5] *Historical Sketches,* Vol III, p. 326. Cf. James Ingram, *Memorials of Oxford,* Vol. III, John Henry Parker, Oxford 1837, article on St Mary the Virgin, p. 4f., footnote i.

[6] An engraving can be found in J. Ingram, *Memorials of Oxford,* Vol. III, John Henry Parker, Oxford 1837, article on St Mary the Virgin, p. 14. The *Littlemore Manuscript* (Bodleian Library, Ms. Auct. D.2.6. folios 156r-200v) is the only book to have survived from the 'Mynchery'. It contains "artistically the finest" copy of St Anselm's Prayers and Meditations according to Otto Pächt: 'The Understanding of St Anselm's Prayers and Meditations' in: *Journal of the Warburg and Courtauld Institutes,* 19 (1956) 68-83, p. 69.

[7] LD II, 63.

[8] LD II, 194.

[9] AW 201.

to Littlemore he either used the time to ponder on his next sermon or to call on parishioners. He soon made a census and counted 452 residents. He asked as early as 1828 for permission from Oriel College to build a church at Littlemore. "My plan is this – ultimately to make Littlemore and St Mary's practically separate parishes – and at present to provide a person who (as dividing the emoluments and labor of the living with me) would take Littlemore entirely or almost entirely to himself, having nothing to do with St Mary's."[10] His request was refused. Littlemore seemed too poor to support a church and vicar of its own. So he had to rent a room where his congregation could meet. He first found one in the house of a Mrs Birmingham. On 8 February 1829 he happily wrote to Jemima: "I began my Littlemore evening catechetical lectures last Sunday."[11]

In 1830 his mother, Jemima, and his sisters, Harriett and Jemima, moved to Rose Hill, close to Littlemore. They were happy to be near to John Henry and soon got involved in the various parish duties at Littlemore. Newman had a set of rooms in their house and so it served as a kind of vicarage for Littlemore. Harriett and Jemima gathered the children of Littlemore together and ran a rudimentary school. They and their mother visited the sick and elderly and started to gather money for the building of a church for Littlemore. In April 1835 his sisters collected a petition for him to present to Oriel College to build a church: practically all the inhabitants of Littlemore had signed it.[12] This time the request met with approval. With joy Newman wrote to his friend Henry Wilberforce: "I am building a chapel at Littlemore. If you know any rich man furnished with ability, I have no objection to be indebted to him. I hope to do it for £500 or £600. The College give ground and £100. Population 470. I want it to hold 200."[13] Mrs Newman had the honour of laying the foundation stone of the church on 21 July 1835. Sadly she died suddenly on 17 May 1836. Newman commemorated her in the new church with a memorial plaque made by his good friend Westmacott. Newman decided that the church should have St Mary and St Nicholas as its patrons, he perhaps wanting to keep the link to the life of the Church at the time of the Littlemore Mynchery. On 22 September 1836 the church was consecrated by the bishop of Oxford, Richard

---

[10] LD II, 162.
[11] LD II, 119.
[12] 295 signatories, "including all but one of the householders": M. Lobel (Ed.), *Victoria County History of Oxfordshire*, Vol. 5, London 1957, p. 212.
[13] LD V, 64.

Bagot. It was a day of great joy for Newman, his parishioners and friends. The children, whom Newman was always fond of, were given buns.[14] Newman wrote to Keble: "Everything has been happy and pleasant."[15] In the succeeding years Newman made the anniversary into an impressive feast.

Littlemore now had a church. From that time onwards it also received a hard working curate as Newman could not give as much time to the village as he found necessary. Bloxam, a fellow of Magdalen College, moved to Littlemore, residing at the house of Mr and Mrs Barnes, and doing his best to improve the situation in Littlemore. In 1838 a small school was built.

Shortly before Lent 1840 Newman informed his brother-in-law Thomas Mozley:

> Tell Harriett I hope to write her soon – but I am very busy just now. I am going up to Littlemore for a while. (Bloxam has resigned the Curacy and Copeland is to be Curate. Meanwhile I want to see how the school is) And hence I have a good many things to get off my hands here. I am afraid my school mistress drinks – and at best she is a do-nothing – which is a perplexity.[16]

Newman took Bloxam's room with Mr and Mrs Barnes and looked after things in the school with determination. At the same time he set himself a strict programme for Lent: reciting the Breviary, abstaining from food and from his books, which he had left in Oriel. John Henry gave catechism classes on Sunday afternoons, for which he prepared the children during the week. These classes became an attraction for the Oxford dons and other people. He found an old violin, tuned it and used it to teach the children to sing hymns in church; he practised with them, often twice a week. He wrote to his aunt: "I am passing a most happy time. I came up here as a sort of penance during Lent; but though without friends or books, I have as yet had nothing but pleasure. So that it seems a shame to spend Lent so happily."[17]

He considered moving to Littlemore for good and wrote to some of his friends, confiding a 'secret' to them:

> Since I have been up here, an idea has revived in my mind, of which we have before now talked, viz. of building a monastic house in the place, and coming up to live in it myself. It rose in my mind from the feeling which has long been growing on me that my duty as well

---

[14] LD V, 358.
[15] LD V, 359.
[16] LD VII, 248.
[17] LD VII, 286.

as pleasure lies more at Littlemore than I have made it. It has long been a distress that I know so little of my Parishioners in Oxford, but tradespeople it is next to impossible to know, considering how they have hitherto been educated – at least impossible to me. It has pained me much to be preaching and doing little more than preach – knowing and guiding only a few, say about half a dozen: moreover from the circumstances of the case, however little I might wish it, preaching more for persons who are *not* under my charge, members of the University.[18]

What Newman of course does not mention, humble as he was, was that his preaching had an enormous influence on Oxford and drew large crowds.

He thought much about the possibility of erecting a μονη.[19] He wrote down his hopes about this *monastic* house (which had to be big enough to host his extensive library) in a Memorandum[20] and admitted to Pusey:

I am sanguine that if we could once get one set up at Littlemore, it would set the example both in great towns and for female societies. Again, perhaps it might serve as a place to *train up* men for great towns. Again, it should be an open place, where friends might come for a time if they needed a retreat, or if they wished to *see* what it was like.[21]

Easter 1840 was celebrated at Littlemore with great solemnity. His sister, Jemima, and his sister-in-law, Anne Mozley, had made him at his request a very ornate altar-cloth for the church. Newman put it up on Easter Eve and wrote to Jemima: "It looks beautiful … Indeed we are all so happy that one is afraid of being too happy. We have got some roses, wallflowers, and sweet briar, and the Chapel smells as if to remind one of the Holy Sepulchre."[22]

After the happy Lent in 1840 Newman returned to his rooms in Oriel College. However, he continued to make plans for his future residence at Littlemore. On 20 May 1840 he bought 10 acres of land at Littlemore and soon planted various trees. But before he could develop his future 'monastery', Newman felt compelled to leave Oxford more quickly than anticipated. The publication of Tract 90 in February 1841 had roused such a great controversy, that he took the lease of the 'Cottages' in College Lane at Littlemore: a stable

[18] LD VII, 264.
[19] 'Place of retreat' (LD VII, 264 footnote 1).
[20] LD VII, 263.
[21] LD VII, 265.
[22] LD VII, 312.

previously used for the Oxford-to-Cambridge coach service which had been linked to some adjoining cottages. The former stable was big enough to accommodate his extensive and valuable library and the cottages could serve for him and for friends, Oxford students, and possibly for candidates for the ministry in the Church of England who would like to share his life for a shorter or longer period. To Pusey he wrote the following note:

> I have given up the notion of a monastic body at present, lest a talk should be made. I have got a room where I can put my books, and myself – also I have a number of spare cottages – If any one chooses to come there from London, Oxford, or elsewhere, for any time he may have a retreat, but without any thing of a coenobitium. It is only in fact furnishing him with lodgings.[23]

During the winter the necessary work of conversion was undertaken, Newman supervising it, partly living in St George, a house close to the Cottages. In Lent his books were transported to Littlemore. On 20 April 1842 we read in his *Letters and Diaries*: "Came up to Littlemore in evening in fly, sleeping for first time in my own cell."[24] In a couple of letters from his new dwelling he writes "from the house of the Blessed Virgin Mary at Littlemore."[25] Soon afterwards John Dobrée Dalgairns, a native of Guernsey, moved in. Together they drew up a schedule for their day. Their source of inspiration and imitation was the Early Church Fathers, whom they had studied intensely.

The prayer of the Breviary, times for frugal meals, study and relaxation followed each other. The day started with prayer at about 6am and ended with prayer at about 10pm. Silence was kept always except in the afternoon until early evening. In the following months others joined them, some for weeks, some for months; at some points there were too many applicants.

The life of Newman and his friends drew a lot of attention in Oxford. Many called it the *monastery* but in a pejorative sense. It seemed too Roman Catholic and a very unusual undertaking. Bishop Bagot inquired about Newman's venture to which he replied in a long letter:

> For many years, at least thirteen, I have wished to give myself to a life of greater religious regularity than I have hitherto led; but it is very unpleasant to confess such a wish even to my Bishop, because it seems arrogant, and because it is committing me to a profession

---

[23] LD VIII, 238.
[24] LD VIII, 508.
[25] LD VIII, 508 and 511.

which may come to nothing. What have I done, that I am to be called to account by the world for my private actions, in a way in which no one else is called? Why may I not have that liberty which all others are allowed?[26]

The reason was that Newman had become such a leading figure in England that his life was not any more 'private'. Rumours were around that he would become a Roman Catholic and this was of great public interest.

Newman was happy to spend his time in prayer, in studies (in particular he continued his work on the Fathers of the Church and on the Lives of the English Saints), in companionship with his friends, and in the pastoral duties of Littlemore.

In summer 1843 William Lockhart decided to be received into the Catholic Church. This was a severe blow for Newman. Lockhart had started to live at Littlemore in summer 1842 with the promise not to 'go over to Rome' for at least three years. Newman had to act. He did what he had contemplated doing for a long time: he resigned his parish. To his sister Jemima he explained: "As to Lockhart's matter, I own that, were there no other reason, it would be sufficient to have made me resign (if left to myself). It is a very great scandal under the circumstances – and I could not hold up my head again as Vicar of St Mary's."[27]

On 25 September 1843, the day on which the anniversary of the consecration of Littlemore church was again celebrated with great solemnity, he preached his famous farewell sermon 'The Parting of Friends'. Edward Bellasis wrote to his wife describing the whole scene in detail concluding,

> Nothing I can say to you can give you the remotest idea of the sorrowfulness or solemnity of the scene. ... And thus the services of the greatest man of our times, the acutest and most laborious, and most energetic of the sons of the English Church is lost to us, he retires into lay communion.[28]

Newman as a layman at Littlemore

The Cottages were no longer a parsonage. They were only a place where a group of men prayed, studied and sought the Lord's will and His truth. Newman lived at the far end of the 'shed' or 'verandah'

---

[26] LD VIII, 505.

[27] LD IX, 504.

[28] E. Bellasis, *Memorials of Mr Serjeant Bellasis. 1800-1873*, Burns Oates and Washbourne LTD, London 1923, third edition, p. 60.

which connected the various cottages. Like the others, he had two rooms for his use. However, he decided to transform one of them into an oratory, where they could pray together. Maria Giberne had to help to make some improvements for the little oratory:

> The small room is hung round with crimson damask – but we want at the end, where the desk is, a white ante-pendium. ... It is to hang from the top downwards till it reaches the desk, on which the lights are, and then to hang over it continuously to the ground. ... The colours white and crimson are St Mary's, to whom Littlemore is especially dedicated.[29]

Newman's conviction, that the Church of Rome was the Church of antiquity, continued to grow in him. In fact, on 25 October 1843 he wrote to Manning: "I must tell you then frankly, that it is from no disappointment, irritation, or impatience, that I have, whether rightly or wrongly, resigned St Mary's – but because I think the Church of Rome the Catholic Church, and ours not a part of the Catholic Church, because not in communion with Rome, and feel that I could not honestly be a teacher in it any longer."[30] However, he did not yet take the step. He felt, that he had to have utter conviction before making such an important decision – important for him as well as for the many people who looked up to him as their spiritual guide and who would be put into confusion in one way or the other.

In 1845 Newman set himself to write a book about a theme which had occupied much of his thoughts. In fact, it had been the theme of his last University Sermon preached on 2 February 1843: the development of Christian doctrine.[31] "The necessity of the theory of development has increasingly pressed upon me," he confided to Pusey.[32] It was a necessity for him in regard to understanding the definition of dogmas in the Catholic Church. He, too, felt compelled to explain to his contemporaries why he would join the Church. From the beginning of 1845 onwards he started to make clear to his family and friends the conviction to which he had come and which would lead him into the Catholic Church. To his sister Jemima who was worried about the outlook for the future he explained:

> As to my conviction, I can but say what I have told you already, that I cannot at all make out *why* I should determine on moving [to the Catholic Church] except as thinking I should offend God

---

[29] LD X, 56.
[30] LD IX, 585.
[31] University Sermons 312–351.
[32] LD X, 592.

by not doing so. I cannot make out what I am *at*, except on this supposition. ... I have a good name with many – I am deliberately sacrificing it. I have a bad name with more – I am fulfilling all their worst wishes and giving them their most coveted triumph – I am distressing all I love, unsettling all I have instructed or aided – I am going to those whom I do not know and of whom I expect very little – I am making myself an outcast, and that at my age – Oh what can it be but a stern necessity which causes this.[33]

The 'stern necessity' was his burning love for God and for the truth for which he had sought and prayed already for so many years. This search for the truth was a question about his eternal salvation, as he conveyed to Jemima: "Suppose I were suddenly dying – one may deceive oneself as to what one should do – but I think I should directly send for a Priest – Is this not a test of one's state of mind? Ought I to live where I could not bear to die? Again, I assure you it makes me quite uncomfortable travelling, lest some accident should cut me off in my present state. Is this a right frame of mind to be in?"[34] At the same time he assured her: "Let us not doubt, may we never have cause to doubt, that He is with us. Continually I do pray that He would discover to me, if I am under a delusion – what can I do more? what hope have I but in Him? to whom should I go? who can do me any good? who can speak a word of comfort but He?"[35]

He made it clear in his letters that already in 1839 he had had the inner conviction that the Church of England was in the same position towards the Catholic Church as the heretical churches towards Rome. At that same time he had taken the decision to wait for seven years before taking a concrete step towards the Catholic Church. He had pledged himself to defend the Church of England as long as he could: "When doubts of our Catholicity came powerfully upon me, I did all I could to throw them from me – and I think I never can be ashamed of doing my utmost as I have done for years, to build up the English Church against hope."[36]

On 11 April 1845 he wrote to Robert Francis Wilson: "I do not think our Church *was* a branch of the Holy Catholic Church in Bishop Andrewes' day."[37] This belief comes out, too, in the following letter of June 1845:

---

[33] LD X, 595 (15 March 1845).
[34] LD X, 596.
[35] LD X, 596f.
[36] LD X, 591.
[37] LD X, 623.

> It is now near six years since I came to a clear conviction that our
> Church was in schism, and the Roman Church the true Church.
> I thought it a duty to set myself against the conviction, (and think
> so still-) I wrote against it, and went on as usual except that I did
> not speak as I had done about the Church of Rome and I told no
> one but two friends [Frederic Rogers and Henry Wilberforce] who
> were about me at the time. In this way I managed to overcome
> the feeling – i.e. by argument on the other side – there was much
> which I could not receive in the Roman system and much that was
> good and holy among ourselves. At the end of 1841 my conviction
> returned strongly – and has been on me without interruption ever
> since.[38]

On 11 July 1845 he wrote to Westmacott: "I suppose I may now tell
you, that it is morally certain I shall join the Roman Catholic Church,
though I don't wish this *told* from me. It has been the conviction of
six years – from which I have never receded."[39]

To his brother Frank he affirmed: "My reason for going to Rome
is this: – I think the English Church in schism. I think the faith of
the Roman Church the only true religion. I do not think there is
salvation out of the Church of Rome."[40]

In September 1845 he sent his book *An Essay on the Development
of Christian Doctrine* to the publisher. His conviction had become so
firm, that no more time could be wasted. On 3 October he resigned
his Oriel College fellowship. Providence intervened through John
Dalgairns who had been received into the Church by Dominic Barberi
of the Mother of God, an Italian Passionist at the end of September.
Dalgairns was astute enough to suggest to Dominic Barberi that he
should stop at Littlemore, on his way to a chapter of his order in
Belgium. Newman agreed to Dalgairn's suggestion, seeing in it God's
guiding hand.

John Henry started to prepare his general confession.[41] Dominic
Barberi arrived at Littlemore on 8 October about one hour before
midnight, soaking wet from the heavy rain all day long. He entered the
library and stood at the fireplace to dry his clothes. What happened
then is best described in Dominic's own words:

> The door opened – and what a spectacle it was for me to see at
> my feet John Henry Newman begging me to hear his confession
> and admit him into the bosom of the Catholic Church! And there

[38] To John Moore Capes, 4 June 1845 (LD X, 690).
[39] LD IX, 729.
[40] LD X, 745 (7 August 1845).
[41] LD X, 778 (5 October 1845).

by the fire he began his general confession with extraordinary humility and devotion. In the morning I betook myself to Oxford to say Mass in a Catholic Church there, and returned to Littlemore once more amid pouring rain. There I terminated Mr. Newman's confession, and then heard the confession of two other gentlemen who were there, namely, Revs. Stanton and Bowles, both of them, like Newman, ministers of the Church of England. That same evening about six o'clock I received the profession of faith of all three, and gave them conditional baptism. ... Those who know Mr Newman and his companions will be in a position to judge and weigh the results of such an event. Newman has been up to now what I might term the Pope of the Protestants, their oracle, the soul of the Puseyite party. ... In my judgement he is one of the most humble and lovable men I have met in my life. Let us hope that the results of such conversions may be incalculable. All that I have suffered since I left Italy is well compensated by such a happy event as this.[42]

Dominic stayed on for a few more days and twice celebrated Mass for them. Not much is recorded about these days. One can imagine that a deep peace and joy prevailed in the hearts of all who were at The College. The outward way of life still remained the same. Two small, but significant changes were made: the Oxford pronunciation of Latin gave way to the Italian and the antiphon to Our Lady after Night Prayer was sung for the first time on 9 October. Dominic advised his young converts not to be too strict with themselves.

After Dominic Barberi had left, the great question arose about God's plan for Newman. He wrote to Jemima on 14 October: "I feel it very doubtful what is best to be done and what is God's will. I have always looked at Littlemore as under the special protection of St Mary, and so many providential circumstances have brought me and fixed me where I am, that I fear to move."[43] Newman decided to approach Bishop Wiseman, as Apostolic Vicar responsible for the Midland District. Wiseman confirmed him on 1st November.[44] Wiseman wrote a few days later: "Newman opened his mind completely to me: and I assure you that the Church has not received, at any time, a convert who has joined her in more docility and simplicity of faith than Newman."[45] He suggested to Newman and his convert friends that

[42] Urban Young, *Dominic Barberi in England. A new series of letters* (London: Burns Oates and Washbourne LTD, 1935), pp. 138–140.

[43] LD XI, 17.

[44] Newman took Mary as his confirmation name (LD XI, 23).

[45] Wilfrid Ward, *The life of John Henry Cardinal Newman*, vol. I (London: Longmans, Green, and Co., 1912), p. 99.

they should move to a house which had served as the seminary of the diocese but which was now empty, 'Old Oscott', or as Newman would call it, 'Maryvale'. Newman prepared his move. The last night he spent at Littlemore was the night of 21 February (his birthday) 1846. On Sunday, 22 February, he went to Mass at St Ignatius's for the last time. At 4pm the fly came to take him and his baggage to his friend Manuel Johnson at the Observatory, where he spent his last night in Oxford. Newman had to tear himself away from Littlemore, as he himself testified: "As you suppose, it was of course a very trying thing to me to quit Littlemore – I quite tore myself away – and could not help kissing my bed, and mantlepiece, and other parts of the house. I have been most happy there, though in a state of suspense."[46] To Mrs Bowden he wrote: "In spite of my having been in such doubt and suspense, it has been the happiest time of my life, because so quiet."[47] In a letter to Henry Wilberforce he put the question: "Shall I ever see Littlemore again?"[48] He saw it only twice more.

On 16 June 1868 Newman visited Littlemore with his close friend Ambrose St John. They took the train from Birmingham to Abingdon from where they made their way to Littlemore. Newman visited some of his old parishioners and was happy to see how Littlemore had become 'green'.[49] He wrote the next day: "It is a great pleasure to me to have seen Littlemore once again – and to see so many persons whom I have not seen for so long – and to see how beautiful the place looks. It will be a pleasant picture in my memory."[50] He returned only one other time, in 1878, again for a very brief stay.

Some years after he had left Littlemore, Newman received a visit from Richard Humphries who had been parish clerk of Littlemore, while Newman was vicar. Newman had taught him as a young boy to play the violin and had married him to his first wife Mary Hanks at St Mary the Virgin in 1839. One day Richard Humphries noticed the advertisement of a cheap trip to Birmingham, and made up his mind to avail himself of it, and go and see his 'dear vicar', although a journey by train was very new to him. On arrival at the Oratory, he rang the bell, and asked the porter for Mr Newman. He was told that Mr Newman was not usually disturbed at that hour. "Well," he said, "will you take him a message? Tell him Richard from Littlemore

---

[46] LD XI, 132.
[47] LD XI, 126.
[48] LD XI, 125.
[49] LD XXIV, 89.
[50] LD XXIV, 87.

has come to ask how he is." He did not have to wait long. Newman did not even wait to put on his boots, but came along in his slippers, and said, "Come in, come in, and tell me all about my dear people." So Richard Humphries went in, and had a long talk with his former vicar and was invited to stay for dinner with the Fathers.

Littlemore today

The evidence of that visit, an article of 1899 in *The Oxford Times*,[51] was recently given to the Sisters of The Spiritual Family The Work, the present guardians of The College at Littlemore, by a great-great-great-grand-daughter of Richard Humphries. She had come with a group of parishioners from a neighbouring parish to see the place where Newman had lived between 1842 and 1846 and to learn more about him and about his affection for Littlemore.

Newman's church still serves as the Anglican parish church. Newman's memory is still cherished, and visitors may see the memorial plaque in honour of Jemima Newman, the list of benefactors, the baptismal font which Newman brought in from St Mary's, and a modern icon depicting Newman as a cardinal.

In the chapel where Newman used to pray with his friends, red and white curtains hang down from the walls just as in his time. There stands now, too, a beautiful statue of Our Lady. She is a reminder to all who come to The College today that Mary had so much an essential role in Newman's spiritual life that he could write in 1848 to his friend Henry Wilberforce: "I have ever been under her shadow, if I may say it. My College was St Mary's, and my Church; and when I went to Littlemore, there, by my own previous disposition, our Blessed Lady was waiting for me."[52]

---

[51] Cf. LD VIII, 625
[52] LD XII, 153–4.

The chapel of the Collegio di Propaganda Fide *in Rome where Newman celebrated his first Mass after being ordained priest in the Catholic Church in 1847.*

Chapter 3

NEWMAN AND ROME

by Brigitte Maria Hoegemann

It is impossible in a short essay to give more than a glimpse of what Rome meant to Newman. Long before the Anglo–Catholic Oxford don actually saw the city, its name must have resonated with him, evoking not just images of the ancient city, kingdom, republic and empire, its history of three thousand years, its rise and fall, but also its huge claim to power and its unique culture of antiquity both pagan and Christian. Rome was not just a subject of deep interest to the young Oxford student, but also the visible centre of the Catholic Church from the time of the apostles. Yet he still had the conviction, learned as a boy at Ealing, that the Christian faith in Rome had, over time, become so corrupted as to be 'the work of Antichrist'. The mere name of the city aroused in Newman notions, emotions and convictions both happy and painful. He tells about an Anglican looking down on the city, who remarked: "the Christian can never survey (it) without the bitterest, the most loving and the most melancholy thoughts."[1]

In the course of time, and his personal development, Newman's attitude to Rome became simpler and more distinct. He visited the eternal city four times, in the early third, the fourth, the fifth and the late seventh decade of his life. These are used as biographical stepping-stones, to trace something of what 'Rome' meant in Newman's life, pointing out some of the main changes in his attitude to the city and the Church. When he visited Rome for the first time, in the spring of 1833, invited by friends to accompany them on a long voyage to Southern Europe, he was a young Oxford scholar, an already famous

---

[1] See the discussion by "two speculative Anglicans" aiming at strengthening their Church in 'Home Thoughts Abroad', published in the *British Magazine* in the spring of 1836, republished under 'How to accomplish it' in *Discussions and Arguments on Various Subjects,* London 1872, pp. 2f.

don of Oriel College, an ordained minister of the Church of England whose preaching and teaching was influenced by his studies of the Early Christians.

Thirteen years later, in early November 1846, he arrived, having been a Roman Catholic layman for just over a year, to prepare for his ordination to the priesthood at the *Collegio di Propaganda Fide* and to find out about his further vocation. When he left Rome in early December 1847, he was ready to set up an English Oratory at Maryvale close to Birmingham on his return.

Another ten years later, from 12th January to 4th February 1856, Dr Newman, the Provost of the Birmingham Oratory and the Rector of the Catholic University of Dublin, was for a short time in Rome "on Oratory business".[2] Differences in the interpretation of the vocation of an English Oratorian by the two English houses in Birmingham and London made it necessary for him to clarify the matter with the *Propaganda Fide* and the Holy See.

Finally, called by the newly elected Pope, he returned to Rome in his seventy-ninth year, for some strenuous weeks from 24th April to 4th June 1879. On 12th May in a ceremony at Cardinal Howard's residence he received the official biglietto that Pope Leo XIII had raised him to the rank of Cardinal and gave his famous Biglietto Speech; on May 15th Leo XIII honoured him with the Cardinal's hat.

I. First Impressions of Rome (1833)

1. Rome is a wonderful place – Rome is a cruel place

As to Rome, it is the most wonderful place in the world. We do not need Babylon to give us a specimen of the old exertions of our Great Enemy against heaven – (who now takes a more crafty way) – it was an Establishment of impiety –. The Coliseum is quite a tower of Babel – and this is but one out of a number of vast buildings, which astound one. Then, when you go into the Museum etc, you get into a second world – that of taste and imagination. The collection of Statuary is endless and quite enchanting. The Apollo is indescribable – its casts give one no notion of it, as *an influence* – it is overpowering. And the great pictures of Raffaello [sic], tho' requiring a scientific taste to criticize, come home in a natural way to the uninitiated. I never could fancy any thing so unearthly as the expression of the faces. Their strange simplicity of

---

[2] *The Letters and Diaries* of John Henry Newman, I-XXXII, ed. at the Birmingham Oratory with notes and an introduction by Charles Stephen Dessain and others, Nelson/Oxford University Press, 1961-2006, vol. XVII, p. 99: From now on abridged e.g. LD XVII, 99.

expression and almost boyishness is their great charm. – Well then, again after this, you have to view Rome as a place of religion – and there what mingled feelings come upon one. You are in the place of martyrdom and burial of Apostles and Saints – you have about you the buildings and sights they saw – and you are in the city to which England owes the blessing of the gospel – But then on the other hand the superstitions; – or rather, what is far worse, the solemn reception of them as an essential part of Christianity – but then again the extreme beauty and costliness of the Churches – and then on the contrary the knowledge that the most famous was built (in part) by the sale of indulgences – really it is a cruel place. (LD III, 240–241)[3]

When writing this sketch on 7th March 1833, Newman was on a long voyage with good friends. Archdeacon Froude had invited him to accompany him and his son, Newman's friend, Richard Hurrell Froude, who needed a change of climate on account of his delicate health. They had set off on 8th December 1832 in the Hermes, a military supply ship bound for the British garrisons in the Mediterranean, that also had comfortable facilities for passengers on board, calling first at Gibraltar, thence to Malta, where they spent a month, before arriving via Naples in Rome in the evening of 2nd March. Newman wrote many letters from the Eternal City, where they stayed all through March and the first week of April 1833.

In most of these letters he puzzles the reader with his contrasting, even contradictory comments when summing up his impressions, demonstrating the complex nature of his initial reactions. In the sketch above he distinguishes three main *views* of Rome. There is first of all the Ancient city and Empire, which Newman brings to his reader's mind less in its political power and importance than in "the heathen greatness" (249) or the revolt of pagan mankind against the one and eternal God – as conjured up in the visions of Daniel. He describes the Coliseum as the tower of Babel, thus comparing "the hateful Roman power" with Babylon or "the 4th beast of Daniel's vision and the persecutor of the infant Church" (253). Another example from his letters from Rome brings that out even more clearly:

The first notion one has of Rome is as of the great Enemy of God, the fourth monarchy – and the sight of the city in this view is awful... the immense size of the ruins, the thought of the purposes to which they were dedicated, the sight of the very arena where Ignatius suffered, the columns of heathen pride with the inscriptions

---

[3] Until stated otherwise, the page numbers after the quotations in the text refer to LD III.

still legible, the Jewish candlestick still perfect in every line on the arch of Titus, brand it as the vile tool of God's wrath and again Satan's malice. (231)

The second view of Rome is that of a world of exceptional beauty. Newman experiences with delight the "intellectual beauty in the scenery" (240) of Rome and mentions famous examples of Ancient sculpture and of Renaissance painting[4] and the beautiful churches, in other letters also the amazing bridges, the fountains and other outstanding samples of architecture, sharing with his correspondents this so different and "fresh world", a world "of taste and imagination" (240). The way in which Newman captures the lively charm of the two fountains in the Piazza of St Peter is enchanting and may serve here as an example. He compares them to "two graceful white-ladies arrayed in the finest and most silvery dresses."

> There is a highest jet in the middle and it is surrounded by a multitude of others, so contrived all, that in falling they do not form a stream or look at all like water, but are changed into the finest and most impalpable spray circling round the jets, like the plumage of a swan or as I say the muslin of the white lady's dress. This dashes against a ledge, and then against another; – so that the whole effect is such as I token by way of comparison – for describe the effect I cannot. When the wind takes them, it is like muslin waving about. (264)

Thirdly he speaks of Rome as a place, which is uniquely marked by its Christian history and the presence of Christian religion. Yet the witnesses of this history evoke in him awe and anger. He experiences awe at the sight of the tombs of the early martyrs, or when remembering his gratitude for St Augustine who brought the faith to England, at the tomb of Pope Gregory I.

Yet other sights make him angry. He cannot fully enjoy the beauty of St Peter's, as it reminds him of the business with indulgences. And then there are the many statues of Saints in the churches and in the streets he is passing through, and not just the statues, but candles before them, people who kneel before them, signs that speak to him about superstitions, and even of "the solemn reception of them as an essential part of Christianity" (241).

When offering his third view of Rome: the city "as a place of religion", notions, impressions, and thoughts, qualifying, opposing, even contradicting one another, follow so quickly upon each other,

---

[4] He had by then already visited the Vatican Museum for the first time.

that Newman no longer forms full sentences, but just names whatever emerges into his consciousness, in this way communicating to the reader his "mingled feelings" evoked by the sights and his interpretation of them.

His refrain on the eternal city in the letters home to friends and family is ever that of praise: "Rome ... is of all cities the first, and ... all I ever saw are but as dust, even dear Oxford inclusive, compared with its majesty and glory" (230) – "Rome grows more wonderful every day" (231). This praise remains, however, interspersed with harsher comments and judgements, primarily evoked by the impression which its gigantic ruins, and what he associates with them, made on him.

During his first visit to Rome Newman had not only all his senses open to the sometimes awe inspiring, sometimes light and charming beauty of the place, but he also suffered, when looking at sights, what to him were manifestations of Antichristian features in what he called 'the Roman system', if not the work of Antichrist[5] himself in the Roman Catholic Church.

2. The Catholic System most loved – the Roman Catholic system loathed

In some of his later letters from that first visit Newman develops a third view of Rome as the Roman Catholic Church: "As to the Roman Catholic system, I have ever detested it so much ... that I cannot detest it more by seeing it, tho' I may be able to defend my opinion better and to feel it more vividly, – but to the Catholic system I am more attached than ever" (273). He actually suggests that the nineteenth century Catholic Rome is "somehow" still "the only remnant of the 4 great Enemies of God – Babylon, Persia, and Macedon have left scarce a trace behind them – the last and most terrible beast lies before us as a subject for our contemplation, in all the visibleness of its plagues" (248/9). He declares:

> I cannot quite divest myself of the notion that Rome Christian is somehow under an especial shade as Rome Pagan certainly was[6] – though I have seen nothing here to confirm it. Not that one can tolerate for an instant the wretched perversion of the truth which is sanctioned here, but I do not see my way enough to say that there

---

[5] Martin Luther for example depicts the Pope as *Antichrist*, who soon after Gregory the Great started to reign over the Church, enthroning himself in God's temple, claiming authority over the word of God. See Schmalkald. Art. IV; (2 Thess 2:3-12; Rev 13:5).

[6] A fuller account of this theory is to be found in the letter to Samuel Rickards on 14th April 1833 from Naples, LD III, 287-290 and in *Discussions and Arguments*, see above, footnote 1.

is anything peculiar in the condition of Rome – and the clergy, though sleepy, are said to be a decorous set of men. (258)

The cautious reservation and prudent restraint, to which Newman submits these thoughts and opinions on Roman Catholicism, now that he is in Rome and has first hand experience of it, are typical of him. His attitude allows the assumption that, in spite of the fact that he is busy developing his, so to speak, inherited negative notions and critical opinions of the Roman Catholic Church into a theory, he keeps, at the same time, his mind and heart open – not only to a possible *new vista,* but, as the future will show, to the intervention of providence.

Newman is fascinated by his discovery that in many of the churches in Rome, "the materials and buildings of the Empire" were turned

> to the purpose of religion. Some of them are literally ancient buildings – as the Pantheon, and the portion of the Baths of Diocletian, which is turned into a church. And all – St Peter's, St John Lateran, etc. – are enriched with marbles, etc., which old Roman power alone could have collected. (235)

That became almost symbolic of the Roman Catholic Church for Newman, which, as he was still convinced at that time, interpolated amidst the great Christian truths more and more deformations of them, finally failing to guard the Christian teaching and the life of Ancient Christianity, that he loved so much, from the influences of the surrounding pagan world.

The notion that Rome, whether Pagan or Christian, whether the Ancient Empire or the Roman Catholic Church as an institution, was and will be under the wrath of God, was nourished by Newman's prejudice, which he had harboured since his early boyhood: his protestant conviction, that Rome is a church system which, by being centred on the Pope, is centred on *the Antichrist.* Thirty-one years later Newman describes in his *Apologia*[7] the slow process of overcoming that core prejudice held against the Roman Catholic system of faith by Protestantism.

In the second chapter of the re-ordered second edition of the *Apologia* (1865) Newman recalls that from the age of fifteen, he knew and defended dogma as the fundamental principle of religion and believed in a visible church with sacraments, rites and an episcopal

---

[7] John Henry Newman, *Apologia pro Vita Sua*, 2nd edition 1865, II pp. 52-54; 64-65. The Roman number refers to the chapter, the first Arabic numeral to the unified edition, the second to the edition in the Penguin classics ed. by Ian Ker 1994.

system. But he also stresses that at the same time he firmly believed "the Pope to be *Antichrist*", preaching on that conviction still ten years later, at Christmas 1824.

Through the influence of Richard Hurrell Froude and of Keble, but more so through his repeated, ever more thorough studies of the Fathers of the Church, by whose writings he learns to love the Catholic Church, he loses some of his bitterness concerning the papacy and Romanism. In 1822/23 he speaks less of the extreme protestant conviction that the Pope takes the role of *Antichrist*, but still claims that by the Council of Trent the Roman Church was "bound up with the cause of *Antichrist*". Later again, he claims that the Roman Church is "one" of the "many antichrists" whom St John foretold and finally that opinion is replaced by an even milder one: that it has something "very Antichristian or unchristian" about it (*Apo.* II, 52, 64). Gradually he even learns to have more "tender feelings towards" the Roman Catholic Church, especially for her "zealous maintenance of doctrine," for the Apostolic "rule of celibacy" and other faithful agreements with Antiquity (*Apo.* II, 54; 65). Yet, in 1833 he still maintains his negative judgment against the Roman Church as an institution (*Apo.* II, 54; 66).[8]

With such convictions in heart and mind, Newman travelled with the Froudes through Italy. No wonder then that they, as he formulated it in 1864, "kept clear of Catholics throughout" their tour (*Apo.* I, 32; 48), and tried to keep away from any Roman Catholic life. All the more important it is to look at the few occasions when he did come in touch with the living Roman Catholic faith in Italy: when attending a pontifical Mass, visiting some churches and shrines, meeting some priests, and observing some young seminarians.

In one of his letters[9] he tells of a Church function, which he attended in Sta Maria sopra Minerva on the Feast of the Annunciation.[10] After describing in about seven hundred words the pomp, the show, the luxurious altar dressings and vestments, the appearance of the Sovereign Pontiff and of the religious "*court* of Rome" with all the sumptuously dressed cardinals and many priests, the manifold and numerous ceremonies, he simply states: "Besides, Mass was celebrated."

---

[8] In 1843 John Henry Newman formally withdrew "all the hard things" which he had said against the Church of Rome (*Apo.* IV, 200; 184).

[9] See LD III, 266-269.

[10] The other two of just three church services, which he seems to have attended, were the afternoon offices on Maundy Thursday and Good Friday at the Sistine Chapel: "the Tenebrae" (272).

After a further three hundred words of description and comment, inevitably leading up again to Daniel's vision of the four beasts and the solemn declaration that the Roman Church united itself with the enemy of God, he concludes:

> And yet as I looked on, and saw all Christian acts performing the Holy Sacrament offered up, and the blessing given, and recollected that I was in church, I could only say in very perplexity my own words, 'How shall I name thee, Light of the wide west, or heinous error-seat?'[11], – and felt the force of the parable of the tares – who can separate the light from the darkness but the Creator Word who prophesied their union? And so I am forced to leave the matter, not at all seeing my way out of it. – How shall I name thee? (268)

For the first time ever, he attended Mass, and it was a highly festive one with much going on to distract him from the central mystery. He describes at length what has fuelled his dislike and detestation. Having, however, gone through that experience, he cannot but recognize and acknowledge the wheat among the weeds. Remembering the Lord's recommendation in 'the parable of the tares', he confesses his perplexity, acknowledging that it is alone God's due to separate the light from the darkness. He signals that he is not the one to see his way out of that difficult matter. He quotes two lines from his first poem on Rome. Repeating the first few words, he changes them into an outcry coming from his heart, a true question addressed to the Roman Church demanding an answer: "How shall I name thee?"

He mentions in the *Apologia* that in Sicily he was most impressed by the shrines and the noble churches, as well as by the devotion of the people. He remembers "the comfort" he had received in visiting the churches and recalls especially how the singing in a lonely church in the wilds of Sicily attracted him when on a stroll around six o'clock in the morning. How astonished he was to find out at that early hour that the church was crowded. He adds: "Of course it was the mass, though I did not know it at the time" (*Apo.* II, 53f; 65).

He and the Froudes met but a few priests on their journey, the Dean of Malta, with whom they talked about the Fathers of the Church, and Abbot Santini in Rome, who furnished Newman with the Gregorian chants, and also Dr Wiseman, then Rector at the English College, whom they heard once preach and on whom Newman called twice before leaving Rome. The only other priest he met in Italy was the one who came to his sickbed in Sicily. Yet, Newman remarks on

---

[11] From his first poem on Rome in a letter to his sister Harriett (232).

the young seminarians he saw in Rome: "I feel much for and quite love the little monks of Rome, they look so innocent and bright, poor boys" and again when he speaks of the "children of all nations and tongues" who at *Propaganda Fide* are educated "for missionary purposes" (273, 279). In spite of his conviction from the age of fifteen that the Lord had called him to a celibate life to be free for His claim on him for the good of many (*Apo.* I, 7; 28), and in spite of the fact that in the *Apologia* he remembers to have had early on respect for the Apostolic rule of celibacy as it was maintained in the Roman Church, his playful comment, "poor boys" seems to imply a criticism. In a letter, written just a few days later, he speaks, indeed, of "the custom of 'forced celibacy of the Clergy'" (289). He obviously does not yet understand that, if God calls someone to priesthood or to consecrated life and if that person in free will obeys His call, that supernatural response in faith, hope, and love enables them, with the grace of God, in free self-giving to follow the example of Jesus Christ, who lived a celibate, virginal life among us. Newman could not have imagined at that time, that some thirteen years later, at the age of forty-six, he would sit among the young seminarians of the College of Propaganda, attending their lectures in preparation for priesthood.

Looking back to his first experience of the city of Rome, only days after he had left the city, which he was convinced he would never see again, he sums up his experience:

> Rome is a very difficult place to speak of from the mixture of good and evil in it – the heathen state was accursed ... and the Christian system there is deplorably corrupt – yet the dust of the Apostles lies there, and the present clergy are their descendants. (287)

And again:

> Oh that Rome were not Rome; but I seem to see as clear as day that a union with her is *impossible.* She is the cruel Church – asking of us impossibilities, excommunicating us for disobedience, and now watching and exulting over our approaching overthrow. (284)

The mere tone of his exclamation, the identification of Rome and Church, the fact that he claims that the Roman Church is "excommunicating" Anglicans of the nineteenth century and that he speaks of demands which she has on them, that cannot possibly be fulfilled, show how deeply he suffers from the centuries old wound of disunity. Less than ever is he able to think about the Church of England without seeing it in relation to the Church it had separated from. His assumption that the Catholic Church expects the imminent overthrow of the Church of England and rejoices in the prospect, speaks volumes.

In the *Apologia* Newman recalls his farewell visit to Wiseman. The Rector had kindly expressed his hope to see them again in Rome, and he answered, "with great gravity: 'We have a work to do in England'" (*Apo.* 34; 50). That solemn expectation of a mission waiting for him in England assumed the character of an existential conviction and need during his serious illness in Sicily. He was convinced that he would not die, crying out: "God has work for me yet!"[12]. On his return to Oxford, he heard Keble preach the Sermon *On National Apostasy* on the next Sunday, 14th July 1833, and had the strong sense that this was the beginning of a movement of revival in the Church of England. Newman recognized the Oxford Movement as "that work which I had been dreaming about, and which I felt to be so momentous and inspiring" (*Apo.* 43; 57). Only very gradually did he realize that what he had meant to be his own work of strengthening the Anglo-Catholicism in the Church of England, thus fighting the forces of liberalism in religion, had been taken out of his hands. He gradually accepted that God was doing His work in him and wanted to do more through him, step by step leading him to ask to be received into full communion with the Catholic Church.

II. At Home in Rome

1. Advised to Prepare for Priesthood in Rome

When Newman had embraced the Catholic Church as the true heir of the Early Church of the Fathers and had been received at Littlemore into full communion with the Catholic Church by the Italian Passionist Padre Domenico Barberi,[13] it was Mgr Wiseman who confirmed him,[14] with St John, Walker and Oakeley on All Saints Day 1845 at Oscott. The former Rector of the English College in Rome, whom Newman had met in 1833, had in the meantime become President of the new Oscott College near Birmingham and the Coadjutor to the Vicar Apostolic of the Midland District. He offered Newman and his fellow converts old Oscott, the former Seminary of the Midland district, "without rent, stipulations, control, or responsibility of any kind" (79).

---

[12] LD IV, 8.

[13] Since 1963, Blessed Dominic Barberi.

[14] In gratitude he took the name of Mary, see LD XI, 23, footnote 1. Until stated otherwise, the numbers in brackets after the quotations in the text refer now to LD XI.

In February 1846 Newman left Littlemore for Maryvale, his new name for Old Oscott, for another spell of shared life with some of his now Catholic friends. It seemed ideal as "a place of refuge", as they "had still to find out the vocation of each and all." The position of the house seemed to be just right, only a few miles from Birmingham, which at that time was one "of the chief nurseries of Catholicism" (79). Though Newman had lived at Oriel College many years beside the chapel, with an entrance from his flat into the organ loft, it was totally different for him to live in Maryvale wall to wall to the Lord in his Eucharistic presence:

> I am writing next room to the Chapel – It is such an incomprehensible blessing to have Christ in bodily presence in one's house, within one's walls, as swallows up all other privileges and destroys, or should destroy, every pain. To know that He is close by – to be able again and again through the day to go to Him. (129)

He could actually open a window in that wall, which allowed him to look down into the chapel and to see the tabernacle below, without leaving his room.[15] This brought home to him the realness of the Catholic faith, where everything falls into place, joy and pain, by the grace of the personal, real presence and closeness of the Lord.

> I could not have fancied the extreme, ineffable comfort of being in the same house with Him who cured the sick and taught His disciples, as we read of Him in the Gospels, in the days of His flesh. (131)

It was providential that the Holy Father, Gregory XVI, sent him and the small community a silver crucifix and a splinter of the True Cross. Cardinal Fransoni, the Prefect of *Propaganda Fide*, added a personal letter to the two precious gifts. Their personal interest in him touched Newman; yet, he was moved even more by the "singular coincidence" as he wrote to Miss Giberne, "that the certificate of the grant of the sacred Relic is dated on the date that No 90[16] came out 5 years ago – and the news of it came to me on the anniversary of the Heads of the Houses bringing out their manifesto against it – so that the process of condemnation was just as long as the time it has taken to do me honour"(139). In the thoughtful personal gesture of the Pope, Rome had come to Maryvale, long before Newman left Maryvale for Rome.

---

[15] The window in that room can still be opened, and the sanctuary light glows beside the tabernacle below in the chapel.
[16] Tract Ninety.

Around Easter, in April 1846, less than two months after Newman's move from Littlemore to Maryvale, Mgr Wiseman advised him to go to Rome for a year of studies at the Collegio di Propaganda Fide. This was, as Newman said "simply my own act", and yet he "wished to leave the whole thing to him." The choice of the college was Wiseman's response to Newman's wish for "a regular education" (152), the wish to go somewhere, where he "might be strictly under obedience and discipline for a time" (283).

On 1st June 1846, the vigil of Trinity Sunday, John Henry Newman, Ambrose St John and three or four of their group[17] received minor orders and the tonsure in the chapel of Oscott. It was not until 9th June that they learned that it had been the very day on which Pope Gregory XVI had died. Newman, who had expected to go to Rome with Dr Wiseman by the end of the month, was content that his departure was deferred until the autumn.

Soon after Pius IX was elected on 16th June, the new pontiff, too, sent a thoughtful sign to Newman, who on 21st July 1846 wrote to Dalgairns: "The new Pope sent me his blessing, and I hear that the last thing he was speaking of before going into the conclave was about Wiseman and me" (212).[18] He also learned from Dr Wiseman in August, that Cardinal Fransoni had assured him that *Propaganda* was ready to comply with whatever Newman might wish for at the college; they wanted "to help the movement" (218). It was Wiseman's suggestion that two from Maryvale should go; Ambrose St John was to be Newman's companion at *Propaganda* (219).

2. At Home in the Roman Faith

The Catholic Religion – a Real Religion

After a short stay in Paris, where he also visited the shrine at Notre Dame des Victoires in gratitude for prayers offered there for him by a Fraternity of the Immaculate Heart of Mary, which had the image of the Miraculous Medal for its badge,[19] Newman and St John spent five weeks in Milan. His letters give a most lively account. He had come home, a Catholic, to the place to which St Athanasius had come "to meet the Emperor, in his exile"; to the see and the tomb of St Ambrose; to the place where St Monica sought her son; the place of

---

[17] This is implied from Newman's letter to the Earl of Shrewsbury on 23 Aug. 1846, LD XI, 232.

[18] See letter to Knox, 20th Aug. 1846, 227.

[19] See LD XI, 245, diary, footnote 1; also the footnotes 21 and 22 of this essay.

the baptism of St Augustine.[20] He got to know and to love, and to be at home, too, with the great Archbishop St Charles Borromeo,[21] who, in the strength of Christ, resisted "that dreadful storm under which poor England fell," saving his country from Protestantism. Newman went almost daily to kneel and pray at his tomb, convinced to find in this great Saint of the Counter Reformation a special helper for his future mission in England. In this simple act of devotion he affirmed the fact that the Catholic Church of all ages had become his home.

More than by anything else, the convert was touched by the presence of the Blessed Sacrament in all the churches. It became a main topic in his letters. In Maryvale he had had the personal experience of actually living with the Lord under one roof. Now in Milan the experience 'I live with God' was broadened and changed to the experience, 'wherever I enter a church the Lord is waiting for me'. He wrote:

> It is so very great a blessing to be able to go into the churches as we walk in the city – always open with large ungrudging kindness – full of costly marbles to the sight, and shrines, images, and crucifixes all open for the passer by to make his own by kneeling at them – the Blessed Sacrament everywhere. (251)

On his first trip through Italy in 1833 Newman had not observed the tabernacle light, nor known its meaning, as he did not understand or attempt to understand Mass (131). But now he saw the sanctuary light flicker and invite him from within the churches he walked by:

> It is really most wonderful to see this Divine Presence looking out almost into the open streets from the various Churches, so that at St Laurence's we saw the people take off their hats from the other side of the street as they passed along; no one to guard It, but perhaps an old woman who sits at work before the Church door, or has some wares to sell. (252)

He was overwhelmed that the Blessed Sacrament is, as it were, "ready for the worshipper even before he enters" (254). By the visible *omnipresence* of the Eucharistic Lord, if it could be named visible, Newman experienced also the unity of the Church:

> There is nothing which has brought home to me so much the Unity of the Church, as the Presence of its Divine Founder and Life wherever I go – All places are, as it were, one – while the friends I have left enjoy His Presence and adore Him at Maryvale, He is here also. (254)

---

[20] See (252f.).
[21] See (250f.).

Something else was brought home to him in Milan by the Real Presence of the Lord in the Eucharist and the way the faithful people react to it: Newman realized that the Catholic faith is a real religion, not just a belief among others. He realized that going to church marks the lives of those who live up to their faith, be they educated or not, rich or poor, old or young. The faith gives their lives a special character, which makes them feel at home in cathedrals, in churches or chapels. It makes them take their religion home after the services – in so many forms of devotion, which give their days a structure, linking the natural events of everyday life to the Creator, the Saviour, the Sanctifier, to the Holy Trinity. There are many signs, symbols and images reminding them that they live in the presence of God, wherever they are, in churches as well as in their homes, at their work places and where they meet their friends. Newman had long realized that faith comes from hearing, listening always more carefully to the message of the Gospels and the teachings of the Apostles, as well as that of the Fathers of the Church. Now he realized that faith becomes a real, a transforming strength in the life of the Christian by being lived, primarily in the simple, set acts of responding to the presence of Christ, in holy Liturgy, in the divine service of holy Mass and in the other sacraments, then – in the strength of these – also in the actualities of daily life. In Newman's own words:

> I never knew what worship was, as an objective fact, till I entered the Catholic Church, and was partaker in its offices of devotion, so now I say the same on the view of its cathedral assemblages. (253)

Few could forget the way Newman describes the life in a Catholic cathedral:

> a Catholic Cathedral is a sort of world, every one going about his own business, but that business a religious one; groups of worshippers, and solitary ones – kneeling, standing – some at shrines, some at altars – hearing Mass and communicating – currents of worshippers intercepting and passing each other – altar after altar lit up for worship, like stars in the firmament – or the bell giving notice of what is going on in parts you do not see – and all the while the canons in the choir going through [[their hours]] matins and lauds [[or Vespers]], and at the end of it the incense rolling up from the high altar, and all ... lastly, all of this without any show or effort, but what everyone is used to – every one at his own work, and leaving every one else to his. (253)

In Milan Newman learned what it meant to be at home in Rome, at home in the Roman Catholic faith and Church. When he was still an

Anglican, he had "studiously abstained from the Church services in Italy." Now, thirteen years later, he attended them and truly "entered into them" (253).

3. Preparing for the Ordination to Priesthood in Rome and Finding a Roman Vocation for England

It seemed providential to John Henry Newman that he and Ambrose St John found Pius IX celebrating Mass at St Peter's Confession,[22] when they visited the basilica after their arrival in Rome:

> the first morning I was here at St Peter's – we went to say the Apostles' Creed at St Peter's tomb, the first thing – and there was the Pope, at the tomb saying Mass – so that he was the first person I saw in Rome and I was quite close to him. People say such a thing could hardly have occurred once in a century, for no one can celebrate there but he, and he went by accident (in private) that morning – no one knew he was going. (282)

The College of Propaganda did their utmost to show their eminent student and his friend their respect and to give the converts a true home in a Catholic community. Newman describes in his letters the great care taken by Cardinal Fransoni, the Prefect of *Propaganda*, Mgr Brunelli, the General Secretary of the *Propaganda* and Father Bresciani, the Rector of the *Collegio di Propaganda* to make him feel at home by making "every thing suitable to English habits"(270).

> We are certainly most splendidly lodged … much better off than even in England. They have cut off by a glazed partition the end of the corridor, and such united two opposite rooms, the intercepted portion of the gallery being at once a room of passage, and of reception for strangers. (269)

In a few of his letters he describes "the very nice rooms" (268) and what they contain; everything seems to be new: the furniture, the wall paper, the curtains, the bedclothes and sheets, even the prie-dieus, the writing tables, and the crucifixes. Another time, when he tells how they found their beds made up, the reader almost sees his smile when he speaks about the absurdity to be thought of having curtains around his bed in England (273). "We are treated as if we were princes, much to our distress," he writes, (272), and again with humour, "like wax dolls or mantle piece ornaments" (273). He affirms that they are "anticipating all our wants in the most provoking way" and again he adds with good humour: "so that we were obliged today

---

[22] See Diary in LD XI, Thursday 29th October 1846 (266).

to smuggle some things in, in our pockets" (269). In addition to the very good meals, they are served tea in the evening, stoves are put into their rooms (276), and they receive "a key of the library" (269) the very first day.

They were quite moved – Newman mentions it several times in his letters – that their windows at the Collegio Urbano looked down on the church of San Andrea delle Fratte, where *Our Lady of the Miraculous Medal* had appeared to Alphonse Ratisbonne on 20th January 1842 (269).[23] In Littlemore Newman realized that his Oxford life had been under the protection of the Blessed Virgin; he renamed Old Oscott Mary Vale; a Miraculous Medal and a prayer campaign for Newman in Paris played a role on his way into the Catholic Church. They must have recognized their closeness to that place of her apparition as a sign of God's loving providence. Maria Giberne's[24] painting shows that awareness, too. She depicts Newman and St John, sitting in one of their rooms in the *Collegio,* and Our Lady of the Miraculous Medal stands in the middle behind the two priests, as if protecting them.[25]

Newman was touched by the kindness he met in Rome and only worried, as it seemed to him that his new friends felt respect for someone who lastly remained a stranger to them, "some imagination of their own which bears my name" (294). But such thoughts brought him closer to God as the one who has known him and has always shown him his love guarding his ways. Thus he could write:

> It is so wonderful to find myself here, in Propaganda – it is kind of a dream – and yet so quiet, so safe, so happy – as if I had always been here – as if there had been no violent rupture or vicissitude in my course of life – nay more quiet and happy than before. I was happy at Oriel, happier at Littlemore, as happy or happier still at Maryvale – and happiest here. At least, whether I can rightly compare different times or not, how happy is this very thing that I should ever be thinking the state of life, in which I happen to be in, the happiest of all. There cannot be a more striking proof how I am blest. (294)

The eminent Anglican theologian, thinker and preacher, then author of already sixteen books, co-author or editor of more, leader of the

---

[23] Also e.g. LD XII, 23.

[24] Maria Giberne – a lifelong friend of the Newman family, convert of John Henry Newman.

[25] See LD X, 658, footnote 2 and the photograph of Maria Giberne's painting of Newman and Ambrose St John at the *Propaganda College* with the information of Fr Gregory Winterton in *Benedict XVI and Cardinal Newman*, Peter Jennings (ed.), Family Publications, Oxford 2005, p. 83. Newman sat for the painting on 9th June 1847.

Oxford Movement, and his learned friend Ambrose St John, both Oxford graduates, now converts, found themselves among the young and very young foreign seminarians and young priests, most of them from the mission countries of the Church. Among the 120 to 150 resident students (277, 296) 32 languages were spoken. Newman mentions "Indians, Africans, Babylonians, Scots, and Americans" (272), and again "Chinese ... Egyptians, Albanians, Germans, Irish" (283), he and Ambrose St John being the only English students.

In an early letter he had expressed his disappointment about finding little theology and philosophy in the present theological schools throughout Italy. He hoped that the Pope would do something about the fact that Thomas was loved and venerated as a Saint, but not taken as an authority. Quoting one of the Jesuit fathers, he wrote: "They have no philosophy. *Facts* are the great things, and nothing else. Exegesis, but not doctrine" (279).

Until Christmas 1846, however, Newman and St John voluntarily ("This too was all left to ourselves.") attended with the seminarians three lectures on five days a week, "two dogmatic, and one moral" (273). When they ceased going, they only did what the professors at the *Collegio di Propaganda* had expected them to do from the very beginning. In a letter to one of his group at Maryvale, interested in studying at the *Collegio*, Newman explains why at his time a post graduate student was not catered for at the *Propaganda*. The teaching, its method even more than its content, was addressed to young beginners only. "The lecturers are men quite up with their subject, but the course takes four years" and it takes "lecture after lecture to drawl through a few tedious pages – All this is quite necessary for boys, but not for grown men."[26]

The two Oxford men replaced the lectures by personal studies, deliberating whether to take a doctorate from the *Propaganda*. Newman, however, considered his first duty to make known his theological thinking, especially on faith and reason. It had brought him into the Church and seemed to him to be Catholic. He could see that the phraseology needed to be altered here and there to facilitate the

---

[26] LD XII, 48. Interesting in this context is the letter written by Newman to the Rector of the *Collegio*, LD XII, 88-90. Today the *Collegio Urbano* is a large seminary for young students from the mission countries, who since 1962 study their philosophy and theology at the *Pontifical University Urbaniana* (situated on the campus on the Gianicolo above the Vatican). The large number of graduate students, who follow post-graduate degree courses for a licentiate or a doctorate at that University in philosophy, theology, canon law and missiology, live outside the seminary.

understanding in a Catholic context of different academic traditions. He therefore wrote an explanatory introduction to the planned French translation of six of his *Oxford University Sermons*, giving background knowledge of his thinking on faith and reason to Catholic readers.[27] Before the beginning of March, he also translated four "dissertations" from his *Athanasius* into Latin for publication (60)[28] to counteract a criticism, which was passed on from one of the colleges in Rome to the other, that a "mere theorist" had written the *Essay on Development* (60). Those dissertations gave evidence to the fact, that he had, indeed, "studied, analysed, sorted, and numbered" the phenomena of the documents of ancient theology, as a critic ought to do."[29]

He and St John attended the monthly disputation at the Collegio Romano, at the invitation by the Rector, Fr Passaglia (61). They participated in weekly theological meetings at the English College, invited by the Rector Dr Grant (27). Newman was also content to discuss some of his ideas on faith and reason and on the development of doctrine with Fr Perrone,[30] then quite a celebrity in Rome, whose theory on faith and reason he liked.

Above all, the two converts allowed time for God to show them in which way their group could serve the Church in England. Dr Wiseman had already encouraged them at Maryvale to consider the possibility of an Oratorian vocation. Soon after their arrival in Rome, they contacted the Oratory, making friends with the learned Fr Theiner. From now on they attended now and then services in the Chiesa Nuova, calling at the Oratory house. They informed themselves about the rule and the history of St Philip's Oratory, but they also looked at other congregations.

Newman had great respect for the self-denying life of the Jesuits, "the most wonderful and powerful body among the regulars" (25), for their holiness and selfless devotion (111), which he experienced first hand at the *Collegio di Propaganda*. He thought highly of the Passionists, so "peaceful" and of the Capuchins, so "cheerful", though the two severest orders (62). They read the rule of the Redemptorists (7f) and were in contact with the Franciscans (10f) and the Rosminians (5). He took an interest in the Dominicans in Rome and later developed

---

[27] See LD XII, 5. Until stated otherwise, the numbers in brackets after quotations in the text refer now to pages in LD XII.

[28] These were his insights related to and published with his translation of Athanasius in the *Library of the Fathers*.

[29] Loc. cit. On 12th May Newman could give the Rector his copy.

[30] See LD XII, 55 incl. footnote 3.

a lifelong love for the Benedictines, yet, he could not imagine himself becoming a monk or a modern regular like the Jesuit. He was aware that it would not only mean at the age of forty-six to give up "property" and "take to new habits" but lastly to part with his whole former life, which had not just been his, private to him. His name, his person, his books were known to many whom he never had met in person. As a regular he would cut off all this, and if he were still speaking and writing, people would not know whether he was passing on what was thought in his community (as "a sort of instrument of others") or whether he was speaking his own words. With one word, he needed what he called *"continuation, as it were, of my former self."*[31]

On the one hand he did not want to become a monk, on the other hand he thought they had "a calling to a life more strict than a secular's." There the Oratorian Rule seemed "a sort of '*Deus ex machina*' to him" (16). On 17th January he began a letter to Mgr Wiseman: "It is curious and very pleasant that, after all the thought we can give the matter, we come round to your Lordship's original idea, and feel we cannot do better than be Oratorians." (19f) That was also the first day of a novena of daily pilgrimages to St Peter from the eve of the Feast of St Peter's Chair, then on 18th January, to that of the conversion of St Paul on 25th January – for light in that matter.

On 21st February, Newman's birthday, Mgr Brunelli, the Secretary of *Propaganda* gained the Holy Father's approbation of Newman's calling to introduce St Philip's Oratory to England. Pope Pius IX expressed his joy by offering the Monastery of *Santa Croce in Gerusalemme* to the future English Congregation of St Philip Neri for the first part of their noviciate from July to December 1847 in Rome. This caused Newman to remark that this meant to live in the centre of the Church. St Helena had not only brought Christ's Cross from Jerusalem to Rome, but with it earth from the Mount Calvary. Santa Croce is Jerusalem in the midst of Rome.[32]

One month before they moved to Santa Croce, on St Philip's day, 26th May, Cardinal Fransoni ordained Ambrose St John and John Henry Newman Subdeacons "in his private chapel" (84).[33] On 29th May they were ordained Deacons in St John Lateran by the Cardinal Vicar. On Trinity Sunday, 30th May, Cardinal Fransoni ordained them

---

[31] LD XI, 306, *italics* by Newman.

[32] See (79).

[33] Recently the altar, where Newman celebrated his first mass and which had been moved to the new Collegio Urbano on the Gianicolo, was returned to the Propaganda Fide on the Piazza di Spagna and a small chapel was set up there.

Priests. This must have been in the Propaganda church (84),[34] as all the students were present and they had the organ play. After the ordination they went to see the house in Santa Croce. On Corpus Christi Newman celebrated his first mass in the Jesuits' chapel on the altar of St Hyacinth, close to his room.

They moved to Santa Croce on 28th June, and on the next day, Newman celebrated the mass for the Feast of Peter and Paul. In the evening all of them walked to St Peter's as in those nine days in January, this time in thanksgiving.

In the centre of the Church, in Santa Croce, Newman would more and more find the heart of St Philip, and under his guidance the Heart of Jesus, the light of his soul, whom he adored in the Eucharist. In the grace of his vocation, and in the sign of the cross, he would become a Father of souls in the new Oratory of St Philip. When Newman left Rome in December, he carried the brief with him.

III. Self-giving and Late Reward

Newman's first stay in Rome was marked by "the bitterest, the most loving, the most melancholy moods and thoughts." Bitterness and melancholy accompanied the many sights of what Newman had called the first and the third view of Rome; they were not evoked by the sights alone, but by all the thoughts and theories, notions and impressions that came with them.

His second stay seemed not at all burdened by that dark, heavy or melancholic reasoning that had marked the first; the bitter and sharp criticism; the restless comparing for the better or the worse. Newman had discovered in the churches of Milan and Rome what gave the people around him light and peace, consolation and joy. Above all it is the Eucharistic presence of the Lord, of which the tabernacles and the sanctuary lamps speak.

Then there are the Saints, of whom the many statues remind the faithful who enter a church. In a letter to his sister Jemima, Newman describes the catacomb of St Agnes in a way, which might have brought home to her that the teaching of the Roman Catholic Church on the practice of Mass, or on the practice of confession, or on the extraordinary greatness of Mary among all the other saints, had been the teaching of the ancient Church.

A glance at Newman's third and fourth time in Rome brings to

---

[34] See there, footnote 2.

mind two more aspects of what Rome meant to him. His third trip in 1856 was undertaken in the immense effort to solve some problems in the interpretation of the Oratorian rule, which had evolved between the two houses in England, before the wound of disunity would start to fester. That mission was most strenuous for Newman at a time when he was burdened with the double task of the Oratory House in Birmingham and the University project in Dublin. It manifests his humble and simple trust in Rome, in the hierarchy, the Holy Father and those in responsibility at the Propaganda, who had helped him with the preparations to set up the Oratories in Birmingham and London.

When Newman travelled again and for the last time to Rome in 1879, the Holy Father had called him. He wanted to honour him for the good of the whole Church by creating him Cardinal. It was once more a homecoming, as the Holy See thus acknowledged his lifelong untiring effort to defend the truth against liberalism in religion and to live for Christ's Body, the Church. Newman accepted that honour in humility and simplicity of heart.

Newman's room at the Birmingham Oratory in Hagley Road.

Chapter 4

NEWMAN AND BIRMINGHAM

by Paul Chavasse

Tuesday 1 July 1879 proved to be a wet day, but the rain could not prevent large crowds from making their way to the Oratory Church on the Hagley Road in Birmingham's prosperous suburb of Edgbaston, in order to witness a remarkable sight. After some delay, caused by a cold which had turned to pneumonia, the newly created Cardinal Newman was expected back from Rome after a long and wearisome journey. He arrived at New Street Station and was greeted there by some of the leading Catholics of the City, who escorted him to his carriage. The Oratory is a little over a mile from the station and this gave the Cardinal time to change from his travelling clothes into his red piped cassock, skull cap and biretta, as well as striking red *ferraiolo* or cloak. The young Henry Bellasis takes up the story: "When the policeman gave us in solemn whisper at the front door the news 'They are here sir!' up drove the carriage (- pouring with rain by the bye -) and the Father got out in – so to speak – full costume."[1]

Eventually the Cardinal reached the Sanctuary of his church, where he received the homage of his community with great affection. Then, sitting down, and leaning his head on his hand, Newman spoke, according to an eye-witness, a most beautiful and touching address and began by saying: "It is such happiness to come *home.*"[2]

For forty-one years Birmingham was the place where John Henry Newman had his home. As a city, it was a place unlike anything with which he had been familiar. Although born in London, his early years had been spent in Alton, Hampshire, followed by the long years of his

---

[1] Meriol Trevor, *Newman, Light in Winter* (Macmillan & Co., London, 1962) p. 574.

[2] These words are as given by Henry Tristram in a private memorandum. A slightly different version will be found in William P. Neville (ed.), *Addresses to Cardinal Newman with his Replies 1879-81* (Longmans, London, 1905), p. 103.

sojourn in the university town of Oxford, a place he was to describe as "nearest to my heart". Eventually, just as other friends came to replace Hurrell Froude, whom he had lost, so Birmingham came to take the place of Oxford, however inadequately.

John Henry Newman first saw Birmingham fifteen years before he took up residence there. His diary for 16 January 1834 records: "Breakfasted at Birmingham" and in later years he added in parentheses "The first time I saw Birmingham."[3] He makes no mention of any impression the city made on him then, although he must have been struck by the fact that it was already a fast-growing industrial centre, a world apart from his usual haunts.

It was not until after the events surrounding his conversion and the decisions for the future of himself and his friends had been made that Birmingham became the place where God's providence determined they should live. Nicholas Wiseman, Vicar Apostolic of the Midland District, had watched Newman's Anglican deathbed from his residence at Oscott College, on the outskirts of Birmingham. When the new converts were looking for a place to settle, Wiseman offered them the property of Old Oscott, a couple of miles from the College, which Newman promptly renamed Maryvale. In those days it was in the country; now it is swallowed up by the suburb of Kingstanding. It was at Maryvale that the English Congregation of the Oratory of St Philip Neri was set up at Vespers on 1 February 1848, with Newman as the first Superior.

The Papal Brief establishing the Oratory in England named Birmingham as the place where it was to be located. Soon after this took place, Newman's original community was noticeably increased in size by the arrival of Fr Frederick William Faber and his group of converts. The eventual division of the community between the Birmingham and London houses led Newman to think seriously about which city should be his home, given that many people thought his talents would be better used in London, where he would have greater access to the more educated and influential classes of society.

Despite the claims put upon him, and despite his passing inclination to move, Newman decided that it was to be in Birmingham that his work for God would take place. Years before, when only a month in the Catholic Church, Newman had realised Birmingham's limitations. Writing to Dalgairns from Littlemore concerning Bishop Wiseman's

---

[3] Ian Ker & Thomas Gornall (ed.), *The Letters and Diaries of John Henry Newman* (Clarendon Press, Oxford, 1980), vol. 4, p. 176.

offer and their future work, he had said: "London is a centre – Oxford is a centre – Brummagem is no centre."[4]

With the decision made to stay in Birmingham, and even though the problem of maintaining Fr Faber's mission at St Wilfrid's at Cheadle in Staffordshire was not resolved, Newman began the search for a more centrally placed property in the city, which would provide a more suitable home for the Oratorian community and a more appropriate setting for their apostolic labours.

On 23 October 1848 Newman recorded in his diary: "closed with the owner of the House, near Deritend, for three years."[5] Preceded by some others of the community, Newman himself moved into the new house on 26 January 1849, and the following day recorded: "Altar set up in Alcester Street for mass – first time."[6] The Chapel was opened for the Feast of the Purification, 2 February, with the Mass being celebrated by Fr Ambrose St John, Newman preaching the sermon, and Mr Hardman providing the music, which was described as "Gregorianized". The sermon later became the first piece in *Discourses addressed to Mixed Congregations*, entitled "The salvation of the hearer the motive of the preacher."[7]

The premises where the Oratorians now lived was nondescript, and had formerly been a gin house or distillery and, more recently, a marine store. This building had an ornate classical façade, rather out of keeping with the surrounding houses. The house itself, which formed three sides of a quadrangle, comprised sixteen bedrooms, three sitting-rooms, a chapel for the community, and a library, where Newman could put his collection of the Church Fathers. It was the ground floor of this house which became the public chapel, and it was immediately filled to overflowing. The first Sunday, they had two services, with Newman telling Faber that in the morning "the chapel full – crammed – but not a good collection ... viz. £1.13s."[8] Two policemen were in attendance for the evening service, as trouble was expected from militant Protestants. Nevertheless, as Newman wrote to R. A. Coffin: "we had 500 or 600 in Chapel last night – a sea (as they say) of heads."[9] On Tuesday 6 February the Fathers began

---

[4] Charles Stephen Dessain (ed.), *The Letters and Diaries of John Henry Newman* (Thomas Nelson and Sons, London, 1961 onwards), vol. 11, p. 30.

[5] Dessain, *Letters and Diaries*, vol. 12, p. 305.

[6] Ibid., vol. 13, p. 16.

[7] J. H. Newman, *Discourses addressed to Mixed Congregations* (Longmans, London, 1849).

[8] Dessain, *Letters and Diaries*, vol. 13, p. 24.

[9] Ibid., p. 26.

giving instructions in the faith, with some 40 children turning up, and Newman heard confessions in the chapel for the first time.[10] So the work of the mission got under way and it soon became demanding: by the summer of 1849 they were preaching four sermons every Sunday; giving a lecture every weekday evening, and the catechism classes were attracting over a hundred children. As well as this Newman was busy drawing up plans for the division of the community – Fr Faber and several others were to be sent to London to open the Oratory there. They departed on 15 April and on 31 May the London Oratory duly opened on King William Street, off the Strand, with Newman preaching at the evening service. Back in Birmingham, the feast of Corpus Christi (7 June) was marked by the mission's first High Mass, with Newman being the celebrant. The work was not all pastoral; some light relief came on 18 June when he "gave a flash Lecture on Poetry – to the Birmingham Catholic Reading Society Association", which met in St Chad's School rooms. Newman said it "was a splendid concern ... for really I quite laughed when I was delivering it. I said absurd things which I knew they would applaud – and when they did, it quite overcame me – *emotion* it certainly was."[11]

What sort of an area had Newman come to? The Victoria County History of Warwickshire tells us that Deritend, where Alcester Street was, had the highest population density in the city and was "an area of piecemeal development on small sites, in courts and narrow streets, while the proximity of the Warwick and Birmingham Canal encouraged the building of workshops and warehouses."[12] Newman wrote to Ambrose Lisle Phillips of "me and mine in Birmingham amid our labyrinth of lanes and beneath our firmament of smoke."[13] Many of the inhabitants would have been recent arrivals and a fair proportion of them Irish Catholics, with poverty being the distinguishing mark. The number of children attending the Oratory services and classes led to early thoughts of some sort of a school, but with little hope of it being realised as city children at that time who were over the age of seven went to work until 8pm In fact much of the Oratory's work in those early days had to be concentrated into two hours between 7 and 9pm, when there was "a rush of all sorts."[14]

---

[10] Dessain, *Letters and Diaries*, vol. 13, p. 26.

[11] Dessain, *Letters and Diaries*, vol. 13, p. 239.

[12] The Victoria County History of the County of Warwick (Oxford University Press, London, 1964), vol. 7, p. 13.

[13] Dessain, *Letters and Diaries*, vol. 13, p. 445.

[14] Dessain, *Letters and Diaries*, vol. 13, p. 44.

Before that busy year of 1849 was over one of the most famous incidents in Newman's early life in Birmingham took place. In early September he fell ill with a heavy cold, which brought on deafness. Despite not being able to say Mass for some days, on 15 September he went, along with Fr Ambrose St John and Br Aloysius Boland, to nearby Bilston, in order to assist the local priest who was struggling to cope with an outbreak of cholera in the town. He stayed a few days, even though the disease was subsiding and there was not too much work to do.[15] The reaction of the congregation at Alcester Street was one of panic, with people in tears and prayers being offered for the safety of those who had gone to Bilston. Fr Joseph Gordon wrote of "the hearts and tears of your most affectionate and devout people"[16] – which shows how quickly Newman and the Oratory had won a large and loyal congregation.

Who exactly was at the Oratory in these early months? Published in 1849, Allen's *Pictorial Guide to Birmingham* has the entry: "The Congregation of the Oratory of St Philip Neri, Alcester Street – consists of sixteen members, of whom eight are priests. The Rev J. H. Newman is Superior of the Community." Two years later, the census of 1851 also gives us a glimpse of the community in those early years: at numbers 39 and 40 Alcester Street there were then six priests, viz. Frs John Henry Newman, Ambrose St John, Frederick Bowles, Henry Austin Mills, Nicholas Darnell and John Joseph Gordon; two church students, John Stanislaus Flanagan and Edward Caswall; and five lay brothers, David Jennings, Bernard Hennin, Charles Gradwick, Thomas Godwin, Francis Davis and Edward Smith. Also resident was the Church organist, James Pitts. In addition to these, at number 37 resided two more church students, Henry Bittleston and Stuart Bathurst and an "errand boy", John Flynn aged 12.[17]

In 1851 an American traveller in England, the Revd A. C. Coxe of Hartford, afterwards Episcopalian Bishop of Western New York, sought out the chapel in Alcester Street in order to hear Newman preach. So he found himself, as he described it,

> in a low and dirty-looking place of worship in which the first object that met my eye was an immense doll of almost ludicrous aspect, representing the Virgin, with the crescent beneath her feet[18]

---

[15] Cf. Dessain, *Letters and Diaries*, vol. 13, pp. 258-60.
[16] Ibid., p. 258.
[17] National Archives, 1851 census, ref. H.O. 107/2060
[18] Ironically, Newman himself had a "perfect hatred" of this statue and contrived to leave it behind when he left Alcester Street.

... [Then] a lank and spectral figure appeared at the door of the chancel, stalked in and prostrated himself before the altar ... I felt a chill creep over me as he mounted his rostrum and turned towards us his almost maniacal visage. There could be no mistake. It was indeed poor fallen Newman. ... I could not learn that he was doing much by all his efforts.[19]

It may well have been that "poor fallen Newman" was doing more than it was given to Coxe to suspect. Although he had no particularly rosy picture about the city in which God and St Philip had placed him, Newman had the greatest hopes that the work of the Oratory in Birmingham would bring in a rich harvest, and that his "efforts" would be blessed.

Writing as early as February 1847, Newman reflected on what Birmingham was like:

the City of Birmingham, a most thickly populated place, remarkable for its recent flock of converts, but full of every sort of heresy, with its youth skilled in the trades but holding a false religion or none at all. This City was for many years the centre of those organisations which were actively hostile to the laws of nature and society; and also of those Associations, the Mechanics' Institutes, devoted to the perverse cultivation of literature (good in itself) and of an unhealthy science, which that English lawyer, Lord Brougham, for these twenty years has spread all over England, in order to teach the people Science, and make them unlearn their religion.[20]

As the years passed Newman's view of his adopted city did not particularly mellow. Writing in 1850 to Philip Howard, who lived at Corby Castle, near Carlisle, he said: "As to Birmingham, it is an odd place and it is certainly not so well inclined to Catholicism as some places in the neighbourhood ..."[21] In similar vein and ten years later, Newman wrote of the city to Canon Estcourt, Bishop Ullathorne's right hand man, saying it was the sort of place "where nearly everyone is a nothingarian, an infidel, a sceptic, or an inquirer ...".[22] But in that same letter to Estcourt, Newman expressed very clearly the fact that in Birmingham, something could be achieved: "Here Catholic efforts are not only good in themselves, and do good, but cannot possibly do any even incidental harm – here, whatever is done, is so much gain."

---

19 Cf. Meriol Trevor, Newman, *The Pillar and the Cloud* (Macmillan & Co., London, 1962), pp. 542-3.
[20] Placid Murray (ed.), *Newman the Oratorian* (Gill & Macmillan, Dublin, 1969), pp. 153-4.
[21] F. McGrath (ed.), *The Letters and Diaries of John Henry Newman* (Oxford University Press, forthcoming),vol. 32, p. 44.
[22] Dessain, *Letters and Diaries*, vol. 19, p. 352.

This positive view of the apostolate in Birmingham echoed what Newman put in a "round robin" letter, sent to all those he thought might be able to contribute financially to the success of St Philip's institute in Birmingham, and which was sent out in the summer of 1850.

> Every order and congregation in the Church has its own work, and ours specially lies among the population of great towns and still more directly with the educated or half-educated or professedly educated portion of it. Here in Birmingham our object will be to influence the tone of thought and opinion prevalent in the various circles of society, high or low; to recommend Catholicism, to expose Protestantism, and especially to take care of young men. We have been here about a year and a half; and have been sufficiently blessed to feel sanguine that St Philip will make use of us here, if once we get established ... .[23]

This letter had been written, because, as Newman put it: "We are collecting subscriptions for a Church". The decision had been made to leave Alcester Street and to find another site for the Oratory, which would become its permanent home. In his Oratory Papers Newman describes the process: "In the years 1848, 1849, our views of buildings were limited to the localities of Deritend, Alcester Street, Smithfield, Carr's Lane and the Moseley and Bristol Roads. In Spring 1850 Mr Tarlton, without our seeking it, found out the ground, which still remains unpurchased, at the corner of Francis Road, Hagley Road ..."[24]

Edgbaston, where this plot of land lay, was a fast developing suburb of Birmingham, and was the home of professional and wealthy citizens. In 1851 a little over 9,000 people lived in Edgbaston; within twenty years that population would nearly double. The adjoining area of Ladywood, much of which would also become part of the Oratory parish, although poorer, was undergoing a similar expansion: in 1851 the population was just over 20,000; by 1871 it would be over 42,000. It was to this burgeoning part of the city that Newman set his sights.

In the event the process of moving would not be easy. Practically the whole of Edgbaston was (and is) part of a single estate, owned by the Calthorpe family, and so available freehold sites were few and far between. The Francis Road plot was soon acquired, as Newman told Faber: "We have just bought a piece of ground at the corner of *two* ways just beyond the Five Ways, at Edgebaston [sic], a mile from the Town Hall, on the high road, in the gentlest neighbourhood, price

---

[23] McGrath, *Letters and Diaries*, vol. 32, p. 43; cf. Dessain, *Letters and Diaries,* vol. 14, p. 33.
[24] Murray, *Newman the Oratorian*, p. 307.

£1400, size 40 yards by 65."[25] Although "everyone in Birmingham is in such raptures at the site,"[26] almost immediately problems began. Newman discovered that, in all likelihood, there was a local act which would prevent them building flush with the road. Sacrificing the requisite amount of land would mean that the space left was virtually useless, a conclusion Newman soon reached after trying to juggle plans for a house and a church, even if the latter were to be circular! Even when the adjoining plot became available in March 1850, the price of £2000 was more than the Oratory could manage.

Fortuitously, in the middle of April 1850 Newman was told that another plot of land was available a quarter of a mile further down the road, on the triangle between Hagley Road, Plough and Harrow Road, and Monument Road. This was purchased in May 1850 for £1800 and the first piece of land was resold. On 22 May the Oratorians voted to start work on building a house and a church on the site. Local interest in what was happening was intense, as Newman wrote to Faber: "The Edgebaston [sic] worthies are in great commotion."[27]

These were busy months for Newman, for not only was he striving to acquire suitable building land for his community, but he was also travelling to and from London, giving his series of talks at the London Oratory entitled *Certain Difficulties Felt by Anglicans in Catholic Teaching*. These began on 9 May and were given twice a week, on Thursdays and Fridays, until 5 July, apart from Whit Week and the last two weeks in June. It is noticeable that the volume of Newman's letters decreases markedly at this time!

Newman's workload now was so intense that he often succumbed to heavy colds, which showed his whole system was overtaxed. The timetables for these Alcester Street days have survived and they reveal Newman taking his turn week after week and month after month with preaching and instructing and confessing. Indeed, at Christmas 1850 he doubled and then trebled his hours in the often bug-ridden confessionals in order to give the other Fathers a respite.

1850 saw the restoration of the Hierarchy in England and Wales and Newman made one of his appearances at St Chad's Cathedral in order to preach at the High Mass of Thanksgiving. He regarded the giving of this sermon, 'Christ upon the Waters', as a penance, but Bishop Ullathorne thought it one of his most remarkable and urged

---

[25] Dessain, *Letters and Diaries*, vol. 13, pp. 438-9.
[26] Ibid., p. 441.
[27] Ibid., p. 447.

its publication. The restoration of the Hierarchy caused great unrest in England, with demonstrations against what was thought of as an act of Papal aggression. This delicate situation coincided with the first death in the Oratorian community. Fr John Cooke, who was 32 years old, had been in the Oratory for only 18 months and was already suffering from consumption when he entered. On 5 November 1850 he was taken seriously ill and a week later he died. The following morning, 13 November, Newman sang a High Mass of Requiem in the Alcester Street chapel in the presence of the body, and in the evening what he called in his diary a "funeral service" was held, in the presence of a "crowd." What actually occurred was reported in *The Times* on 15 November, and revealed the volatile nature of the Birmingham crowd, who presumably suspected foul play surrounding Fr Cooke's death.

> A tumult of an unusual description occurred at the chapel of the Oratorians (an order of Monks), in Alcester-street, in this town on Wednesday night ... the body [of Fr Cooke] was exhibited in the chapel ... In the evening a large number of persons congregated in Alcester-street and the chapel was soon crammed to suffocation by a most miscellaneous assemblage ... although the congregation within was as far as possible orderly, the mob without was somewhat tumultuous ... Many persons in the street, attracted by curiosity, if not by other less worthy motives, attempted to force an entrance into the edifice... .

Newman sent for the police, who restored order, and the service was concluded behind closed doors.[28]

By the time of Fr John Cooke's death, the plans for the Edgbaston house had been submitted, and building began. What was on foot did not escape observation. The architect of the house, Terence Flanagan,[29] not unnaturally, included cellars in his plans for the building. When news of this got out the neighbourhood was seized with alarm: in the popular imagination the cellars became cells, obviously designed for sinister purposes. Newman was giving his lectures on the "*Present Position of Catholics*" at the Corn Exchange on Birmingham's High Street and took the opportunity to defuse the situation with humour, addressing a "large and respectable" audience on the misconceptions that abounded concerning Catholicism. He made some of his points so amusingly that it was reported that the laughter could be heard on the street outside. On the national scene the rumours about the nature of the Oratorians' dwelling continued, with W. Spooner MP (maternal

---

[28] Dessain, *Letters and Diaries*, vol. 14, p. 126.
[29] See note, Dessain, *Letters and Diaries*, vol. 13, p. 447.

uncle of Newman's good friends the Wilberforces), denouncing in the House of Commons the "underground cells" in Edgbaston. Newman wrote to the papers pointing out the true nature of the buildings, but the correspondence gained the heading: "The Apostate Newman's defence of Underground Cells in Convents"!

Through it all the construction work went on; as Newman wrote: "Our house is rising at Edgbaston – we have been able to build all through the winter. It is quite frightful, the space of ground it covers."[30] He records that some 1,700,000 bricks would be used in the building of it, and in his diary he makes mention of visits to the site (including one on Good Friday 1851) to inspect the progress being made.

On 15 February 1852 Newman wrote to Dalgairns: "Tomorrow morning at 10 I say the first Mass in the new house – a Missa cantata[31] – the two Frederics and the choir astonishing the corridors, the workmen, and the public of Edgbaston with their voices. The altar at the end of the cross corridor ..."[32] He took up his quarters in the new house and on 3 April was able to note in his diary: "finished getting in all my books and papers into my room at Edgbaston", although later on he added to the entry: "all the time thinking I might have to leave them for prison!"[33] Newman is here referring to the Achilli trial and its expected outcome. He was also in the middle of preparing lectures on University Education to be delivered in Dublin – an indication of the new work soon to begin with the founding of the Catholic University there. On 13 April Cardinal Wiseman came to inspect the new house, and two days later Newman left the Alcester Street mission for good, although one Father was to keep the church going until the Bishop finalised other arrangements. On the feast of St Philip, 26 May, the community finally took full possession of its new, permanent, home.

After the house, the great need was for the building of a church. Newman had already given some thought to this – his diary for 18 December 1851 reveals that he had had some plans drawn up by the French architect Louis Joseph Duc (1802-1879).[34] However, Newman soon found himself in a quandary. He had practically no resources of

---

[30] Dessain, *Letters and Diaries*, vol. 14, p. 232.
[31] Appropriately it was a Mass in honour of St Philip Neri, founder of the Oratory. Cf. Dessain, *Letters and Diaries*, vol. 15, p. 48.
[32] Ibid., p. 32.
[33] Ibid., p. 62.
[34] Dessain, *Letters and Diaries*, vol. 14, p. 476. It has since been shown that the architect involved was not Viollet le Duc, as indicated in the footnote on that page.

his own to draw upon, and it was difficult to launch a public appeal for funds, as even then subscriptions were coming in from all over the world to meet the heavy costs of the Achilli trial. He therefore decided to abandon for the time being designs for an ambitious church building and contented himself with putting up something sufficient for immediate needs. Even so, his letters reveal the great care he took in finding suitable fittings – candlesticks, pictures and statues, crucifixes, relics and vestments – to adorn the church. On 31 March 1853 the contract was settled for "our temporary chapel", as he called it, and on 4 April 1853 the first stone was laid. Work took longer than expected – a poor summer's weather, delays with plasterers and painters – and so the hoped for opening date of 1 November, All Saints Day, was not possible. It was not until the feast of St Cecilia, 22 November, that the church was finally opened. As usual, Newman was recovering from a bad cold, getting up in order to say Mass himself and then to preach at the High Mass celebrated by Bishop Ullathorne and welcome the guests afterwards.[35]

The church had no pretensions to being architecturally beautiful; in fact it consisted of nothing more than four plain brick walls and a roof, and the roof itself was bought, ready-made and second-hand, from a disused factory. During the next few years Newman's attention was occupied with setting up the Catholic University in Dublin, but when he returned to Birmingham for good in 1857, he realised that the church was inadequate to the growing demands of the neighbourhood, and so almost immediately he enlarged it by the addition of an aisle, while the roof was raised at the same time. These alterations were completed by 8 August 1858, and Newman, the only priest in the house that Sunday, celebrated the first Mass. Immediately afterwards work began on converting two small rooms into what would become St Philip's Chapel, the only part of the original church complex to survive to today. Two years later a transept and an apsidal sanctuary were added, and the opening ceremonies to mark these additions took place on 10 February 1861, a cold, sleety Sunday. There was a High Mass in the morning and a Te Deum in the evening, with instrumental music. The architect employed for these alterations was John Hungerford Pollen, who designed the University Church in Dublin in accordance with Newman's wishes.

The church contained eight altars in all, one of which, somewhat set apart, was in the Bona Mors Chapel, and it was here that Newman

---

[35] Dessain, *Letters and Diaries*, vol. 15, p. 482.

regularly celebrated Mass, as its seclusion and privacy appealed to him. Fr Henry Tristram, who knew the "old Church" as it came to be called, recollected "the church with which Cardinal Newman was forced through lack of means to content himself for all his days, dingy, shabby and dowdy, although quaint and attractive in many ways, and entirely devotional."[36]

With both House and Church completed, the remaining architectural endeavours which concerned Newman were to do with the Oratory School, which he founded and which was opened on 2 May 1859. The present "Cloister Buildings", designed by Henry Clutton[37], and which form such a distinctive part of the Oratory's Hagley Road frontage, date from this time.

Newman's work for education, both with the Oratory School and the later St Philip's Grammar School, which began in 1887, are important contributions to the story of Newman's connections with Birmingham, although this is not the place to examine them in detail.

It is interesting to note that, given all the work Newman undertook to establish the Oratory – the house and church, the schools and the orphanage, the work done in parish, prison and workhouse – he still felt detached from his adopted city. Writing to Dean Church in 1864, he said: "This very town of Birmingham, of course, knows nothing of me ...".[38] Again, in 1866, when a group of Birmingham notables asked him to sit for a portrait, he hesitated because he was "deeply conscious" that he had "been of no use whatever to this great Town"; indeed he had "almost been a stranger amid its large population."[39] In 1867, when he finally acceded to the renewed request, he remarked again that he had "done nothing" for Birmingham – "I have paid my rates as an honest man, but have no claim on the place for any sort of service done for it of any kind."[40] In the book "Nine Famous Birmingham Men", published in 1909, J. H. Muirhead, who was Professor of Philosophy at Birmingham University, makes a similar

---

[36] Henry Tristram, Cong. Orat., *Cardinal Newman and the Church of the Birmingham Oratory* (The British Publishing Co., Gloucester, 1934), p. 33.

[37] Henry Clutton (1819–1893), notable church architect in the early French Gothic style; runner-up in the design competition for Westminster Cathedral. He was the brother-in-law of Fr Ignatius Ryder of the Birmingham Oratory.

[38] Dessain, *Letters and Diaries*, vol. 21, p. 100.

[39] Dessain, *Letters and Diaries*, vol. 22, p. 230.

[40] Dessain, *Letters and Diaries*, vol. 23, p. 379. Another reason was admitted to later on – see Dessain, *Letters and Diaries*, vol. 28, p. 178:"I had no wish at all to be put in a collection together with a set of liberal party men or town celebrities with whom I had nothing in common."

point. He wrote of Newman and Birmingham: "He owed it little but a resting-place. He lived, it is true, for the last forty years of his life in Birmingham, but he took no part in its business or government. He was as effectively cut off from its busy life as was the quiet chamber in which he thought and wrote, behind those great iron railings, from the noise and traffic of the Hagley Road ... [he was] in it, but not of it; yet perhaps of it too as far as it was possible for one like him to be of any earthly city ... ."[41]

Muirhead has a point, we may say, but it would not be true to say that Newman had no interest in some of the wider aspects of Birmingham's life. His famous retort to Mgr George Talbot, when declining the invitation to preach a series of sermons in Rome, "Birmingham people have souls"[42], indicates how he saw his real work in the city. On occasion in later life he did engage in city matters. In November 1889 he interceded in a dispute when the female work-force at the local Cadbury chocolate factory refused to attend their Quaker employers' daily Bible classes. When appealed to, although thick snow lay on the ground, Newman drove to Bournville to see the Cadbury brothers, who were "charmed by the loving Christian spirit with which he entered into the question."[43] As a result a room was set aside especially for Catholic prayers.

Less controversial was his involvement in an aspect of Birmingham's cultural life. Newman's love of music is well known and he was proficient as both a player and a composer. He took great care over the music performed at the Oratory, running the Choir himself for a time, and drawing up precise rules for the organist. In 1877 he preached a memorable sermon on church music, the occasion being the blessing and inauguration of a new organ in the church.[44] It comes as no surprise, therefore, that he was interested in the musical life of his adopted city, telling the Fathers in 1856: "Music is one of the special characteristics of the Oratory, and it is the art for which Birmingham is famous."[45] The basis for this remark is the fact that Birmingham hosted, every three years, a Music Festival, which was of international renown, with many composers writing new pieces especially for it. The Festival began in 1784 and from 1834 was held at the Town Hall, with the proceeds helping the finances of Birmingham's General

[41] J. H. Muirhead (ed.), *Nine Famous Birmingham Men* (Cornish Brothers Ltd., Birmingham, 1909), pp. 183, 205-6.
[42] Dessain, *Letters and Diaries*, vol. 21, pp. 165-7.
[43] Dessain, *Letters and Diaries*, vol. 31, p. 278, note.
[44] See *The Tablet*, 25 August 1877.
[45] Murray, *Newman the Oratorian*, p. 309.

Hospital. Usually taking place over three or four days in the last week of August, the Festival drew large crowds. Newman makes mention of it in his letters, and after he became a Cardinal in 1879 he was invited to become one of the (many) Vice-Presidents, an office he fulfilled for the festivals of 1882, 1885 and 1888, donating £5 on the first two occasions. It is recorded that he attended rehearsals as well as the actual performances, but he was not an uncritical listener. At the 1879 Festival a piece by Wagner (*The Supper of the Apostles*) he described as all "sound and fury", and in 1882 *The March to Calvary*, part of Gounod's oratorio *Redemption*, Newman likened to "the bombardment of Alexandria." More to his taste was Rossini's *Mosé in Egitto*, which he heard on 27 August 1879, and Cherubini's *Requiem in C minor,* performed on 29 August the same year. Some years later, in November 1886, it was twice performed in the Oratory church and the old Cardinal said afterwards: "It is magnificent music. That is a beautiful Mass, but when you get as old as I am, it comes rather too home."[46]

Attending the Festival on 1 September 1882, in company with Edward Bellasis, the programme commenced with Mozart's *Symphony in G minor*; a woman behind the Cardinal talked throughout. It was followed by Brahms's *Triumphlied,* which Newman disliked, but the din of which drowned the talker's voice. Newman whispered: "Brahms is a match for her". That was followed, to his relief, by Cherubini's *Mass in C*, which he thought beautiful, and Beethoven's *Mount of Olives.* The talkative woman tried to engage Newman in conversation when the morning concert ended around 3pm; he was then trapped by a second woman, "who detained him upon questions relative to the state of the soul after death, what St Thomas had said, etc. Meanwhile sweepers, uninterested in this ill-timed discussion, were pursuing their avocation in the emptying hall, and stewards were set wondering as to when His Eminence would be released"![47]

Newman's connection with the Triennial Festival was maintained, albeit posthumously, through his famous poem, *The Dream of Gerontius*. This had been written at the Oratory in January 1865, was first published in the May and June numbers of *The Month*, and then independently in November that same year. The poem was dedicated to Fr John Joseph Gordon of the Birmingham Oratory, who had died in 1853. The Oratorian Fathers wished to have the poem set

---

[46] Edward Bellasis, *Coram Cardinali* (Longmans, Green & Co., London, 1916), p. 21.

[47] Ibid., pp. 20-1, note.

to music and offered it, in German translation, to Antonin Dvořák, who ultimately declined the commission.[48] It was Edward Elgar who eventually accepted the task, and having selected some three hundred of the nine hundred words Newman wrote, produced an oratorio for the Triennial Festival of 1900. The first performance on 3 October was a disaster, due to a combination of factors, including insufficient rehearsals. Nevertheless, within a decade it had become a firm favourite with choral societies everywhere, and it serves to link forever the names of Newman and Elgar.[49]

When Cardinal Newman came to die in August 1890 the reaction from Birmingham showed that, for all his talk of being unknown and having done nothing for the city, he had become part of the fabric of the place. His years of quiet, unassuming pastoral work – visiting the housebound, finding jobs for the unemployed, giving coal to the poor, paying for medicines for the sick, hearing confessions, preaching and saying Mass, his enormous correspondence – had left their mark, and many came to pay their respects at his lying-in-state. The *Leicester Daily Post* reported that: "A stream of visitors passed through the Oratory yesterday, to view the body of the late Cardinal lying in state. At one time the crush was so great as to become almost unmanageable... ."[50] These visitors to the church comprised almost every class and every age, as the *Daily Mail* put it: "from the venerable gentleman of affluence, to the butcher-boy with his basket on his arm." Another paper, the Dublin-based *Freeman's Journal*, wrote: "No peer, or prince, or priest, or merchant who ever walked the crowded streets of Birmingham is so missed or mourned as the Roman Cardinal."[51] On 19 August, the day of the funeral, an estimated fifteen to twenty thousand people lined the streets as the cortege wound its eight-mile journey to Rednal, for the peaceful burial. Many of the houses passed en route had black drapes hanging from their windows.

What was the secret of it all? Many of the visitors who came to the Oratory over the years and experienced Newman's gracious

---

[48] It is interesting to note that his setting of the *Requiem Mass*, which had its first performance at the Triennial Festival of 1891, was dedicated in memory of Cardinal Newman.

[49] The Birmingham Oratory Archives possesses the original manuscript score of Elgar's *Dream*, signed, after the first performance, by the composer, the principal singers, the orchestra and others. When Elgar presented the score to the Oratory in 1902, he wrote: "Nothing would give me greater happiness than to feel that the work, into which I put my whole soul, should be, in its original form, near to where the sacred author of the poem made his influence felt."

[50] *Leicester Daily Post*, 14 August 1890.

[51] *Freeman's Journal*, 20 August 1890.

hospitality, felt that they were in the presence of a truly great and holy Christian man and that their meeting had changed them for good. The *Leamington Chronicle*, quoting from a sermon delivered by Mgr Longman in St Peter's Church, Leamington, said: "He did not court public applause, and when he retired from public life he tried to hide himself and lived, in Birmingham, in the most humble way."[52] The effect of this hidden work, whether in Birmingham, or anywhere he laboured for God and the Church, was summarised after his death when the *Birmingham Daily Post* wrote: "Men thought he was the servant of the unseen and eternal powers, and when they came near him it was easier for them to believe in God and in God's nearness to mankind."[53]

---

[52] *Leamington Chronicle*, 23 August 1890.
[53] *Birmingham Daily Post*, 12 August 1890.

Chapter 5

NEWMAN AND DUBLIN

by Angelo Bottone

John Henry Newman spent seven years of his life assisting with the foundation, and then guiding, the Catholic University of Ireland. He travelled to Ireland for the first time in 1851 and since then he crossed the Irish Sea fifty-six times. During the years of his Irish enterprise Newman wrote his most interesting and, even today, most relevant pages on university education.

1. The Catholic University in Ireland

At the beginning of the nineteenth century, Trinity College, the sole constituent college of the University of Dublin, was the only institution that provided third level education in Ireland. When it was founded in the year 1591 it was open to students of any religious denomination. From 1637, with the Statute of Charles I, Catholics were excluded from being members of the College. With the Catholic Relief Act of 1793, the English Parliament abolished the religious tests and a Royal Letter of 1794 allowed Catholics to proceed to the degree levels in Trinity College, though scholarships and fellowships were reserved for members of the Church of Ireland, and there was no religious teaching for Catholic students.

In 1845 the Secretary of State for the Home Department introduced into Parliament the project of erecting three new colleges that might well unite in forming a new university. They were to be in Belfast, Cork and either Galway or Limerick. These new colleges were open to students of every denomination, and non-sectarian programmes were provided according to mixed education. There would be no religious tests for admittance, no religious topic introduced into the curriculum, and no religious instruction would be given except at the expense of each denomination.

The Catholic bishops held different and opposing positions on the proposal. A minority was inclined to give the plan a trial, whilst the majority of the bishops were disposed to stand out for a solution on definitely denominational lines. It is important to note that during this period Ireland was suffering from the Great Famine; the population of the country was virtually halved as hundreds of thousands of people were starving to death or forced to emigrate. Hence survival, rather than education, was the main concern for the majority of them.

The Irish bishops appealed to Rome and on 9 October 1847 the Sacred Congregation of Propaganda Fide decided in favour of the majority party among the bishops opposing the plan. Towards the close of the Rescript that they issued, there occurred the first reference to the project of founding a Catholic University in Ireland. The decision of Propaganda Fide was not regarded by either the minority bishops, or by the Government, as final, and indeed, its terms invited further representations in Rome where consultations took place between 1847 and 1848. On 11 October Propaganda Fide responded with a second Rescript stating that, having considered the revised statutes and the opinions of bishops, the Holy See was unable to mitigate the previous decision "on account of the grievous and intrinsic dangers of the same Colleges." Additionally, a further reference to "the erection of a Catholic University" can be found in the document.

In spite of the Papal pronouncements, the Government proceeded with preparations for the opening of the three colleges in Belfast, Cork and Galway, although Limerick was excluded. They were called Queen's Colleges, they opened their doors in October 1849, and Presidents were appointed to two of the colleges. Fifty-three of the sixty professors were Protestants, and this fact was perceived as further corroboration of the anti-Catholic nature of the Government project.

On 6 April 1849, Dr William Crolly, Archbishop of Armagh, who was the most determined member of the minority and was inclined to accept the plan, died. Dr Paul Cullen, Rector of the Irish College in Rome, was chosen to replace Dr Crolly as the new Archbishop of Armagh. Dr Cullen was the senior and official Irish presence in Rome where he had been living since the age of seventeen, initially as a student at the Urban College of Propaganda, then as Vice-Rector and finally Rector of the Irish College.

Some bishops were inclined to allow their clergy to accept appointments in order to provide a guarantee for the few Catholics who had enrolled in the colleges. However, on 18 April 1850, Rome prohibited the clergy from holding any office in the colleges, laying on the bishops the obligation of discouraging their subjects from entering them. The bishops met in Thurles on 22 August of that same year and condemned the Queen's Colleges, adopting a number of measures in order to assure practical results from the resolution. A mere condemnation, however, was not enough to ensure the non-involvement of Catholic students in the Queen's Colleges. In order to prevent this it would be necessary to provide instruction for the potential student body of Catholics, and therefore imperative that an alternative plan to the Queen's Colleges be implemented. A Catholic University Committee was appointed to examine the project of a new university. The Committee drew up an *Address to the People of Ireland*, urging that funds be raised with a view to founding an institution that could "provide for the Catholic youth of Ireland education of a high order."[1]

On 15 April 1851 Dr Cullen wrote a letter to John Henry Newman asking for advice on how to set up a university, and requesting him to deliver 'some lectures on education' in Dublin. Newman accepted the invitation, and on 30 September 1851 he travelled to Ireland for the first time. During this brief visit he met some bishops, discussing with them the university to be founded, and he also assisted a subcommittee in writing a *Report on the Organization of the Catholic University of Ireland*. The report was presented to the Catholic University Committee on 12 November 1851, and at the same meeting Newman was appointed on acclamation President of the University.

2. University Discourses

Newman gave the first of his lectures on University Education on Monday, 10 May 1852 in the Rotunda in Dublin, and he delivered four additional lectures on consecutive Monday afternoons. All the important intellectual figures were in attendance, thirteen Trinity Fellows, eight Jesuits, a great many clergy and also some ladies. Joseph John Gordon, one of his fellow Oratorians, wrote him in a prophetic vein: "you are writing for the world and for posterity, though speaking to an audience."[2]

---

[1] Quoted in Fergal McGrath, *Newman's University: Idea and Reality* (Dublin: Browne & Nolan, 1951), p. 100.
[2] Letter from Joseph John Gordon, May 19th 1852; reported in McGrath, *Newman's University: Idea and Reality*, p. 160.

Newman's Discourses were written under considerable mental stress due to legal trouble. Giacinto Achilli, an apostate Italian Dominican, had been attacked by Newman in the fifth of the talks he gave in Birmingham, which were subsequently published under the title *On the Present Position of Catholics in England*. On 4 November 1851, with the help of the Evangelical Alliance, Achilli brought a criminal action for libel against Newman who was required to provide evidence of his charges, and later forced to stand trial. The process went on until June 1852, exactly the period after Newman's lectures in Dublin. In January 1853, the final verdict only required Newman to pay a fine of £100, and although he was not imprisoned, the stress of the trial had severe consequences on his work and health.

In the introductory *Discourse*, which is also the shortest one, Newman made a preliminary remark about the confessional character of the claims he would put forward. Even if his purpose to found a Catholic university was clear, he stated that his proposed principles could also be accepted by non-Catholics, and furthermore, that Protestants would accept them more easily. In a letter sent to his dear friend Henry Wilberforce on the 17 April 1852, referring to this first *Discourse*, Newman wrote: "I am going to treat my subject merely as a matter of philosophy, not of Catholic duty."[3] Even though the project of the Catholic University of Ireland eventually failed to endure, the success of the *Discourses* lies in the universal character of Newman's vision of a university, and in his attempt to avoid arguments to support this vision by directly appealing to faith. One could conclude that if the *Idea* is still considered a classic in education theory today, it is because of its schematic arrangement, which overcomes the narrow limits of specific religious tenets.

In *Discourse II* Newman defines theology as a science of the intellect, not of faith, common to every reasoning person. On this ground he defends the teaching of theology in a university. His argument is very simple: if theology is a branch of knowledge, and if a university is by definition a place for universal teaching that should take into account all the sciences, to exclude one of them would imply a severe injustice.

In *Discourse III* Newman discusses the relationships between theology and other forms of knowledge. He puts forth a holistic conception: knowledge is a whole in which each discipline has its dignity and its role: all sciences are connected and interrelated, so

---

[3] See John Henry Newman, *Letters and Diaries*, vol. XV, p. 70.

it is impossible to teach any one of them without taking them all, theology included, into consideration. Although he accords great value to theology in the organisation of the studies, philosophy is for him, in some sense, the science of sciences. He believes unity of knowledge, which keeps man away from errors and deviations, is guaranteed by the employment of this integrating faculty.

> The comprehension of the bearings of one science on another, and the use of each to each, and the location and limitation and adjustment and due appreciation of them all, one with another, this belongs, I conceive, to a sort of science distinct from all of them, and in some sense a science of sciences, which is my own conception of what is meant by Philosophy, in the true sense of the word, and by a philosophical habit of mind, and which in these Discourses I shall call by that name.[4]

Originally only three lectures had been planned. Two further lectures were given, while another five *Discourses* were written but never delivered. *Discourse IV* deals with the consequences of the exclusion of theology from the university curriculum, and Newman suggests that all the other sciences will feel the effects of this in as much as they have as their own object the human person.

Discourse V of the final edition gave Newman the most trouble, and harsh criticism caused him to revise the work many times.[5] Newman conceives of knowledge as a system where the intellect works in order to seal in one form the data given by sensibility, science, and tradition. The ideal of knowledge introduced in this *Discourse* is a vision capable of catching everything as a whole. The field of knowledge is a universe, an ordered cosmos where everything has its own definite meaning. There is a harmony in things springing from their being part of Creation, but also a unity given by the intellect that, by contemplating them, inserts them in the horizon of sense. "To have mapped out the Universe is the boast, or at least the ambition, of Philosophy."[6]

In the next three *Discourses* Newman touches upon three main questions: the relation of intellectual culture to mere knowledge, to professional knowledge and to religious knowledge.

In *Discourse VI* Newman defines a university as being the place where universal knowledge is taught. "It educates the intellect to reason

---

[4] John Henry Newman, *The Idea of a University* (Oxford: Oxford University Press, 1976), p. 51. (Hereafter *Idea*).
[5] See Ian Ker, 'Introduction' to John Henry Newman, *Idea*, p. xxxii.
[6] *Idea*, p. 113.

well in all matters, to reach out towards truth, and to grasp it."[7] Even if born inside Christianity, the university institution has a universal value, namely the cultivation of the intellect. Newman claims that its primary end is not research, he would leave that to the academies, instead, the aim of the university would be one of teaching. For this reason, at the centre of his idea of a university, he places the student and his life amongst his fellow students and teachers. For Newman, the end of intellectual training, and of a university, is not learning or acquisition, it is thought or reason exercised upon knowledge. This is what Newman calls philosophy.

In *Discourse VII* Newman means to contrast the concept expressed firstly by Locke, and later by the *Edinburgh Review*, according to which education should be confined to some particular and narrow end, and should issue in some definite work, which can be weighed and measured. According to this utilitarian view, if everything has its price, and if there is a great outlay in education – either from a social or an individual point of view – we have the right to expect a return of a kind that justifies it. Newman replies that intellectual culture is its own end. He believes that liberal education reaches at the same time, even if not directly, the personal utility that Locke pursued, and the social utility, which the *Edinburgh Review* aimed for.

The final two *Discourses* discuss the relations between mental culture and religion. In *Discourse VIII* Newman presents the mutual benefit of the cultivation of the mind and of moral virtues. A cultivated mind will feel scorn for vices, and a religious man will be more disposed to the pursuit of knowledge. There can be found here the famous definition of a gentleman as "one who never inflicts pain."[8]

Newman, having celebrated in the previous Discourse the virtues of the cultivation of the mind, in the last one analyses the possible damage to religion that liberal education may involve and indeed perpetrate. Liberal institutions may be hostile to truth derived from religious revelation because they have a tendency: "to impress us with a mere philosophical theory of life and conduct, in the place of Revelation."[9] The educated man risks judging everything, mystery and miracles also, according to his knowledge, closing himself to Revelation. If our mind is the measure for everything there will be no space for any truth that is not intelligible, that does not enter into

---

[7] *Idea*, p. 126.
[8] *Idea*, p. 208.
[9] *Idea*, p. 217.

our categories, that does not satisfy our expectation, all with serious consequences for religion.

3. Occasional Lectures and Essays

The Catholic University of Ireland was formally opened on 3 November 1854. The lapse of three years since the appointment of Newman as President of the University was initially caused by the opposition of Dr Daniel Murray, Archbishop of Dublin, to the project. Murray's fear was that a University in Dublin would potentially increase anti–Catholic sentiments in England and thereby threaten Maynooth seminary. He eventually died on 26 February 1852 and the difficulty was overcome, particularly because he was replaced by Dr Cullen, who was the strongest supporter of the new University. Even after Murray's death, however, Irish bishops were divided on the enterprise. Its strongest opponent was Dr John MacHale, Archbishop of Tuam, who was opposed to Newman's wish to appoint English professors to the University, and who viewed the University mainly as an expression of Cullen's interests.

The Achilli trial was the second reason for the late opening of the University. Moreover, Newman complained in his letters about the lack of communication between Cullen and himself. This is better understood if we consider the delicate political situation, and the difficult relationships amongst the bishops. Colin Barr holds that Cullen was rude to Newman for reasons of strategy, i.e. that he was stalling for time and desired to be perceived as holding a position between Newman and Dr MacHale.[10]

This strategy proved useful, as in March 1854 Pius IX formally appointed Newman as Rector and required the Irish bishops to meet in Synod, along the lines Cullen had originally suggested. In the meantime, Cullen purchased a magnificent Georgian House on St Stephen's Green which is today called Newman House. During this same time Newman, who had been in Ireland since February, was travelling intensively and beginning to establish important connections with strategically placed prelates.

The Synod opened on 18 May and closed two days later, following the granting of approval for the establishment of a university on the model of Louvain. The statute allowed Cullen to open the University

---

[10] Colin Barr, *Paul Cullen, John Henry Newman, and the Catholic University of Ireland, 1845-1865* (Herefordshire, 2003), p. 109.

with the Rector he wished, but he also alienated many bishops in the process.

The University was ultimately to possess the four faculties of arts, medicine, law and theology, but at first only the faculty of arts could be founded. From October 1853 Newman began to make appointments to the various university positions. Of the fifteen names that Newman submitted for the archbishops' consideration, seven were English and had their professional origins in Oxford or Cambridge. Of the fifteen appointments, there were to be six professors and nine lecturers. In order to attract students, Newman urged that it was essential that celebrity professors should be chosen to fill professorial chairs in relation to the more important subjects. Newman conceived education to comprise a balance between personal influence and organised discipline, with personal influence being the priority. Students were to be separated into small communities of twenty or so, with each community having a Dean and two or three young men serving as tutors. A certain number of bursaries should also be provided, to be obtained by *concursus*.

Newman, as Rector, gave some inaugural lectures and wrote several essays addressed to the members of the Catholic University of Ireland. They were collected and published in London in 1859 with the title *Lectures and Essays on University Subjects*. This was a companion volume to the first English edition of the *Discourses*, which had been previously published in Ireland. Since 1873 the two works have always been published together under the title: *The Idea of a University Defined and Illustrated*.

The lectures and essays are not arranged in chronological order but according to their contents, which are somewhat lighter than the content of the *Discourses*. Three essays concern Letters, in themselves and in relation to Christianity; three regard methods of teaching and learning; the other three deal with the proper relation between Christianity and Science; and one is about the challenge that Positivism offered to religion.

In the first lecture of this collection, titled 'Christianity and Letters', Newman presents the standards of education in ancient and modern civilizations, and traces analogies between them and Christianity. It was read as the opening lecture of the Faculty of Arts courses, on 9 November 1854, six days after the opening of the Catholic University of Ireland.

Newman arranged a programme of Inaugural Lectures to be

delivered by the professors in order to open and introduce the new institution to the city of Dublin. After the first lecture, all the university teachers gave a lecture each in his own field every Thursday evening until the end of the term. The project was so successful that Newman planned a more ambitious programme for the second term to include two types of course, an academic one in the morning and a more popular one in the evening. The evening classes were intended to extend the advantages of the University as far as possible by involving the working young men of Dublin who were unable to attend during the day, and who were unlikely to be able to afford regular university tuition. In providing an intellectual cultivation for the Catholic working class of the time Newman was also compensating for a cultural deficit that prevented them from playing an active part in civil society. Ladies too could attend them. It can be said that in spite of the limitations common to all the universities of the time, due to these evening lectures, from the outset, women could take advantage of the new Catholic University of Ireland.

'Literature', the second lecture of the collection, was read on 3 November 1858, the day before Newman's definitive departure, at the opening of the academic year of the Faculty of Philosophy and Letters. It is perhaps the best known of these lectures, where Literature is defined as "personal use or exercise of language".[11]

The third essay concerning Letters is titled 'Catholic Literature in the English Tongue' and it deals with the particular relationship between English literature, 'formed on Protestantism', and Catholicism. Newman recommends its study, in spite of the presence of authors, like Milton and Gibbon, proud and rebellious creatures of God but endowed with incomparable gifts. The next essay, 'Elementary Studies', brings together some articles from the *Catholic University Gazette*. It is the longest of the essays and provides an illustration of Newman's methods as a teacher. He critically analyses, and sometimes satirises, the statements of educational theory of his time, while long passages are devoted to translations from Greek and Latin.

The essay 'A Form of Infidelity of the Day' treats of the exclusion of theology from the University. The next essay is 'University Preaching'. For Newman, the pulpit was an essential part of university life and for this reason this essay, which is rich with guidance for composing sermons, finds its place among university subjects. The occasion of the essay was the initiative whereby sermons were delivered in University

---

[11] *Idea*, p. 275.

Church, Dublin, by distinguished preachers.

After the three essays regarding the methods of teaching and learning we find two lectures dealing with the relationship between religion and science, which was already discussed in *Discourse IX*.

The Medical School of the Catholic University of Ireland was opened on 2 November 1855, in the second year of the University's existence. The Inaugural Lecture was given not by Newman, who was unable to attend due to illness, but by the Dean of the faculty. In the following month Newman presented a lecture that later was published with the title 'Christianity and Physical Science'. The next essay, 'Christianity and Scientific Investigation', was never delivered, although it contains the famous passage on the imperial intellect, where Newman explicitly compares his Dublin enterprise to the Roman Empire:

> We count it a great thing, and justly so, to plan and carry out a wide political organization. To bring under one yoke, after the manner of old Rome, a hundred discordant peoples; to maintain each of them in its own privileges within its legitimate range of action; to allow them severally the indulgence of national feelings, and the stimulus of rival interests; and yet withal to blend them into one great social establishment, and to pledge them to the perpetuity of the one imperial power; – this is an achievement which carries with it the unequivocal token of genius in the race which effects it. [...] What an empire is in political history, such is a University in the sphere of philosophy and research.[12]

The evening classes, which began in 1854, were suspended at the end of the academic year, but due to the requests of a number of young men engaged in business in Dublin they were reopened with great success in April 1858. The statute passed in 1857 enabled students attending these evening classes to sit examinations and to graduate. The lecture 'Discipline of Mind' was given by Newman in University Church on 2 November 1858, two days before his final departure from Dublin.[13] He proudly recalls:

> I can truly say that I thought of you before you thought of the University; perhaps I may say, long before; – for it was previously to our commencing that great work, which is now so fully before the public, it was when I first came over here to make preparations for it, that I had to encounter the serious objection of wise and good

---

[12] *Idea*, pp. 458-459.

[13] In his diary Newman wrote 'Nov. 4 … off for Bm. [Birmingham]' and there is the added note: 'Never been in Ireland since (Sept. 3, 1874).'; see McGrath, *Newman's University: Idea and Reality*, p. 473.

men, who said to me, "There is no class of persons in Ireland who need a University;" and again, "Whom will you get to belong to it? who will fill its lecture-rooms?" This was said to me, and then, without denying their knowledge of the state of Ireland, or their sagacity, I made answer, "We will give lectures in the evening, we will fill our classes with the young men of Dublin."[14]

'Christianity and Medical Science', the last lecture of the collection, was read the very day Newman left Ireland for the last time 4 November 1858. After the lecture he distributed prizes and gold medals to the successful medical students.

4. The Catholic University Gazette

One of the first tasks Newman undertook at the onset of the University actually being established was the setting up of the *Catholic University Gazette*, a small weekly periodical, consisting of just eight pages, published from 1 June 1854. Newman wrote more than fifty articles for the *Catholic University Gazette* and used most of them in his later books. Twenty historical articles on the University were collected from the *Gazette* and published by Newman in 1856 with the title *Office and Work of Universities*. They were renamed *Rise and Progress of Universities* in the 1872 edition.

It must be noted that, unlike the *Discourses*, the *Occasional Lectures and Essays* and the articles later collected in *Rise and Progress of Universities* were written when the Catholic University had already been established, and Newman's projects were met with both admiration and refutation. Compared to the other two publications, *Rise and Progress of Universities* was not directed towards an intellectual audience, which was the one attending his preparatory discourses, but to a wider and more heterogeneous lay public.

In *Rise and Progress of Universities* Newman chose to present the life of higher education in its development from ancient Greece to modern times. Newman represents in an imaginative but plausible way the realisation of an ideal type: the *universitas*, and he provides a variety of examples, with each one embodying it in a different way.

The two fundamental aspects of university living for Newman are discipline and personal influence; these two aspects are manifested in the communal life within the college and in the person of the teacher respectively.

---

[14] *Idea*, p. 480.

5. Sermons

Newman exercised profound influence as a preacher and leader of the Tractarian Movement while he was Vicar of St Mary's, the university parish in Oxford. The pulpit was for him an essential part of university life, and he wished to introduce in Dublin the Oxford tradition of sermons given by distinguished preachers. His idea was realised when University Church was opened in May 1856, and he was the most notable preacher. Eight of his sermons, preached in 1856 and 1857, were published in London in 1857 under the title *Sermons Preached on Various Occasions*.

The importance of these sermons is not comparable with the fortune Newman had as a preacher in Oxford, but nevertheless, they were conceived to play a particular and undeniable function in the education given by his University. In the first sermon, preached the Sunday after the opening, Newman clarifies the essential place of University Church in his project:

> I wish the same spots and the same individuals to be at once oracles of philosophy and shrines of devotion. [...] Devotion is not a sort of finish given to the sciences; nor is science a sort of feather in the cap. [...] I want the intellectual layman to be religious, and the devout ecclesiastic to be intellectual.[15]

6. The end of the Catholic University in Ireland

The Catholic University of Ireland eventually went into decline for many different reasons. Firstly, this was due to the limitations of its own promoters. Newman, for instance, had little knowledge of the political and social situation of post-famine Ireland, and because of his English origin it was often difficult for his Irish contacts and peers to accept him. Moreover, he worked under a great personal stress due to the Achilli affair. He had not given up his position in the Oratory in Birmingham and this twofold allegiance, which involved frequent travels between England and Ireland, affected his achievements in Dublin. He said that he expended two times more effort than should have been required in order to achieve what needed to be accomplished while he was in Ireland. It is not necessary to stress how the attractiveness of the new University was linked to Newman's reputation, so that when he finally left forever, the University had much less to offer to prospective students and professors. Irish bishops

---

[15] John Henry Newman, *Sermons Preached on Various Occasions* (London, 1874), p. 13.

never reached an agreement on the Catholic University of Ireland, and the tension between the two principal figures, Cullen and MacHale, and their followers, prevented the Catholic University from being identified as a common enterprise of the whole Irish Church. Even if the historian Colin Barr has successfully proved that Cullen always acted according to the best possible intentions, his strong personality, at least as it was perceived by Newman, negatively affected the development of the University.[16]

Besides the human limitations of those involved in the University, it must be added that the historical realities of the situation also contributed to its failure. The Catholic University never had enough students; this was due to a lack of secondary schools functioning as feeder institutions for the University, and the fact that the Maynooth seminary absorbed all ecclesiastical students. In addition, the Irish Catholic elite and middle class were not sizeable enough to provide a sufficient number of pupils.

In being envisaged not only for Irish people, but for any Catholic of the English-speaking world, the Catholic University of Ireland represents an exception amongst the new universities born in the nineteenth century, and it is probably the first supranational university institution of the modern era. This is also one of the reasons for its failure as it was not able to attract students from other countries, especially one of the most likely recruiting grounds, i.e. England. Oxford and Cambridge, in 1854 and 1855, abolished religious tests for matriculation and the BA degree, with a corresponding diminution of English Catholics' interest in an institution overseas. From the beginning of his project Newman was well aware of these problems, and before the University was opened he wrote in a letter to his dear friend William Froude:

> The great difficulty, between ourselves is, that, what with emigration, campaigning, ruin of families, and the pusillanimity induced by centuries of oppression, there seems to be no class to afford members for a University – and next, there is a deep general impression that this is the case, which is nearly as hopeless a circumstance as the case itself, supposing that case to be a fact.[17]

The final, but nonetheless important, reason for the failure of the Catholic University was its lack of a charter, or formal licence by

---

[16] See Colin Barr, *Paul Cullen, John Henry Newman, and the Catholic University of Ireland, 1845-1865* (Herefordshire: Gracewing, 2003).
[17] John Henry Newman, *Letters and Diaries*, vol. XVI, p. 66. See also ibid. p. 68.

the State to confer degrees. In fact, only the Medical School, which did not need a charter because it was linked to the Royal College of Surgeons, survived. Arthur Dwight Culler in his study *The Imperial Intellect* writes:

> The lack of a charter for granting degrees, the division and hostility among the bishops, the dearth of pupils, and the simple poverty of the land – these are the reasons for the relative failure of Newman's university. But although the university languished and the nations of the world never came flocking to Dublin for their education, there did go forth from Dublin a conception of education which has deeply influenced the universities of the English-speaking world. And in this sense one might say that the institution at Dublin did become an 'Imperial University'.[18]

---

[18] Arthur Dwight Culler, *The Imperial Intellect: A Study of Cardinal Newman's Educational Ideal* (New Haven and London: Yale University Press, 1955), p. 170.

Newman House and the entrance to the University church
on St Stephen's Green in Dublin.

Part II

The pulpit used by Newman in St Mary's University Church, Oxford.

Chapter 6

NEWMAN THE PREACHER

by Paul Chavasse

Our Victorian forebears, whether Anglican, Catholic or Nonconformist, were all of them used to experiencing sermons the length of which is virtually unheard of nowadays. A famous example concerns William Bernard Ullathorne, the Benedictine Bishop of Birmingham. Called upon at very short notice to preach at the funeral of Mother Margaret Hallahan, foundress of the Dominican Sisters at Stone in Staffordshire, he managed to talk for an hour and three-quarters![1] Many preachers had their collected sermons published, so that people could read them at greater leisure; nowadays we can mostly find these volumes in the unvisited corners of libraries or in the shops of second-hand booksellers.

There is one notable exception to this: the sermons of John Henry Newman. Constantly in demand in his own lifetime, his published sermons appeared in several editions. Since his death in 1890, selections of them have appeared at regular intervals; some have been included in anthologies; in 1987 eight volumes were republished under one cover and in 2006 fifteen University sermons of his appeared in a critical edition.[2] What is the abiding appeal of these sermons, and others of his, many of them now over a hundred and fifty years old?

It is recorded of the late Fr Henry Tristram of the Birmingham Oratory that he would tell scholars always to think of John Henry Newman under the title "Father of Souls"[3]. That would give them

---

[1] Archives of the Archbishop of Westminster; Ullathorne correspondence; Ullathorne to Manning, 15 May 1868.

[2] John Henry Newman, *Parochial and Plain Sermons* (Ignatius Press, San Francisco, 1987); *Fifteen Sermons Preached Before the University of Oxford* (James David Earnest and Gerard Tracey, ed., Oxford University Press, Oxford, 2006).

[3] This was the title given by Fr H. J. Coleridge to his appreciation of Cardinal Newman. See 'A Father of Souls', *The Month*, vol. 70, no. 316, October 1890, pp. 153–164.

the key to understanding his whole life and mission. As a "Father of Souls", as a pastor of God's people, therefore, we approach Newman the preacher.

Newman preached his very first sermon in the little church at Over Worton, near Banbury, on 23 June 1824. His ministry of preaching became continuous after that, always preaching on Sundays and feast days, sometimes both morning and evening, whether at St Clement's or St Mary's in Oxford, or at Littlemore, as well as, on occasion, preaching for friends or others elsewhere. All in all, in these nineteen Anglican years, Newman entered the pulpit around 1,270 times. Meticulous as ever, each of his sermons was given a number – his last Anglican sermon, preached at Littlemore and entitled 'The Parting of Friends', was numbered 604. Many of these sermons were used on more than one occasion, in some instances as many as seven or eight times over a span of up to seventeen years. It is interesting to note that, in re-using a sermon on later occasions, Newman made many revisions and alterations, so much so that the sermon was virtually re-written. These changes also help map for us his theological development. In this regard, it is interesting to note Newman's own comments on his earliest sermons. In the Archives at the Birmingham Oratory there is a collection headed: "Packet of Sermons, St Clement's, 1824-1826", on which Newman has written: "May 17th 1881. None of these sermons are worth anything in themselves, but those preached at St Clement's 1824-6 will show how far I was an Evangelical when I went into Anglican Orders."

From this large number of pastoral sermons about one third have been published and they are established as one of the great classics of Christian spirituality. In sermon 290, called 'On the objects and effects of Preaching', and dating from March 1831, Newman told his hearers: "In Scripture to preach is to do the work of an evangelist, is to teach, instruct, advise, encourage in all things pertaining to religion, in any way whatever."[4] Preaching for Newman was the means to an end, it was meant to be an incentive to praying better and to living better. When Newman was appointed as Vicar of St Mary's, Oxford in 1828, he was able to use the pulpit of the University church to build up in a new and far-reaching manner the faith of those who came to him. Until then the Sunday sermon was delivered in the morning by the clergyman whose turn it was to preach that particular day. The

---

[4] John Henry Newman, *Sermons 1824-1843, Volume 1* (Placid Murray ed., Clarendon Press, Oxford, 1991), p. 25.

method of selecting these preachers need not concern us here, but more often than not what they offered was dry and remote from the few who bothered to hear them. Newman felt that the needs of his own parishioners were not being met, and so he instituted an afternoon service, which was held at 4pm, and at which he would preach. To start with the numbers attending this afternoon service remained small, but as news of the quality of Newman's sermons spread, so numbers increased, so that eventually the congregation numbered five or six hundred, drawn from the parish and the University. As Bishop Wilberforce recalled: "From that pulpit he reached the heart of young Oxford. Man after man, in whom was the receptive faculty, received the living force of his words, and reproduced so far as he was able, the Master's spirit in himself."[5]

On average these sermons covered some fourteen pages and would have taken about 45 minutes to deliver. The way he preached them was thought to be the antithesis of normal oratory, and yet it had a power all its own. We will examine the effects of his preaching below, but for now we should note that, apart from the use of long pauses, which perhaps revealed the intensity of his thoughts, he contented himself with reading the sermons "with hardly any change in the inflexion of his voice and without any gesture on the part of the preacher, whose eyes remained fixed on the text in front of him."[6] By the time he began to give these sermons Newman's study of the Fathers of the Church had led him to a deeper grasp of the sacramental principle in Christianity, in particular the regenerating force of Baptism, the mystery of the Resurrection and the significance of the indwelling of the Holy Spirit. These elements, distilled from the teaching of the Fathers and from his own musings on the Scriptures, gave an extraordinary force to his sermons. Their dogmatic, patristic origins, coupled with their liturgical setting – they arose out of a particular celebration, with a particular congregation in view – meant that they were unlike anything most of his hearers had ever heard before. His use of the Scriptures was fresh and showed no evidence of a debt to any one school or system of interpretation; Newman brings to bear his own native intelligence, and this, coupled with his deepening theological insights, resulted in a quality and quantity of preaching unsurpassed by any other preacher at that time. The method he used

---

[5] R.D. Middleton, 'The Vicar of St Mary's', *Newman Centenary Essays* (Burns, Oates & Washbourne, London, 1945), p. 130. The quotation originally appeared in *The Quarterly Review*, 1864.
[6] Ian Ker, *John Henry Newman* (Oxford University Press, Oxford, 1990), p. 91.

in his preaching also distinguished him from his contemporaries. He explores themes and harmonies in a new way, uses the Old Testament (especially the Prophets) to explain the New, and applies the lessons drawn not in any vague way, but to the needs of the church and the individual hearer in particular. His call was one to greater holiness, coupled with a realisation that people sin, and sin because they want to. What he taught of prayer was realistic; a combination of shrewdly practical psychology and highly idealistic spirituality. He called on his hearers to practice self-examination of their consciences – not in an introverted way, but in an attempt to open themselves more and more to the workings of Christ. "His aim was to speak to each individual soul, to open to each the secrets and needs of the heart, to reason of righteousness, of temperance and of the judgement to come. No one could have attended St Mary's regularly for any length of time without learning the teaching of the Church given in as clear a manner as the preacher was able to present it."[7]

Some found the realism of the sermons disconcerting, even shocking, especially when Newman preached on the Crucifixion. James Anthony Froude, the historian, recalled the delivery of the sermon 'The Incarnate Son, a Sufferer and a Sacrifice', given on 1 April 1836.[8]

> Newman had described closely some of the incidents of our Lord's Passion; he then paused. For a few moments there was a breathless silence. Then in a low, clear voice, of which the faintest vibration was audible in the farthest corner of St Mary's, he said, 'Now I bid you recollect that He to whom these things were done was Almighty God.' It was if an electric stroke had gone through the church, as if every person present understood for the first time the meaning of what he had all his life been saying. I suppose it was an epoch in the mental history of more than one of my Oxford contemporaries.[9]

It is no wonder that the 4pm sermons at St Mary's came to be seen as the most powerful spiritual force of the Oxford Movement. On 26 October 1840 Newman wrote to Keble describing what his aim was: "my sermons are calculated to undermine things established ... I am leading my hearers to the Primitive church if you will, but

---

[7] Middleton, 'The Vicar of St Mary's', pp. 133-4.

[8] John Henry Newman, *Parochial and Plain Sermons* (Rivington, London, 1868) vol. 6, no. 6, pp. 69-82.

[9] J. A. Froude, *Short Studies on Great Subjects* (Longman, Green & Co., London, 1894) vol. 4, p. 286.

not to the Church of England."[10] It is no wonder that the Heads of the Oxford Colleges became alarmed at the influence these sermons were having and took steps – like changing the time of dinner in their halls – in order to prevent their undergraduates attending. Of course, such measures had little effect. Week by week and month by month, Newman's hearers imbibed an important doctrinal message, centred in and around the mystery of the Incarnation of God's Son. This fact led on to considerations in many sermons on the Church as a divinely constituted society, founded by our Lord as a visible entity, with its government vested in the Apostles and maintained by the Bishops in apostolic succession, which enables the Church of today to be linked with the whole Church spread throughout the world. His study of the Fathers led him to teach without hesitation the Presence of Christ in the Holy Eucharist – our Lord began His ministry by a miracle, the turning of water into wine; He closed it by a greater miracle, the gift of His Body and His Blood in Holy Communion.[11] Newman also teaches the doctrine of the sacrament of Penance, saying that the Christian "has his original debt cancelled in Baptism, and all subsequent penalties put aside by Absolution."[12] The priest has the power to do this as a result of a "plain divine commission to do so."[13] No wonder his words were regarded as revolutionary, serving to wake the Church of England from what has been described as its "long sleep." Just as revolutionary was the practice of a daily service and a weekly celebration of the Eucharist, even though numbers at the former tended to be low and Newman often found these smaller services dreary.

In March 1834 the first volume of his sermons appeared in print and more followed in the years up to 1842. In 1843 he contributed a volume to the Tractarian series *Plain Sermons*. Two further volumes appeared that same year. *Sermons on Subjects of the Day*, as the title indicates, brought together in one volume a number of sermons, edited for publication, which dealt with religious issues which preoccupied the Church of the day. The other volume, *Sermons preached before the University of Oxford*, Newman was to regard as collecting together some of the best things he had written. The majority of these sermons

[10] G. Tracey (ed.) *The Letters and Diaries of John Henry Newman* (Clarendon Press, Oxford, 1995), vol. 7, p. 417.
[11] John Henry Newman, *Sermons on Subjects of the Day* (Rivington, London, 1868), sermon no. 3 'Our Lord's Last Supper and His First', p. 38.
[12] Newman, *Parochial and Plain Sermons*, vol. 3, no. 24, p. 362.
[13] Newman, *Parochial and Plain Sermons*, vol. 2, no. 25, p. 309.

concern the theory of religious belief and the relationship between faith and reason, and can be viewed as partly an autobiographical description of Newman's own theological and philosophical development.

Newman's last sermon as an Anglican was preached at Littlemore on 25 September 1843. He called it 'The Parting of Friends' and most of the large congregation that packed into the church knew that they were listening to him for the last time. People were in tears, including Edward Pusey, Newman's friend and fellow Tractarian, who was the celebrant. After that sermon a great silence fell, and then two years later Newman became a Catholic. Another year passed before Newman, the great preacher, spoke again. The contrast could hardly have been greater. It was 4 December 1846 and Newman, now in minor orders and a student at the College of Propaganda in Rome, was asked to deliver the funeral oration for a niece of the Countess of Shrewsbury, who had died suddenly. Somewhat reluctantly, Newman did as he was asked, preached extempore, and spoke quite strongly on the need we all have for conversion, presumably hoping to influence some of the Protestants present. Afterwards he said: "I assure you I did not like it at all"[14] and certainly some present took offence at what seemed his lack of tact. The Pope himself was said to have been displeased. This first Catholic sermon has not been preserved, and there is no record either of the sermon he gave to the students at Propaganda on 31 October 1847. Newman's real Catholic preaching begins with his return to England at the end of that year, when the Oratory was set up at Maryvale. He began by writing out and numbering his sermons, just as he had done when an Anglican. The very first was given at St Chad's Cathedral on 23 January 1848; the text has not survived. Seven subsequent ones, all given in St Chad's, the last on 26 March, have all come down to us.[15] Although the series is incomplete (Newman went to preach at Southwark Cathedral at the end of Lent), they are revealing insofar as they show that Newman was preaching much in the style he had used in St Mary's — the concrete illustrations, the psychological insight, the use of Scripture, the stress on moral preparation in order to receive the truth — all is authentic Newman, but all is given with humility and docility and all

[14] Charles Stephen Dessain, *The Letters and Diaries of John Henry Newman* (Thomas Nelson & Sons, London, 1961), vol. 11, p. 290.
[15] *The Catholic Sermons of Cardinal Newman*, ed. at the Birmingham Oratory (Burns & Oates, London, 1957), pp. 19-104.

is entirely Catholic. The big departure from his Anglican days came with his decision, after the second sermon had been given, to conform himself to Catholic custom and not read his sermons. He noted on the manuscript: "preached, not read at St Chad's." One of Newman's great gifts as a preacher was that of being able to enter into the minds of others, and the simplicity of these early Catholic sermons shows him striving to do this for a congregation in a large industrial town, with many ordinary Irish folk listening to him and following him with ease. A world so different to that of St Mary's in Oxford, and yet one that once again reveals Newman as a true "Father of Souls."

This simple style would have marked the sermons preached at the Oratorians' chapel on Alcester Street and later on at Edgbaston. There are very few of the Catholic sermons that have a full text, and these are ones which were given on very special occasions, such as 'The Second Spring', preached at the Synod of Bishops at Oscott College in 1852, or 'The Infidelity of the Future' given for the opening of St Bernard's Seminary at Olton in 1873. Newman was always very cautious about accepting invitations to preach to groups with whom he was unfamiliar. He did not like these 'set-piece' events, and he made his thoughts plain when he wrote: "I can preach to people I know, but anything like a display is quite out of my line."[16] Indeed, he must have felt anxiety about the giving of such sermons, given that he wrote on one occasion of having had "my usual dream about having to preach before the University of Oxford without a notion what I was to preach about … ."[17]

As a Catholic, therefore, Newman preached without a text. This does not mean, however, that he preached extempore. He was always extremely wary of such seeming eloquence, and had told his congregation at St Mary's that he would not "dishonour this service by any strangeness or extravagance of conduct or constraint of manner."[18] He considered public extempore prayer "plainly irreverent" and maintained that "for the sake of decency, and reverence, all public prayer, the whole of the priest's liturgy, should be settled beforehand and known."[19] This is the principle he applied to his Catholic sermons. On 2 March 1868 he wrote to an unnamed student at Maynooth College, that a great deal of prior preparation was necessary before

---

[16] Dessain, *Letters and Diaries*, vol. 12, p. 198.
[17] Dessain, *Letters and Diaries*, vol. 20, p. 255.
[18] Newman, *Parochial and Plain Sermons*, vol. 8, p. 164.
[19] Newman, *Sermons 1824-1843*, vol. 1, pp. 67-74.

entering the pulpit to preach. He told the seminarian "to have your subject distinctly before you; to think it over till you have got it perfectly in your head."[20] This was not to be just a mental process – the thoughts should be put down on paper even in note form. The sermon should be known by heart, and the preacher should take care to efface himself and let the truth he wished to convey speak. To his enquirer from Maynooth he wrote:

> Humility, which is a great Christian virtue, has a place in literary composition – he who is ambitious will never write well. But he who tries to say simply and exactly what he feels and thinks, what religion demands, what Faith teaches, what the Gospel promises, will be eloquent without intending it, and will write better English than if he made a study of English literature.[21]

As he exemplified it in his own preaching, so Newman advises the student "to take care that it should be one subject, not several; to sacrifice every thought, however good or clever, which does not tend to bring out your one point, and to aim earnestly and supremely to bring home that one point to the minds of your hearers."[22]

A collection of Newman's sermon notes exists for the period 1849 to 1878. These were first published in 1913 and in the preface, written for the book by Fr Joseph Bacchus of the Birmingham Oratory, we discover that the notes were almost without exception written down by Newman after he had preached the sermon, thus preserving in note form what he had said in church. He did this until about 1884 when, his memory beginning to fail, he took to reading some of his old Parochial Sermons, but "touched up a little bit" for his Birmingham congregations.[23]

With Newman being regarded for so many years as foremost amongst England's preachers, it is hardly surprising that there are a great many recollections in print recording the impression that his preaching made.

Matthew Arnold wrote:"Who could resist the charm of that spiritual apparition, gliding in the dim afternoon light through the aisles of St Mary's, rising into the pulpit, and then in the most entrancing of voices, breaking the silence with words and thoughts which were religious

---

[20] Dessain, *Letters and Diaries*, vol. 24, p. 44.

[21] Dessain, *Letters and Diaries*, vol. 24, p. 45.

[22] Dessain, *Letters and Diaries*, vol. 24, p. 44.

[23] Fathers of the Birmingham Oratory (ed.), *Sermon Notes of John Henry Cardinal Newman, 1849-1878* (Longman, Green & Co, London, 1913), Introduction, p. 6.

music – subtle, sweet, mournful?"[24] It was the effect of Newman's voice which left an indelible impression on the hearers; low and soft, it was at the same time both piercing and thrilling.

The same points were made by Charles Wellington Furse, who was an undergraduate at Balliol College, and who began to frequent the afternoon service at St Mary's in 1839. Many years later he began making visits to Newman at the Oratory in Birmingham and attended the Cardinal's funeral in 1890. Furse left a forty-nine-page memorandum of his recollections of Newman and remembered very clearly what it was like to hear him preach. Newman, he wrote, had "a look of concentration and strong will in every gesture. The only sweetness was in his voice and even that was rather clear and fine, and thrilling with vibrations of metallic force, than soft, with a penetrative and steely vibrating power which I have never known equalled." The immediate effect on this particular hearer was extraordinary:

> It was vivisection practised by him on me. He began at the less vital organs, sometimes at the extremes and worked upward and inward. The practical application of the sermon was made in successive paragraphs. The first paragraph stuck you and fastened you to your seat with a nail. The second clinched it. The third seized another link and another nail was driven. And when you thought he could not possibly come closer to you, he took up a finer drill and a sharper point and absolutely impaled you, till you became, not paralysed, but quickened in every fibre into more vivid sensibility, but fixed invincibly to your seat with neither power nor will to move.

Furse remembered that there was "nothing hard-hitting, no exaggeration, no transcendentalism – you never resented a word, nor evaded it, nor appealed from his judgement to a higher court."[25]

Along similar lines were the recollections of Dean Lake. He regarded Newman as the greatest moral and intellectual force in the University of Oxford and thought his sermons unequalled.

> There was first the style, always simple, refined and unpretending ... marked by a depth of feeling which evidently sprang from the heart and experience of the speaker. His language had the perfect grace which comes from uttering deep and affecting truths in the most natural and appropriate words. Then, as he entered his subject

---

[24] Matthew Arnold, *Discourses in America* (Macmillan, London, 1885), pp. 139-40.
[25] Birmingham Oratory Archives, Furse Papers. Charles Wellington Furse (1821-1900) was Vicar of Staines, Principal of Cuddesdon Theological College (1873-83) and Archdeacon of Westminster. His first wife was Jane Monsell, a cousin of William Monsell, Lord Emly, Newman's friend and fellow convert. The memorandum will appear as an appendix in the forthcoming volume 32 of the *Letters and Diaries of John Henry Newman*.

more fully, the preacher seemed to enter into the very minds of his hearers, and, as it were, to reveal them to themselves, and to tell them their very innermost thoughts. There was rarely, or never, anything which could be called a burst of feeling; but both of thought and of suppressed feeling there was every variety, and you were always conscious that you were in the hands of a man who was a perfect master of your heart, and was equally powerful to comfort and to warn you. Is it too much to say of such addresses that they were unlike anything that we had ever heard before, and that we have never heard or read anything similar to them in our after-life.[26]

That Newman lost none of this force in later years is also attested by different witnesses. One such was Edward White Benson, who heard him after Newman had become a Catholic, and was both attracted and repelled by what he experienced:

He is a wonderful man truly, and spoke with a sort of Angelic eloquence ... sweet, flowing, unlaboured language in short, very short, and very pithy and touching sentences ... he was very much emaciated, and when he began his voice was very feeble, and he spoke with great difficulty, nay sometimes he gasped for breath; but his voice was very sweet ... it was awful – the terrible lines deeply ploughed all over his face, and the craft that sat upon his retreating forehead and sunken eyes."[27]

Another impression of hearing the elderly Newman preach was left by C. H. P. Mayo, who wrote:

Only once did I hear him preach, and the memory of the scene is imperishable. It was an evening service, in the semi-darkened church all faces were upturned to the small frail figure which stood in the pulpit high above their heads. On the steps behind him stood a priest: but the Cardinal, though over 80 and very thin and worn, almost ethereal, needed no help; nor was his eyesight dimmed; he read without glasses a small Bible in which the type must have been minute. In that quiet beautiful voice which had stirred England to its very depths 40 and more years ago, whose echoes had not yet ceased to reverberate in the bitter religious controversies of the day, he said nothing that could not (except for the way of saying it) have been spoken in any professedly Christian place of worship.[28]

James Anthony Froude recalled that

---

[26] Katharine Lake (ed.), *Memorials of William Charles Lake, Dean of Durham 1869-94* (Edward Arnold, London, 1901) pp. 41-2.

[27] A. C. Benson, *The Life of Edward White Benson, sometime Archbishop of Canterbury* (Macmillan, London, 1899), vol.1, p. 62.

[28] C. H. P. Mayo, 'Memories of Birmingham Forty and Fifty Years Ago', *The Cornhill Magazine*, March 1930, pp. 352-62.

I had then never seen so impressive a person ... He told us what he believed to be true ... No one who heard his sermons in those days can ever forget them. Newman, taking some Scripture character for a text spoke to us about ourselves, our temptations, our experiences. His illustrations were inexhaustible. He seemed to be addressing the most secret consciousness of each of us, as the eyes of a portrait appear to look at every person in a room. He never exaggerated; he was never unreal. A sermon from him was a poem, formed on a distinct idea, fascinating by its subtlety, welcome – how welcome! – from its sincerity, interesting from its originality, even to those who were careless of religion: and to others who wished to be religious, but had found religion dry and wearisome, it was like the springing of a fountain out of the rock.[29]

There are other testimonies equally as powerful. Professor Shairp, who remembered Newman's voice as being like a bell tolling, said that "he laid the finger how gently, yet how powerfully, on some inner place in the hearer's heart, and told him things about himself he had never known till then."[30] William Lockhart wrote that Newman had the power of "so impressing your soul as to efface himself, and you thought only of that majestic soul that saw God."[31] This view was confirmed by the Oratorian, Fr Joseph Bacchus, who wrote that "it was only afterwards, if something had struck home and kept coming back to the mind, that one realised that it was not the words only, but something in the tone of the voice, in which they were said, that haunted the memory."[32]

The inexpressible quality of Newman's voice was referred to not just in the context of his sermons alone, but also for the reading of the Scriptures on which his own words were to be based. Canon Furse remembered that "his reading [of the Scriptures] was a commentary."[33] Another hearer recalled that "it is hardly necessary to mention the wonderful charm of Newman's voice and manner as a reader. I once heard him read the Gospel of the lilies of the field before preaching on it. So impressive and suggestive was his modulation of the words that it rang in my ears for days, and seemed to suffice for a sermon by itself."[34] Another testimony speaks of "an indescribable charm of touching

[29] Froude, *Short Studies*, vol. 4, pp. 278–84.
[30] J.C. Shairp, *Studies in Poetry and Philosophy* (Edmonton & Douglas, Edinburgh, 1876), p. 17.
[31] W. Lockhart, *Reminiscences of Fifty Years Since* (Burns & Oates, London,1891), pp. 26–7.
[32] *Sermon Notes*, Introduction, p. 8.
[33] Birmingham Oratory Archives, Furse Papers.
[34] G. E. Phillips, 'Early Reminiscences of Cardinal Newman and of his First Fellow Oratorians', *The Ushaw Magazine* (s.d.) pp. 16–38.

beauty" which surrounded his reading of the Anglican service.

> His delivery of scripture was a sermon in which you forgot the human preacher; a drama in which the vividness of the representation was marred by no effort and degraded by no art. He stood before the sacred volume as if penetrating its contents to their very centre, so that his manner alone, his pathetic changes of voice, or his thrilling pauses, seemed to convey the commentary in the simple enunciation of the text. He brought out meanings where none had ever been suspected ... .[35]

Regular worshippers at St Mary's found their attention riveted and looked forward to hearing their favourite passages, especially some of the Old Testament lessons. There were some who, in years to come, could never listen to the reading of the prophet Isaiah and other passages of scripture without hearing Newman's voice reading them.

This marvellous reading voice continued in his Catholic days as well. At the Sunday High Mass at the Oratory, so Fr Joseph Bacchus recalled, the church notices would be read by one of the other Fathers. Then

> when these were disposed of, [Newman's] voice was heard like a soft piece of music from a distance reading the Epistle. He read it, so far as can be remembered, with very little variation in his voice, except perhaps a barely perceptible lingering over the last words, in which they seemed to die away. His manner of reading the Gospel was different. There were of course the pauses required to mark off the purely narrative portions from the words of different speakers, accompanied by slight changes in the voice. But the marked thing, which cannot be described, was the increased reverence in the reader's voice which culminated when he came to the words of our Saviour. Before and after these there was a kind of hush. A most wonderful thing about it all was the complete elimination of the personality of the reader. He seemed to be listening as much as reading. The words were the living agent, he but their instrument.[36]

Fr Bacchus tells us that for Newman "every sermon [was] a sermon on the objectivity of Revealed Truth."[37] Throughout his long life in the service of the Gospel that was surely his aim as a preacher: to prepare people for conversion, for the acceptance into their lives of the saving truths of revelation. His consummate English style, the extraordinary gift of his voice, his psychological insights, made the legacy of his

[35] Frederick Oakeley, *Historical Notes on the Tractarian Movement 1833-1845* (Longman & Green, London, 1865), pp. 25-6.
[36] *Sermon Notes*, Introduction, pp. 11-12.
[37] *Sermon Notes*, Introduction, p. 12.

sermons one treasured by people all over the world. When he ceased preaching in 1843 many felt utterly bereft and "these withdrew into themselves [and] on Sunday forenoons and evenings, in the retirement of their rooms, the printed words of those marvellous sermons would thrill them till they wept 'abundant and most sweet tears.' Since then many' voices of powerful teachers they may have heard, but none that ever penetrated the soul like his."[38] Canon Furse recounts in his memorandum that one of his daughters could think of nothing she wanted more as a wedding present than all the volumes of Newman's sermons. The influence he wielded from his Anglican and Catholic pulpits was truly extraordinary and has lasted from his own day to this and has helped to reveal him as that sure guide for Christian men and women in their efforts to lead holier and more prayerful lives. His sermons and the ample spiritual riches they contain reveal John Henry Newman to be a supreme Father of Souls.

It would be difficult to find a more explicit statement of his dedication to this God-given work which Newman had taken up than some words from his last sermon as a curate at St Clement's in Oxford, preached on 23 April 1826:

For this at least I can thank God that from the first I have looked upon myself solely as an instrument in His hand, and have looked up to Him for all the blessing and all the grace by which any good could be effected. For I have felt and feel now that it is only as He makes use of me that I can be useful – only as I put myself entirely into His hands that I can promote His glory, and that to attempt even the slightest work in my own strength is an absurdity too great for words to express. He has been pleased to bring me into His ministry and to lay the weight of an high office upon me – and wherever His good providence may lead me I trust I shall never forget that I am dedicated and made over entirely to Him as the minister of Christ, and that the grand and blessed object of my life must be to promote the interest of His cause, and to serve His church, and contribute to the strength of His Kingdom, and make use of all my powers of mind and body, external and acquired, to bring sinners to Him, and to help in purifying a corrupt world – In this good work I willingly would be spent; and I pray God to give me grace to keep me from falling, and ever true to that vow by which I have bound myself to Him that I may at length finish my course with joy and the ministry which I have received of the Lord Jesus to testify the gospel of the grace of God ... .[39]

---

[38] Shairp, *Studies*, p. 256.
[39] Birmingham Oratory Archives, unpublished sermon no. 150, ref. A.17.1.

F. Newman in 1852, returning to Birm^{ham}
in F. Faber's French coat
N.B. The coat is brown, with black
braid, and a hood of bright light blue

SKETCH OF FR. NEWMAN IN FR. FABER'S COAT   *From an album at the London Oratory*

A sketch of Fr Newman in Fr Faber's coat kept at the London Oratory.

Chapter 7

NEWMAN THE EDUCATOR

by Paul Shrimpton

Newman once remarked:"Now from first to last, education, in this large sense of the word, has been my line."[1] Though he wrote this when he was at his lowest ebb, the observation identifies one of the recurring strands of his life. According to conventional wisdom a successful educator is someone who excels either at teaching or at inspiring or organising others to teach; someone who possesses a special talent for dealing with children, adolescents, students or adults in a particular setting, which might be either personal or institutional. What is unusual about Newman as an educator is that over a seventy-five-year period he dealt with every age group, instructing them both individually (in person and by letter) and collectively (in tutorial classes, lecture halls, the schoolroom and the pulpit). The range of his contributions to the organisation of teaching and learning is equally impressive. He reorganised a parish school; founded the first Catholic public school in England; played a leading part in the nineteenth-century revival of Oxford University; and was the chief founder and the first vice-chancellor of a Catholic university. As for his written legacy, Newman's writings have inspired the educational world, above all his best-known work, *The Idea of a University*, which a leading historian of education describes as "unquestionably the single most important treatise in the English language on the nature and meaning of higher education."[2]

It is not a simple task to summarise such a busy and productive life

---

[1] 21 January 1863, *John Henry Newman: Autobiographical Writings*, ed. H. Tristam (London: Sheed & Ward, 1956), p. 259.
[2] S. Rothblatt, 'An Oxonian "idea" of a university: J. H. Newman and "well-being"', *The History of the University of Oxford*, vol. vi, ed. M.G. Brock & M.C. Curthoys (Oxford: Clarendon Press, 1997), p. 287.

and to do justice to such a range of accomplishments; nor is it easy to illustrate how intellectual genius and down-to-earth practicality combined in the same person. By focusing on his literary output, and overlooking the man of action, the reader of Newman can acquire a distorted impression of him as an educator. Consider for a moment the *Idea of a University*. Many people have been hypnotised by the brilliance of the prose and the force of the rhetoric, only to conclude that, however wonderful, the book is ultimately an unworkable ideal. The mistake comes from ignoring the broader picture: that Newman was using the Dublin lectures (that the book is based on) for a specific purpose, to rally support for a new university in a complex political situation. Other writings from Newman's time in Dublin – articles, memoranda, letters – fill out the themes developed in the *Idea* and provide a useful counterbalance; and actual practice at the Catholic University illustrates how his erudite discourses could be translated into action, even in very difficult circumstances. Any reader of Newman's educational writings would do well to remember that he was immersed in the practice of education all his life, and that his thinking derived from constant exposure to learning environments as well as from reflection on how best to shape education to match man's deepest needs.

Born into a happy and secure family, Newman received a stimulating education at home until the age of seven, when he was sent to Ealing School, a large, successful private boarding school. Ealing was quite unlike the great public schools of England: it had first-class facilities, a homely atmosphere, a broad curriculum, specialist teachers and small classes. Newman excelled in his studies and participated enthusiastically in school life, acting in Latin plays, taking part in debates, playing the violin, leading a boys' society and editing several school magazines. His lifelong stress on the role of personal influence in education can be traced back to his formative days at Ealing, where he was befriended by the headmaster and deeply influenced by the sermons, conversations and reading advice of a Classics master. Going up to Trinity College Oxford at the age of 16, after what he called his 'seven years of plenty', was a chastening experience, for he learnt little from his tutors and suffered from the lack of guidance. Almost despite Trinity and its undergraduate rowdiness, Newman continued to pursue a wide range of interests, as well taking on his first (voluntary) educational assignment, the tutoring – by post – of his three sisters and two brothers.

After winning one of the coveted Oriel fellowships in 1822 and receiving Anglican orders, Newman was briefly vice-principal of the tiny St Alban Hall, where he acted as the dean and only tutor of the half-dozen undergraduates. On becoming a tutor at Oriel in 1826, he gave up the curacy of St Clement's, a working-class parish, justifying his decision on the grounds that the tutorship was a *spiritual* office, and one way of fulfilling his Anglican ordination vows. He soon became worried by the "considerable profligacy" of the undergraduates, most of whom were from well-connected families, and by the lack of "direct religious instruction" for them.[3] In doing battle with those privileged young men, whom he considered to be the ruin of the place, Newman and the other three Oriel tutors implemented various reforms: expelling students who they considered beyond reform; tightening up the admissions system; introducing written work into termly college exams; reviving the Chapel sermon at Eucharist; and making changes to the lecture system to favour serious students.[4]

The background to these changes is important. By the 1820s Oxford was in the process of rousing itself after over a century of academic torpor, and Oriel was at the forefront of reform. The problem was that for the majority of Oxford students there were few incentives to work, and so they spent most of their time socialising and in outdoor pursuits. The main academic incursion into their leisure-time was the daily requirement to attend 'college lectures' for two or three hours; during these a tutor would oversee a group of up to fifteen students translating Latin and Greek texts, to which he might add a commentary of a grammatical, historical or philosophical nature. It was an unwieldy system, as the tutors were expected to tackle far too many subjects and the pace was reduced by the presence of many backward and idle students. As a consequence, there had emerged a parallel semi-official system in which the serious students engaged private coaches for individual tuition. Along with the other Oriel tutors, Newman offered the more deserving pupils as much time and attention as the best private coaches, thus eliminating the need and expense of the duplication; in doing so the Oriel tutors provided "the germ of the modern tutorial system" at Oxford.[5]

However, the Oriel tutors were unlike modern-day tutors in that

---

[3] Newman's diary, 7 May 1826, *Letters and Diaries of John Henry Newman* [hereafter abbreviated to LD], vol. i, p. 286n.

[4] K.C. Turpin, 'The ascendancy of Oriel', *History of the University of Oxford*, vol. vi, pp. 188–89.

[5] M.G. Brock, 'The Oxford of Peel and Gladstone, 1800–1833', *History of the University of Oxford*, vol. vi, p. 61.

their principal aim was moral, rather than intellectual; they shared Newman's view that secular education should, if conducted properly, be "a pastoral cure". Arguing from the Oxford statutes, which stressed the pastoral role of tutors, Newman held that "a Tutor was not a mere academical Policeman, or Constable, but a moral and religious guardian of the youths committed to him."[6] In a sermon to the Oriel undergraduates at Easter 1827, he spoke of his responsibility for their welfare: "Account of us as thinking much and deeply of your eternal interests, as watching over your souls as those who must give account."[7] These ideas were not unusual for the time, as families of the lesser gentry, clergy and professional classes were eager to find educational settings which were conducive to moral growth: indeed, one of the reasons for parents employing private tutors in Oxford was so that they could oversee their charges and act *in loco parentis*. This pastoral responsibility was an additional function of the private tutor that Newman had integrated into his role as college tutor, and which rendered it still more effective. By finding extra time for the more worthy undergraduates, Newman "cultivated relations, not only of intimacy, but of friendship, and almost of equality, ... seeking their society in outdoor exercise, on evenings, and in Vacation."[8] The interest he showed was contagious, one tutee describing him as "an elder and affectionate brother".[9] However, the Provost of Oriel became uneasy with what he saw as the 'proselytising' influence of his Tractarian tutors,[10] and feared that the college might lose its connections with wealthy families, and after a dispute over the tutors' role – strictly disciplinary in the Provost's view, fully pastoral in theirs – he simply refused to assign them any more students from the summer of 1830 onwards.

Though Oriel's academic reputation slumped after their departure, Newman's influence on the University's tutorial system did not decline but grew. The explanation for this surprising turn of events forms part of the story of the Oxford Movement, which spread in

---

[6] Newman, memoir, 13 June 1874, *Autobiographical Writings*, p. 91.

[7] Newman, sermon, 15 April 1827, *Sermons, 1824-1843*, vol. i, ed. P. Murray (Oxford: Clarendon Press, 1991), p. 341.

[8] Newman, memoir, 13 June 1874, *Autobiographical Writings*, p. 90.

[9] T. Mozley, *Reminiscences: chiefly of Oriel College and the Oxford movement*, vol. i (London: Longmans, Green, and Co., 1882), p. 181.

[10] For use of the term 'Tractarian' as early as 1829 see P.B. Nockles, "'Lost causes and ... impossible loyalties": the Oxford Movement and the University', *History of the University of Oxford*, vol. vi, p. 202.

grass-roots fashion to the undergraduates and younger graduates of the University through the more personalised form of tuition initiated by Newman and continued by his immediate successors and followers. While the spread of Tractarian ideals and principles was fostered by what Newman called "the force of personal influence and congeniality of thought,"[11] the educational value of the new tutor–pupil relationship was prized even by those who were unsympathetic to the Tractarian cause; over the two decades after Newman's dismissal a growing number of tutors came to regard their office as a pastoral one. Valued as an intellectual training, individual tutorial instruction eventually became the norm at Oxford – and to this day this ideal sets it (and Cambridge) apart from the rest of the educational world.

Newman's influence on university education was felt again, long after his departure from Oxford, when his educational writings appeared in the 1850s. Though what came to form the *Idea of a University* is easily his most widely-read and influential educational work, his historical articles sketching the organic growth and development of what we call a 'university' are vital for grasping his educational ideal, as they illustrate the role played by the 'college'. In these essays (usually printed together as the *Rise and Progress of Universities*[12]) Newman looks at the traditional division of labour at the two ancient universities – however distorted it was in practice – which concerned both methods of teaching (lecturing at the university, tutoring at the college) and the purpose of education (the pursuit of knowledge at university, the formation of character at college). By giving this distinction a new twist, Newman makes his own original contribution. Once he has identified the communication of knowledge as the 'essence' of a university, he goes on to say that the purpose of the college (or its equivalent) is to bring about its harmonious functioning and give it 'integrity': in other words, the role of the college complements that of the university, and stretches the 'strict idea' of a university – what is essential to its 'being' – into 'well-being' and fullness of life.[13] Viewed in this way, the university is the place of progress, movement, and professorial influence; the college of stability, order, and discipline.

Though the *Idea* is usually quoted for its purple passages on the cultivation of the intellect, Newman was at the same time a champion

[11] Newman, *Apologia pro Vita Sua* (London: Longmans, Green & Co., 1864: 1908), p. 40.

[12] *Rise and Progress of Universities* forms the major part of *Historical Sketches*, vol. iii (London: Longmans, Green & Co., 1872: 1909).

[13] S. Rothblatt, 'An Oxonian "idea" of a university', *History of the University of Oxford*, vol. vi, p. 293.

of education outside the lecture hall. He recognised that wherever students gathered, "they are sure to learn one from another, even if there be no one to teach them; the conversation of all is a series of lectures to each, and they gain for themselves new ideas and views, fresh matter of thought, and distinct principles for judging and acting, day by day." Convinced that half the education a student received was derived from the self-perpetuating tradition of the place of learning, Newman attributed great importance to the *genius loci*, or 'spirit of the place'; it constituted "a sort of self-education" which "haunts the home where it has been born, and which imbues and forms, more or less, and one by one, every individual who is successively brought under its shadow." This "ethical atmosphere" amounted to "a real teaching" – and its impact, naturally, was all the greater in a residential university.[14]

Newman's historical sketches illustrate the perennial dangers and hardships that students are exposed to when living away from home. In penning these sketches he tried to illustrate the need for a second home and to show how a collegiate house or hall of residence could provide the necessary paternal oversight, discipline and order. No doubt influenced by memories of Oxford, Newman spoke of the collegiate residence in rousing images of security and sanctuary as "the shrine of our best affections, the bosom of our fondest recollections, a spell upon our after life, a stay for the world-weary mind and soul."[15] When setting up the Catholic University in Dublin, he gave careful thought to the question of student accommodation, and for those living away from home he oversaw the provision of lodging-houses. Each residence was to have its own private chapel and chaplain, one or two lecturers, resident tutors, and up to twenty students, presided over by a dean. Their number and size would "make the large body of students *manageable*", and their variety was intended to "introduce a spirit of emulation".[16] Since the university was only partly residential, Newman grappled with the problem of how to extend collegiate living to those living at home or with local relatives. He tried various schemes for attaching 'externs' to the lodging houses, such as stipulating their presence there for certain hours or meals, so that they might benefit from some aspects of collegiate living rather than simply attending lectures at the university.

Newman also wanted the 'externs' to benefit from collegiate

---

[14] Newman, *Idea of a University* (London: Longmans, Green & Co., 1873:1907), pp. 146–47.
[15] Newman, *Historical Sketches*, vol. iii, p. 215.
[16] Newman to Cullen, 14 August 1852, LD, vol. xv, p. 146.

teaching, as he regarded the tutors – not the lecturers – as the engine of the university. The tutors were to be two or three years older than their pupils, "half companions, half advisers ... thrown together with them in their amusements and recreations ... gaining their confidence from their almost parity of age."[17] As well as conferring academic benefits, tutors would be able to exert "those personal influences, which are of the highest importance in the formation and tone of character."[18] To an Oxford friend, Newman explained that the tutor's work was

> more of influence than of instruction. But at the same time influence is gained *through* the reputation of scholarship etc, and the very duty which comes on a Tutor is to do that which the pupil cannot do for himself, e.g. to explain difficulties in the works read in lecture, and to give aid in the higher classics, or to cram for examinations.[19]

No stranger to the student scene, Newman saw the need for tutors to anticipate in many of their tutees "little love of study and no habit of application, and, even in the case of the diligent, backwardness," and to make adjustments accordingly. The reason he laid such emphasis on the idea of a college tutor was because he saw in it

> that union of intellectual and moral influence, the separation of which is the evil of the age. Men are accustomed to go to the Church for religious training, but to the world for the cultivation both of their hard reason and their susceptible imagination. A Catholic University will but half remedy this evil, if it aims only at professorial, not at private teaching. Where is the private teaching, there will be the real influence.[20]

In proposing guidelines for dealing with students "in that most dangerous and least docile time of life, when they are no longer boys, but not yet men," Newman laid down the guiding principle that "the young for the most part cannot be driven, but, on the other hand, are open to persuasion and to the influence of kindness and personal attachment." University residence (which began, for some, at the age of 16) he saw as "a period of training" linking boyhood and adulthood, designed "to introduce and to launch the young man into the world." This was an enormously important office, because "nothing is more perilous to the soul than the sudden transition from

---

[17] Report for the Year 1854–55, *My Campaign in Ireland, Part I: Catholic University reports and other papers*, ed. W.P. Neville (Aberdeen: A. King & Co., 1896), p. 41.
[18] Newman, Report read to the Thurles Committee, 12 November 1851, *My Campaign*, pp. 84–85.
[19] Newman to T. W. Allies, 6 November 1857, LD, vol. xviii, p. 164.
[20] 'Scheme of Rules and Regulations,' April 1856, *My Campaign*, pp. 117 & 120.

restraint to liberty." Consequently, it was both duty and privilege for the authorities to lead the young men

> to the arms of a kind mother, an Alma Mater, who inspires affection while she whispers truth; who enlists imagination, taste, and ambition on the side of duty; who seeks to impress hearts with noble and heavenly maxims at the age when they are most susceptible, and to win and subdue them when they are most impetuous and self-willed.

This being the case, Newman thought university discipline should be characterised by "a certain tenderness, or even indulgence on the one hand, and an anxious, vigilant, importunate attention on the other."[21]

These words are not the polished phrases of a distant administrator, but those of a rector who had to deal with disciplinary matters personally when he found himself without a vice-rector. Not content with devising the structure of the Catholic University and its degree courses, engaging the academic staff, and undertaking the general administration, Newman led the way by establishing the rector's house (called St Mary's) as one of the first three collegiate houses. While he could easily have distanced himself from the residences and the problems they threw up, instead Newman wished to deal with individuals rather than retreat into academic and administrative isolation. He personally oversaw the servants, the kitchen staff and all the domestic finances at St Mary's, and in addition undertook the duties of dean, chaplain and tutor, alongside those of university rector – and all this while continuing to act as Provost of the Birmingham Oratory. And although he had anticipated that St Mary's would receive sons of Englishmen of the professional classes, he found himself presiding over a cosmopolitan household with considerable social prestige. The vigilance he exerted over his charges – which can be seen in his correspondence – reflected his conviction that the University undertook a grave responsibility of oversight for those who entered its doors; that it acted as a surrogate parent to the students, "an Alma Mater, knowing her children one by one, not a foundry, or a mint, or a treadmill."[22]

In 1857, just as he was about to leave the University, Newman became involved with a different, though equally significant, educational foundation. The Oratory School, Edgbaston opened in May 1859 and during three decades – a third of Newman's long life

---

[21] 'Scheme of Rules and Regulations,' April 1856, *My Campaign*, pp. 114–17.
[22] *Idea of a University*, pp. 144–45.

– it was nurtured and formed by him. The school was a remarkable foundation in a number of ways, both within the Catholic system and on the national stage. It was founded because the converts from the Oxford Movement were unimpressed with the boarding education available to Catholics: they disliked the arrangements at the Catholic colleges (such as Oscott and Ushaw) where those intended for the priesthood were mixed with lay boys in what were effectively minor seminaries. They also disliked their 'un-English' customs: the close supervision of pupils, the impossibility of providing female care for young boys, and the reliance on novices and seminarians as teachers. What they wanted for their sons was an English public school – a Catholic one, but a real one. In the spring of 1858 a group of converts led by the parliamentary barrister Edward Bellasis petitioned Newman to found such a school, promising financial backing and pupils. The Birmingham Oratory sanctioned the plan, and a year later the new school opened its doors to seven boys, aged between eight and twelve, all sons of converts. By the mid-1860s it had grown into a boarding school for seventy boys aged up to eighteen.[23]

Several of the converts called the new foundation 'a Catholic Eton'. If the phrase now brings to mind schools like Ampleforth, Stonyhurst and Downside, it would have made little sense to mid-nineteenth century Victorians, since the Catholic colleges of the time were strictly run, like seminaries, while the public schools were characterised by the wide liberty given to the boys and by the delegation of power through the prefect system. The gulf between the two systems – Catholic college and the Anglican public school – is illustrated by the comments of the convert W.G. Ward twenty years *after* the foundation of the Oratory School, when he declared that "the evils of a public school are inseparable from its very essence"; and he added dismissively that "A 'Catholic Eton' is (to our mind) a contradiction in terms."[24] The fact that Newman was attempting the impossible partly explains why every bishop but Newman's own opposed the school, and why a campaign of gossip against the school continued for over a decade.

Besides creating the first Catholic public school, Newman was also a pioneer within the Catholic system in forming the first *lay* boarding school in England. The Catholic colleges were run either

---

[23] For the story of the school in Newman's lifetime, see P.A. Shrimpton, *A Catholic Eton? Newman's Oratory School* (Gracewing: Leominster, 2005).
[24] 'Catholic colleges and Protestant schools', *Dublin Review*, vol. 31 (October 1878), pp. 313 & 315.

by the secular clergy or by the religious orders, and the education given was generally suited to those boys aspiring to the priesthood or religious life. Most of Newman's convert friends had been educated at the public schools, and what they wanted was a purely *lay* school; they were concerned that the high moral standards at the colleges – which they recognised as important – were "apparently purchased at the expense of many valuable qualities of manliness, energy and readiness to face the world."[25] Their desire for a greater stress on the natural or human virtues met with Newman's full approval, and the statement in his draft manifesto that the Oratory School was intended "for youths whose duties are to lie in the world"[26] incorporated this concern and signalled an important shift in emphasis. This emphasis on 'facing the world' can also be seen in the advice Newman gave boys who thought they might have a priestly vocation, for he invariably urged them to be patient and avoid narrowing their options too early; his attitude shows that he regarded preparation for 'the world' on the same footing as preparation for the priesthood, as one calling for serious and appropriate training. Whether leaving for further study or for the world of work, the boys were prepared by the Oratory School for life in a non-Catholic environment and trained to hold their own in a Protestant society. The number of leavers going into the priesthood – twenty-three in Newman's own time – vindicated, besides, his belief that a curriculum consisting mainly of secular studies would not deter those truly called to Holy Orders.

The fact that the school was the result of parental initiative responded to Newman's conviction that a school's main task is not to replace but to assist parents in their duty to care for and educate their children. This idea was not explicitly stated in school documents, but it showed itself in practice, shaping the Oratory School's attitude to the boys and their parents. Newman declared that the care of schoolboys was "a pastoral charge of the most intimate kind. ... No other department of the pastoral office requires such sustained attention and such unwearied services," because those with pastoral responsibilities live in close contact with their pupils, see them grow up, and "are ever tenderly watching over them, that their growth may be in the right direction."[27] At the same time, when Edward Bellasis told Newman that the school had been a great success for his sons,

---

[25] J. Simeon to Newman, 30 April 1857, Birmingham Oratory Archives.

[26] Draft school manifesto, n.d. [November 1858], Birmingham Oratory Archives.

[27] 'To the members of the Oratory School Society', 20 July 1879, *Addresses to Cardinal Newman with his replies*, ed. W.P. Neville (London: Longmans, Green & Co., 1905), pp. 121-22.

Newman replied that it could only take a "due portion of credit ... seeing the patterns and guidance they have at home"[28] – in other words, a school had to build on the education received in the family.

To make his idea of partnership with parents something real, Newman sent them reports about their sons twice a year – not a common practice for the time. Besides writing reports, he personally undertook the task of dealing with parental demands, a task which kept him busy in term and out. His (highly educated) convert friends badgered him about the curriculum, teaching methods, textbooks – even the boys' pronunciation of Latin. When parents visited the Oratory or passed through Birmingham, and particularly when they came to drop off or collect their sons at the beginning and end of term, Newman used the opportunity to speak to them at length. This degree of parental contact was unknown elsewhere, either at the public schools or at the Catholic colleges.

In order to make the school a second home for the younger boys, Newman placed a 'dame' in charge of them outside school hours. The dame arrangement was largely borrowed from Eton, where dames ran some of the boarding houses and were responsible for the comfort and well-being of the boys in them; in Newman's more elevated vision, her role included overseeing the acquisition of good habits and virtues. Unfortunately the first Oratorian headmaster had his own ideas of what a Catholic public school should be, and as a result he and the entire teaching staff resigned after a disagreement with Newman about the role of the dame; but Newman's closest friends rallied to him, and together they rescued the situation. Ambrose St John, Newman's right-hand man at the Oratory, also played a crucial role by stepping in as headmaster and over the next ten years he and Newman re-formed the school between them.

One effect of the staff mutiny of 1861 at the Oratory School was that Newman's involvement with the school was much closer in the years following. What did this entail? Perhaps the key point was the tone Newman managed to set, and which reflected his lifelong insistence on the pastoral role of the educator. He pulled together observations and opinions from the whole staff to provide a balanced overview in his school reports; the insights they contain show that he had a real gift for judging individuals and a keen understanding of what boys were like. (A theme Newman repeatedly emphasised to parents was the need for patience with their sons. He calmed their eagerness for quick gains, insisting that the

---

[28] Newman to E. Bellasis, 4 September 1865, LD, vol. xxii, p. 42.

phases of growing up be respected and that irritating but passing habits be overlooked: boys could not be forced like plants.) One concrete expression of this pastoral role was the introduction of 'characters' after the end-of-term exams. At these individual interviews St John, as headmaster, would read out an account of the boy's progress and behaviour; then Newman would give a few words of encouragement or approval – or, if necessary, a telling-off. (A similar procedure had existed at the Catholic University, where once a year students were summoned one by one to appear before the rector and listen to a report of behaviour and progress read by his dean and lecturers.) Newman attached great importance to hearing the termly 'characters', refusing to depute the task to others. Nor was he satisfied with a mere acquaintance with the boys; he aimed to know them well and even to make their personal friendship – and this in spite of the age–gap, for he was fifty-eight when the school began. A clue to his ability to relate to boys comes from Oscar Browning, educational reformer at Eton and King's College Cambridge. Browning stayed overnight at the Oratory in 1866 and was struck by "Newman's marvellous copiousness of language and abundant fluency, also with his use of harmless worldly slang, that he might not appear priggish or monkish."[29]

Unlike the students in Dublin, who held Newman in great awe, the youngsters at the Oratory School generally regarded him with affection. One pupil described 'Jack' or 'old Jack' (as Newman was rather irreverently known) as a gentle, understanding and approachable figure for whom nothing was too trivial: thus when the editorial of the *Weekly Wasp* (a school magazine run entirely by boys) criticised the lack of school facilities, Newman saw to it that their grievances were met. In chapel the younger boys found him very quiet and given to rather long quotations from Scripture, but they were held spellbound by his readings from the Bible, and at times his silvery voice and beautiful intonation moved them to tears. Half a century after Newman's death, one old boy could still recall the distinct, deliberate manner in which he intoned the *Pater Noster* during Mass, full of deep devotion.[30]

From the outset Newman had insisted that relations between staff and boys should be characterised by trust, and that they should dispense with the surveillance system used at the Catholic colleges. Thus when the boys were granted an hour a week during school time

---

[29] O. Browning, *Memories of sixty years at Eton, Cambridge and elsewhere* (London: John Lane, 1910), p. 269.
[30] [E. Howard, Viscount FitzAlan] 'Reminiscences of an old boy', *Oratory School Magazine*, no. 98 (July 1940), p. 2.

to write letters home, Newman preferred to trust that the boys did so, rather than check up – even though he knew that some would abuse the privilege. The Oratory School incorporated a full public-school prefect system: senior boys were appointed as prefects not only to play a part in the smooth running of the school, but also to set the younger boys an example – and the boys themselves elected the school captain. Reliance on older boys as prefects was part and parcel of Newman's overall strategy of achieving a new balance in that precarious transition from boyhood to manhood, by placing a premium on trust.

As one might expect, Newman attempted to impart a truly liberal education. The school, he felt, ought to make good scholars out of good boys – he declared to one parent, "it is not simply our aim, but our passion to do so."[31] From the advice he gave, it is clear he considered there was no substitute for hard graft. Yet he was *equally* insistent – particularly with parents – that boys needed their play; his normal reaction to parents who asked for extra tuition for their sons was to remind them of the boys' natural reluctance to forfeit free time outside lessons. He also ensured that sporting enthusiasms were respected: for example, he would rearrange the afternoon timetable in summer, to allow for longer cricket matches. Organised games coexisted with a large variety of other outdoor pursuits; and extra-curricular activities such as music, journalism, debating and acting thrived. Newman himself oversaw the production of the annual Latin play, and he sometimes joined boys in their music recitals, playing second violin.

Newman's arrangements for religious training and instruction are interesting, bearing in mind that the Oratory School was a lay school. Before breakfast the boys said their prayers and attended Mass; at the end of morning school they prayed the Angelus; after tea there was optional Rosary; and at night there were joint prayers followed by a reading from a spiritual classic. In Holy Week all the boys made a three-day retreat. The school had two spiritual directors, whose main duty was to hear the boys' confessions, as well as being available in their rooms for boys to chat to. The boys were taught to say their prayers; they learnt their catechism thoroughly and tested each other in pairs every week, in the presence of Newman or St John; and there were instructions and sermons for the whole school. Newman himself gave the catechetical lectures to the older boys, and he carefully marked and annotated the essays they were required to write afterwards. And in order to stimulate boys' piety, he involved

---

[31] Newman to J. Simeon, 22 August 1864, LD, vol. xxi, p. 205.

them in devotions throughout the liturgical year.

One feature which is common to all Newman's ventures is that in Christianising education he was careful not to distort it; rather than over-stress the Christian dimension, he respected the inner autonomy of education; he understood the connaturality of education and religion, while recognising that "Knowledge is one thing, virtue is another."[32] His harmonious synthesis of the secular and religious in education – "to fit men for this world while it trained them for another"[33] – explains why Christians and non-Christians alike admire him. Nevertheless Newman recognised the ultimate supremacy of holiness over intellectual attainment. This is evident from his words of consolation to the mother of a boy, who died just five years after leaving the Oratory School: "what was your mission ... except to bring him to heaven? That was your very work, – not to gain him a long life and a happy one, but to educate him for his God."[34]

How, then, does Newman rank as an educator? It is inappropriate to compare him with nineteenth-century figures like Arnold of Rugby, because Newman's influence derived from dealing with boys and students separately or in small groups, rather than from addressing them *en masse*. Indeed, his mind instinctively recoiled from an identical treatment of individuals, for he felt that "an academical system without the personal influence of teachers upon pupils, is an arctic winter."[35] While his educational activity shows his insights and reforms to have been both wide-ranging and ahead of his time, his contribution to education cannot be measured simply in terms of new arrangements, but by a variety of indirect means. His sensitivity to both the ideals and the foibles of adolescents and young men enabled him to make demands of them in a way that they would respond to. Newman's original contribution to the ever-present dilemma of an authentic Christian presence in the world is reflected in the down-to-earth training for the challenges and duties of life that he provided in Dublin, in Edgbaston and elsewhere. The principles that guided him in his educational tasks owe much to his understanding of the condition of lay Christians, and their need for an education suited to their condition. If Newman's university and school appear strangely familiar to modern eyes, it is because his insights into the truth about the human condition enabled him to anticipate a future age. And yet, when we

---

[32] *Idea of a University*, p. 120.
[33] *Historical Sketches*, vol. iii, p. 152.
[34] Newman to Mrs F.R. Ward, 22 September 1866, LD, vol. xxii, p. 292.
[35] *Historical Sketches*, vol. iii, p. 74.

see in contemporary education the effects of educational policies pursued in the name of 'efficiency' and 'good management', and the intellectual poverty resulting from production-line learning, we would do well to heed Newman's shrewd observation that while the world is "content with setting right the surface of things," the Church aims "at regenerating the very depths of the heart."[36]

---

[36] *Idea of a University*, p. 203.

The Oratory house on the Hagley Road in Birmingham.

The community of the Oratory in Birmingham. Newman is sitting second from the left.

Chapter 8

NEWMAN THE ORATORIAN

by Daniel Seward

For over half of his life, John Henry Newman's vocation as a son of Saint Philip animated everything else that he did. He wrote so much during his lifetime and achieved so many different things, that the most important is often overlooked. From 1848 until his death in 1890, Newman was first and foremost an Oratorian. Despite founding the Catholic University in Dublin, writing 'Gerontius', being made a Cardinal, and everything else for which he is famous, his life remained that of an Oratorian priest. That is why this chapter is about Newman's home life: his life as a Father of the Oratory.

It would not be an exaggeration to say that after St Philip himself, Newman has been the most important figure in Oratorian history. Nearly all the Congregations of the Oratory which have been founded in the last one hundred and fifty years have been inspired, or strongly influenced, by Newman. Thus for example, the German, North American and South African Oratories founded in the twentieth century were begun by priests who had great devotion to Newman. Newman the Oratorian continues to be a deeply attractive figure. Like St Philip Neri, the founder of the Oratory, John Henry Newman caught souls on the fishing rod of personal influence that is the charism of the Oratorian. Newman's letters are extraordinary because of the variety of people with whom he had profound personal contact. This is exactly the same as St Philip, who used to leave the door of his room on the latch so that anyone could come to him for confession at any time. Newman said that the Confessional was St Philip's great instrument of conversion. With Newman too, so many souls were brought into the Church not by polemics and controversy but by personal kindness and influence.

The Oratory is a community of secular priests who live together without vows. An Oratorian generally remains in the same community for the whole of his life. The 2006 *Annuario Pontificio* describes the work of the Congregation of the Oratory thus: "The individual formation of spiritual culture and piety, by means of instruction, personal contact, spiritual direction, the ministry of the confessional, familiar preaching and the liturgical apostolate, especially among students and young people." This was John Henry Newman's work. In the Brief of Blessed Pope Pius IX of 26th November 1847 establishing the English Oratory we also read:

> We highly approve of the intention of Newman and his companions, who, while performing all the functions of the sacred ministry in England, have at the same time this specially in mind, to aim at doing whatever they think will best promote the cause of religion in the bigger cities, and among those in the higher ranks, the more learned and generally among the more educated.[1]

Thus the English Oratory was given the special role of ministering to the more educated. St Philip drew men to God by attracting them with the good things of this world, especially music, art and good humour. It was said of Philip that he drove men to heaven in coach and four, so simple and winning were his ways. The Oratory as founded in England by Cardinal Newman consciously replicated the Roman customs and the cultural traditions of St Philip. We can see this in the strong musical and liturgical practices of the Oratory that endure to this day in all three English houses. Baroque architecture and polyphony are not essential parts of the Catholic faith, but today as in the sixteenth or nineteenth centuries they are the means of drawing souls to holiness.

In Newman's own lifetime and afterwards, people sometimes have asked why he hid himself away in Birmingham, surrounded by what some saw as second-rate men. It is when we examine what it was about St Philip and the idea of the Oratory that attracted Newman, and why he chose this particular way of life in the Church, that we can properly answer this question and understand what Newman was about. In a sermon for St Philip's Day at the Birmingham Oratory, Mgr Ronald Knox asked this same question. He said that to many, it seemed typical of the Catholic Church that two little slices of

---

[1] The Brief of Pius IX authorising Newman to establish the Oratory in England is published as an appendix to *Newman the Oratorian: His unpublished Oratory Papers*, Placid Murray OSB, ed. (Dublin: Gill and Macmillan Ltd, 1969), pp. 421–429.

Italy "reeking of the Renaissance" should have been transplanted to Brompton and to Edgbaston. Why didn't Cardinal Newman found something of his own, or revive some defunct English religious order, like the Gilbertines, rather than shipping in the Oratory?

In fact, Mr Newman had originally considered founding an entirely new Congregation. There exist some notes that he made in June 1846 about a proposal to begin the 'Congregation of the Most Holy Trinity'. The members would live together, in the country, with a substantial library. Its one object would be

> to practise and promote the loving adoration of the mysteries of Religion – especially that of the most Sacred Trinity.
>
> Considering the rationalistic tone of the times, which is all based or exhibited in denial of mysteries, it seems of special importance to teach the contrary.
>
> Hence the work of the Congregation will consist in reading, teaching, catechising, preaching, controverting, all with a view to enforcing the mysteries of faith, and subjecting reason to faith.[2]

Newman seems to have intended that the members of this congregation would have gone out to preach courses of sermons and would have had an essentially intellectual apostolate. So it already had some things in common with the Oratory, but was not identical with it. Yet by February of the next year (1847), Newman had abandoned this idea, and was full of enthusiasm for the notion of founding an Oratory in England. Looking back, we can see God's Providence at work. St Philip always denied that he was the founder of the Oratory, saying that only the Blessed Virgin could claim that distinction. So also, Newman didn't go to Rome with the intention of founding the English Oratory, but he 'met' St Philip, was captivated by his spirit and won by his influence.

Although it seems that Newman had heard of St Philip while he was still an Anglican, he does not appear to have known much about him. It was Nicholas Wiseman, later the first Cardinal Archbishop of Westminster, and then Vicar Apostolic of the Midland District, who later took the credit for introducing the idea of the Oratory into Newman's head. Certainly, Wiseman had been a Brother of the Secular Oratory when he had been Rector of the English College in Rome, and he had a great devotion to St Philip. All the same, Newman seems to have ignored the suggestion at the time, and only returned to it later. This is what Fr Newman wrote in 1878:

---

[2] *Newman the Oratorian*, pp. 149-150.

When I got to Rome, my first (and very crude) thought was to form and devote myself to the establishment of a theological College in England of secular priests. Then I said 'Shall I be a Jesuit?' and I mentioned the idea to my friends out of Rome as to Stanton, Dalgairns, A. Christie etc., and then, after other inquiries and speculations, I said..., 'Dear me! I have forgotten St Philip,' and then at once I began acquaintance with him, finding out his Church as the first step.[3]

As early as November 1846, Father Theiner from the *Chiesa Nuova* called on Newman and his friend Ambrose St John, who were living at the College of Propaganda and preparing for their ordinations, studying with the Jesuits. Then in December Newman made his first visit to the Oratory, and he recorded his impressions to his erstwhile companion at Littlemore, JD Dalgairns, who was studying in France, and was later to cause Newman much grief, both as a member of the Birmingham and London Oratories. Newman wrote:

We have seen the *Chiesa Nuova* (St Philip's Church) and the Casa adjoining, with Theiner – who said Mass with and for us and communicated us in the small room where St Philip had his ecstacies [sic]. The *Casa* is the most beautiful thing of the kind we have seen in Rome – rather too comfortable, i.e. fine galleries for walking in summer, splendid orange trees, etc, etc. If I wished to follow my bent I should join them, if I joined any. They have a good library, with handsome sets of rooms apparently. It is like a College with hardly any rule. They keep their own property, and really I should not wonder if at last I felt strongly inclined to it, for I must own I feel the notion of giving up property tries my faith very much.[4]

The *Chiesa Nuova* – 'New Church' – is so-called because it was built by St Philip on the site of a previous church. The magnificent house designed by Borromini is next door, and Newman was able to see the Fathers living there before their eviction in the political turmoil of nineteenth-century Italy. (Today the Oratory has the use only of a small portion of the house.)

For a while, the Oxford converts continued to look around at other possibilities. In a letter of January 1847 to Dalgairns, Newman said that they had read the Redemptorist rule, and discovered that it would not do for them. Then he said, "the more we see, the more it seems to lie between our being Jesuits or Seculars – (though *of course* we are not giving up the Oratorians yet.)"[5] Part of the problem seems

---

[3] Memorandum of 10th May 1878, quoted in *Newman the Oratorian,* p. 390.

[4] *Letters & Diaries* Vol. XI, 31st December 1846, pp. 305-6.

[5] Letter to Dalgairns, 10 January 1847, *Letters and Diaries*, vol. 12, p. 8.

to have been that Newman was not particularly impressed with the reality of the Roman Oratory: "By the bye we went to the Oratory last night, and were very much disappointed to find it a *simple concert*, with hardly anything religious about it – a short sermon – a few prayers, people sitting the while… We were this evening at St Andrea, the Theatine church, to hear Father Ventura. The whole was just what we had hoped the Oratory would be."[6] Yet only a week later, Newman wrote to Bishop Wiseman: "It is curious and very pleasant that, after all the thought we can give the matter, we have come round to your Lordship's original idea, and feel we cannot do better than be Oratorians."[7] There were still some difficulties to overcome; the Oratorian rule was very specific about the religious practices to be undertaken, so that Newman thought "the rule, I say, was in almost all its parts perfectly unsuited to a country of heretics and Saxons."[8] Such difficulties were overcome when it was realized that the rule could be adapted to English conditions, and indeed Pope Pius IX gave the English Oratorians their own specific rule and Brief. In his lifetime, St Philip was generally opposed to the foundation of Oratories outside of Rome, mainly because he didn't want to see his own spontaneous response to the action of the Holy Spirit transformed into a religious order. Although the Oratories of San Severino, Naples and Palermo were founded while Philip was still alive, the larger spread of the Oratory began only after Philip's death, and it was soon established that each would be entirely independent from all the others. The genius of the Oratory is that it is able to adapt itself to the particular location and becomes part of the place itself. Newman wrote a hymn to St Philip which quaintly describes the unexpected arrival of St Philip in the industrial midlands of England:

> And when he died, he did but go
> In other lands to dwell,
> A traveller now, who in his life
> Ne'er left that one dear cell.
>
> He travelled, and he travelled on,
> He crossed the swelling sea.
> He sought our island's very heart,
> And here at length is he.

Newman was ordained priest on 30th May 1847, and by the end of

---

[6] Ibid., p. 7.
[7] *Letters and Diaries*, vol. 12, pp. 19-20.
[8] Letter to Dalgairns, 22 January 1847, *Letters and Diaries*, vol. 12, p. 22.

the following month, he and six companions had gone to *Santa Croce*, where they were to perform their Oratorian noviciate under one of the Roman Fathers, Fr Rossi. He doesn't seem to have set the English converts on fire – Newman later remarked, "How dreary Fr Rossi and Santa Croce"! In fact Rossi had ideas of change to the Oratorian constitutions, of making the congregation more centralized, with which Newman had no sympathy. Newman really learnt the idea of the Oratory not from any existing Oratorian, but from his reading of Oratorian history. It was providential that he should have done so, for Fr Rossi's ideas eventually bore fruit in the 'Sicilian Movement' of the 1930s when Fr Nanni of the Roman Oratory, supported by Bishop Arista of Acireale, wished to create a centralized structure for the Oratory with a General to form a 'benevolent dictatorship'. Such a notion was very attractive because it would mean that dwindling Oratories could be propped up by Fathers from flourishing houses elsewhere. However, as soon as the London and Birmingham houses got wind of these plans, they sent off a solemn Protest against this incursion on their traditional freedoms. It was their influence, together with the Fathers of the Barcelona Oratory, which saved the Confederation of the Oratory from becoming a structured religious order. Fr Denis Shiel of the Birmingham Oratory, who had been a boy at the Oratory School, and was the last novice to be clothed by the Cardinal, led the opposition to the reforms at the Congress in Rome. So we see how important it was to be that Newman did somehow pick up the idea of the Oratory, mainly from his reading of the Rule, of the *Excellences* and of Oratorian history.

Newman found in the Oratory much that was already familiar to him. He thought that St Philip was extremely like Keble, and said that the Oratory "seemed more adapted than any other for Oxford and Cambridge men." This does not mean though that Newman simply imposed his own character on an institution that he called the Oratory. His careful study both of the life of St Philip and of the traditions of various houses makes this impossible to believe. He set forth what he considers to be the 'object' of St Philip's institution in his third Chapter Address. First of all, Newman observed that the Oratory came about, as if by accident, in particular circumstances because of the Church's needs in the sixteenth century. (We notice that Newman does not attribute to St Philip any organised plan that Philip never had.) Newman wrote that "the priests of the Oratory formed centres round which a more zealous ministry collected itself after a time of relaxation."[9] From this he abstracted what he calls the 'object' of the Congregation: "the formation of good secular priests, who shall at once be a blessing to the population among which they are placed, and a standard of the parochial clergy or missioners."[10] In other words, the Oratory exists simply to promote holiness, and Newman records some examples of astonishing sanctity amongst the early Fathers. The second feature of Oratorians which is drawn out is one to which Newman returns often – that they are "gentlemen". By this, at least for nineteenth century England, he means that they are educated men. Hence Newman believes that a particular charism of the Oratory is that "refinement ... should have been one of the means by which the Oratory acted in the reformation of both clergy and laity at the time of its establishment."[11]

Newman returned to England in time for Christmas 1847, and arrived at Maryvale on New Year's Eve. It was there, on the evening of 1st February 1848 that the English Oratory formally began, at First Vespers of the Purification. Newman admitted nine members, and then later in the month took on Fr Faber's community at Cotton. There were many problems as a result: the Earl of Shrewsbury was aggrieved that the Oratory wished to withdraw from Cotton, which he had entrusted to Faber, but it was quite unsuitable as a location, being in the country, when Oratories are always situated in towns. For a time, the community was very large, and in 1850 Fr Faber went with half of the Fathers to found the London Oratory, which eventually settled on the Brompton Road. The Birmingham Oratorians settled in Edgbaston in 1852 and the house in which Newman lived is still the home of the Birmingham Oratory. The beautiful church which was built in Newman's memory was of course not known by him. In his lifetime there was only the temporary church, which was really just a utilitarian box. The decision to build the house first and the church later was very deliberate. Newman realized that people would always give money to build a noble church, but not always for a community house. The value of the house is much more hidden, but it is central to the Oratorian life. As Newman told the Fathers in 1878, on the thirtieth anniversary of the foundation of the English Oratory, "an Oratory is a family and a home; a domestic circle, as the words imply,

---

[9] *Newman the Oratorian*, p. 187.
[10] Ibid., p. 188.
[11] Ibid., p. 191.

is bounded and rounded."[12]

Like St Philip, Newman had a tremendous sense of place. Once St Philip had arrived in Rome, he never left it, and he achieved the transformation of that city simply by inhabiting the place, and so filling it with his spirit. Before 1845, Dr Newman had considered the snapdragon on the wall of Trinity to be a symbol of his permanence in Oxford. Now that he had been uprooted from there, he found the stability offered by the Oratory attractive. He stressed that the Congregation is the *home* of the Oratorian, and observed that the Italian Fathers even make an equivalent of this very English concept by using the Italian word *nido* – 'nest' – to describe their rooms. The Oratorian, we are told, is to have 'comfort' and there should be no "meanness, poverty, austerity, forlornness, (or) sterness" either in the church or in the house. That this commitment to stability was real is shown by the fact that Newman persevered to his death in Birmingham, even though he considered London to be more of a centre. We see again Newman's belief that each Oratory must have its own character when he says that, "the Oratory is thus emphatically a local institution; it acts on and is influenced by the town in which it is found, it is the representative of no distant or foreign interest, but lives among and is contented with its own people."[13]

Related to this principle is what we might call the quietness of the Oratory; that it avoids controversy, remembering St Philip's maxim, *Amare nesciri* – 'Love to be unknown'. In his Chapter Address of 9th February 1848, Fr Newman compared the Oratory with the Jesuits, saying that, "the debt which Catholics owe them is vast. They are a body of men, as hardworking as they are devout; their houses breathe the spirit of religion. Their renown is far higher than that of the humble Oratory."[14] The Oratorian does not have the glamorous role on the world stage that the Jesuit has; instead he contents himself with "influence". Fr Giulio Giustiniani of the Roman Oratory said that a priest of the Congregation should die on one of three wooden places: the predella of the altar, the confessional, or the chair used to preach in the Oratory. Newman did not spurn the humble scope of the Oratorian vocation. He saw that the absence of vows in the Oratory was not merely a curious feature or irrelevant quirk, but it was central to the whole spirit of the Congregation. He argued that, in some

---

[12] *Newman the Oratorian*, p. 387.

[13] Ibid., p. 196.

[14] Ibid., p. 210.

senses at least, a voluntary obedience is actually superior to a vowed one, since it demands greater perseverance. Instead of laws, it is charity that holds an Oratorian community together: "Instead of vows or forcible impositions, they held it was enough to have Christian love, and they cultivated that love, towards God and man and each other, in the spirit of that great Apostle to whose inspired writings St Philip had so special a devotion."[15] This is why Newman devotes so many of his thoughts to the nature of community life. Indeed, in his 'Remarks on the Oratorian Vocation', written in 1856, Newman argues that it is almost only in the Oratory that true community life is found, since it is unvowed, and yet permanent. He quotes the maxim *Vita communis, mortificatio maxima* – the common life is the greatest mortification – to show that the common life is the greatest feature of the Oratory, both in bringing about sanctity and obtaining influence.

Newman's Oratorian life certainly had its ups and downs, but he is an example of that perseverance for which the son of St Philip prays daily. At times of stress and isolation, it was his community that sustained him, as we can see in the moving conclusion of the *Apologia*:

> I have closed this history of myself with St Philip's name upon St Philip's feast-day; and, having done so, to whom can I more suitably offer it, as a memorial of affection and gratitude, than to St Philip's sons, my dearest brothers of this House, the Priests of the Birmingham Oratory, AMBROSE ST. JOHN, HENRY AUSTIN MILLS, HENRY BITTLESTON, EDWARD CASWALL, WILLIAM PAINE NEVILLE, and HENRY IGNATIUS DUDLEY RYDER? who have been so faithful to me; who have been so sensitive of my needs; who have been so indulgent to my failings; who have carried me through so many trials; who have grudged no sacrifice, if I have asked for it; who have been so cheerful under discouragements of my causing; who have done so many good works, and let me have the credit of them; – with whom I have lived so long, with whom I hope to die.[16]

Blessed Antony Grassi of the Oratory in Fermo said on his deathbed, "Oh what a joy to die as a Son of St Philip!", and we have a saying that an Oratorian is known at his death, because only then do we know that he has persevered to the end. The familiar affection that Newman expressed for his brethren is a reminder of the depth of friendship he found in his community. At the clothing ceremony of an Oratorian

---

[15] *Newman the Oratorian*, p. 204.
[16] *Apologia pro Vita Sua*, 1864 edition, pp. 429–30.

novice, which Newman devised, the postulant is asked: "Will you love us with brotherly affection, without particular friendship or party combination, being gentle with the impetuous, winning the froward and bearing the perverse?" It is in this constant and deliberate exercise of charity that sanctity is to be found. Newman's attachment to his home and to his brethren is shown in his anxiety that being made a cardinal would necessitate residence in Rome. Only when he was reassured that he could remain in Birmingham was he happy to accept this honour.

One of Newman's setbacks was the frustration of his plan to found an Oratory in Oxford. This was thwarted by the opposition of the Roman congregation *Propaganda Fide* and of the English bishops to any foundation which might encourage English Catholics to attend Oxford University. *Propaganda Fide* attached a secret condition to any foundation of an Oratory in Oxford that Newman should not live there, a direction that caused profound resentment in him when he found out about it. Newman had actually purchased some land in Oxford, on the site of the present Wellington Square, with the aim of building an Oratory there, but he sold the land in 1867 when his plans came to nothing. When we see failure in the lives of saints and holy men it can be encouraging for us to realise that they too had disappointments and reversals and that Providence disposes in ways that seem unclear at the time. In the centenary year of Newman's death, 1990, Oratorians did go to Oxford, and the Oxford Oratory was established as an independent house in 1993. In all three English Oratories, as well as in others abroad, we can see the continuation of Newman's mission given him by Pius IX.

The simplicity of the Oratory was for Newman one of its chief beauties, because the road to perfection was clearly visible. In 1856, he gave a Chapter Address, which, slightly adapted, could serve as a way for all of us, priests and laypeople alike, to become saints. This Address is worth quoting from at length because it gives us a very precise picture of John Henry Newman's daily life, and even of the struggle to find perfection in his vocation. It has been entitled, 'A Short Rule to Perfection':

> It is the saying of holy men that, if we wish to be perfect, we have nothing more to do than to perform the ordinary duties of the day well ...
>
> We must bear in mind what is meant by perfection − it does not mean any extraordinary service, anything out of the way, or

especially heroic in our obedience. Not all have the opportunity of heroic acts and sufferings, but it means what the word perfection ordinarily means. By perfect we mean that which has no flaw in it, that which is complete, that which is consistent, that which is sound. We mean the opposite to imperfect. As we know well what imperfection in religious service means, we know by the contrast what is meant by perfection.

He then is perfect who does the work of the day perfectly – and we need not go beyond this to seek for perfection. You need not go out of the round of the day. We are perfect, if we do perfectly our duties as members of the Oratory.

I insist on this, because I think it will simplify our views, fix our exertions on a definite aim. If you ask me what you are to do in order to be perfect, I say – first – Do not lie in bed beyond the due time of rising – give your first thoughts to God – make a good meditation – say or hear Mass and communicate with devotion – make a good thanksgiving – say carefully all the prayers which you are bound to say – say Office attentively, do the work of the day, whatever it is, diligently and for God – make a good visit to the Blessed Sacrament. Say the Angelus devoutly – eat and drink to God's glory – say the Rosary well, be recollected – keep out bad thoughts. Make your evening meditation well – examine yourself duly. Go to bed in good time, and you are already perfect.[17]

What Newman says here is really just the same as St Thérèse of Lisieux taught in her 'Little Way': it is not doing great things, but doing little things with great love. This in the end is why Newman as an Oratorian proves to be a continual inspiration today. His way of holiness, like that of St Thérèse, is one that is accessible to everyone, because it simply means going about our ordinary lives, doing ordinary things, but doing them all as well as we can and with a supernatural motive, that of giving glory to Almighty God. If Cardinal Newman ever seems a remote, intellectual figure to some, then it is important always to recall the concrete way in which he lived out his pilgrimage on earth: by the daily routines, the community living and the pastoral care of a Father of the Oratory.

---

[17] Chapter Address, 27th September 1856, in *Newman the Oratorian,* pp. 359-60.

And grant that to Thine honor, Lord,
Our daily toil may tend;
That we begin it at Thy word,
And in Thy favor end.

And, lest the flesh in its excess
Should lord it o'er the soul,
Let taming abstinence repress
The rebel, and control.

To God the Father glory be,
And to His Only Son,
And to the Spirit, One and Three,
While endless ages run.

J. H. Newman. *c. 1842.*
J.J.D. May. 12. 1843.

The second half of a translation by Newman of a Latin hymn from the Parisian breviary, done in Littlemore in 1842 and published as number 139 in Verses on Various Occasions.

Chapter 9

NEWMAN THE LETTER WRITER

by Joyce Sugg

The nineteenth century was a time for the writing of letters. The educated were accustomed to write regularly and often copiously, and the improvement in the means of sending letters encouraged them. By the early part of the century there was a carefully regulated postal service in England and, with Rowland Hill's reforms and the use of the railway and the steamship, the post became more speedy and efficient. Eminent Victorians such as Gladstone and Dickens have left a weighty correspondence, a valuable source for historians and biographers.

The correspondence of John Henry Newman is extraordinarily extensive. Father Charles Stephen Dessain of the Birmingham Oratory, writing the introduction to the first volume of the published letters in 1961, explained: "He lived so long, he had so many friends, he was engaged upon such various enterprises, for so much of his life he carried on an intense apostolate by means of letters, that his output became enormous."[1] Father Dessain also explained why he thought it necessary to publish every extant letter of Newman's. There are so many different kinds of people likely to want access to the letters of the great polymath, for instance historians, educationists, philosophers, theologians, students of English literature, that a selection of the letters would not serve. Moreover, only a complete publication really allows Newman to speak for himself. It was decided to publish in the same volumes Newman's brief diaries and quotations from letters to Newman where they were necessary for the understanding of his own letters. Father Dessain died in 1976, having edited twenty one volumes, and other editors have since completed the great task, so

---

[1] LD XI, p. xvii.

these letters are accessible to all and it is not only the specialists who will relish them. "Those interested may see him pursuing his ideal, may admire the serenity, the humour, the shrewd observation and the naturalness that went with such deep feeling and affection, and may form their own judgment of him."[2]

Newman himself had a great opinion of letters as the best form of biography. He wrote to his sister, Jemima Mozley, on May 18 1863:

> It has ever been a hobby of mine (unless it be a truism and not a hobby) that a man's life lies in his letters... . Biographers varnish; they assign motives; they conjecture feeling; they interpret Lord Burleigh's nods; they palliate or defend. For myself, I sincerely wish to seem neither better nor worse than I am... .[3]

He knew that one day a biography would be written and hoped that his friend, Ambrose St John, would be the writer and present his life by means of the letters. After Ambrose St John's premature death he had to look again for a biographer and editor of his letters and chose Anne Mozley, Jemima's sister-in-law, who was intelligent and had shown her skill and judgment in a published selection of her brother's letters. An Anglican herself, she made her selection from Newman's letters written in his Anglican years and they were published together with a memoir that he had written. There was no plan for a second book covering the later part of his life, presumably with a Catholic editor, because, as he said, "toes might be trodden on". This little piece of biographical history explains why Father Dessain began his big publication of the letters with those of the Catholic period. The Anglican letters had already had an airing.

We might wonder how letters could be assembled so readily but the nineteenth century was the age of letters not simply because they were frequently sent but because they were cherished: it was customary to keep drafts, to make copies, to put away letters received. Newman looked after his correspondence and, in the 1863 letter to Jemima, refers to his custom of going at times to his pigeon-holes of letters to "do a little work in the way of sifting, sorting, preserving and burning." There are other references over the years to this regular task so it seems that Newman did it sometimes, just as a good housewife might sort out cupboards when there were a few spare hours. When the Birmingham Oratory asked for a loan of Newman's letters, after his death, thousands poured in and lay in stacks around the desk of Father

---

[2] LD XI, p. xvii.
[3] LD XX, p. 443.

William Neville, Newman's literary executor. Faithful Oratorians continued the Cardinal's sorting work and many collections were added to the first.

The massive volumes of letters are a splendid record and Father Charles Stephen Dessain was right to go for a complete publication but there is also much to be said for making selections: few will read all the letters and even the most assiduous might pass lightly over some dry business notes, the general reader flinch at the size and number of the volumes. All the modern biographies quote from the letters extensively and the reader will do well to dwell on letters that appeal or touch or surprise. With the collected letters it is interesting and instructive to follow a particular episode in Newman's life, for instance the letters that chronicle his disappointment at his poor degree and then his successful application for the Fellowship at Oriel, the period when he was threatened with imprisonment for denouncing Achilli or (the best story) the letters written when he knew he might be made a cardinal but when all was in doubt. This kind of selection gives some taste of what it is to read history as it unfolds day by day. The narrative is immediate, instinct with possibilities and filtered through the sensibility of the main protagonist. Even a handful of letters will instruct and delight and enable the reader to hear Newman's voice. Some groups of letters will give an idea of the possibilities.

The first letters of a child who will grow to be a great letter writer have a particular interest. John Henry Newman seems to have known that letters were the way to communicate with distant friends before he could write a word. When his sister Jemima was born he was three. The nursemaid wrote, with difficulty and wild spelling, to Mrs Newman and reported (this is a corrected version) "that Master John desires his duty to you and his papa, and wished me to send you some violets. He desires I would say he was very well and very happy."[4]

His first letter was written from school and simply gives a formal statement of the date of the beginning of the holidays. It could have been dictated by an usher. However, a later letter about the coming Christmas holidays, written to his aunt, is certainly from the boy's heart and mind as well as from his quill pen:

Ealing December 6th 1811

Dear Aunt,

The joyful 21 again approaches when our books are closed

---

[4] LD I, p. 3.

according to delightful custom, and when I hope for the additional pleasure of seeing you all well and happy at home.

Already in my imagination I pay respects to the mince Pies, Turkies, and the other good things of Christmas.

In the mean time the Notches on my wooden Calendar diminish apace, but not the duty and affection with which I am

Dear Aunt, Your's ever John H. Newman[5]

When he became an Oxford undergraduate at the age of sixteen, of course his circle widened and his mind was filled with new impressions, new possibilities. He thought much on religious matters for he was now a committed Christian. The days had passed when only his family would receive his letters but he did write to them frequently and warmly and he continued to do so as the years went on and his responsibilities multiplied. In March 1826 he was an ordained priest of the Church of England and had "done duty" at St Clement's church, as Fellow and Tutor at Oriel he had administrative and teaching duties and he was writing on Apollonius. A letter to his sister Harriet in March 1826 shows how seriously he took himself at this time:

> I am up to my chin in Apollonius, and very cross, as you may suppose. I *must* send him off by the very beginning of next week, and I have three sermons to write.
>
> I am just transported into rooms in College with my books in disorder all over the room …
>
> I feel pleased you like my Sermons – I am sure I need not caution you against taking anything I say on trust. Do not be run away with by any opinions of mine. I have seen cause to change my mind in some respects, and I may change again. I see I know very little about any thing, though I often think I know a great deal.
>
> I have a great understanding before me in the Tutorship here. I trust God may give me grace to undertake it in a proper spirit, and to keep steadily in view that I have set myself apart for His Service for ever … .[6]

In a sense the adult Newman never left his childhood behind. He remembered with startling clarity the details of all the places he had lived in as a small boy and, like Wordsworth, he believed that it was in such recollections that "one seems almost to realize the remnant of a pre-existent state."[7] We know from letters written at various times that in 1805 he lay in bed at Grey Court House, Ham, and

---

[5] LD I, p. 9.
[6] LD I, pp. 280–281.
[7] LD III, p. 172.

watched the candles burning in the windows to celebrate the victory of Trafalgar, that a magnolia flowered up the house and that the child in his crib in the summer heard the mower's scythe cutting the grass. He remembered his grandmother's house at Fulham and the breakfast things on the table gleaming in the early sunlight. There was a loft in the house with apples on the floor and a mangle. He could have passed an examination in knowledge of the houses of his earliest years, and an observer of the child's responses to the world around him might have prophesied that he would be a poet.

There is one letter from Newman's youth that reads like a prose poem that could have been written by Keats or by Hopkins. It was written from Devon where Newman was visiting the family of his friend Hurrell Froude in 1831. It is not a set piece worked up for publication but a letter home, done freely and at speed:

> What strikes me most is the strange richness of everything. The rocks blush into every variety of colour - the trees and fields are emeralds, and the cottages are rubies. A beetle picked up at Torquay was as green and gold as the stone it lay on and a squirrel which ran up a tree here just now was not a pale reddish brown, to which I am accustomed, but a bright brown red. Nay, my very hands and fingers look rosy, like Homer's Aurora, and I have been gazing at them with astonishment ... . The scents are extremely fine, so very delicate, yet so powerful, and the colours of the flowers as if they were all shot with white. The sweet peas especially have the complexion of a beautiful face – they trail up the wall, mixed with myrtles, as creepers ... .[8]

In 1833 Newman sent long descriptive letters, travellers' tales, of his one great holiday abroad to the Mediterranean with the Froudes, Hurrell and his father. This was the time he took off, dangerously, on his own into the wild places of Sicily. This travel was an unusual luxury and the descriptive writing, from Devon or Italy, something special. He was to be content to spend years in smoky Birmingham where God wanted him to be.

It has been said that Newman wanted only two things, after God: books and friends. This is another way of expressing the paradox about him that he loved to be alone and also loved to be with friends. Many people find it easier to visualise him as Harriett did when she received the letter from Oriel: there he is, with books about him, having sent off a learned essay and about to write some sermons. The letters in bulk give a complementary picture for they are a great monument to

---

[8] LD II, pp. 343.

friendship. In the *Parochial and Plain Sermons* Newman gave his views on the subject:

> We find our Saviour had a private friend; and this shows us first, how entirely he was a man, as much as any of us, in his wants and feelings; and next, that there is nothing inconsistent with the fullness of Christian love, in having our affections directed in an especial way towards certain objects ... . The best preparation for loving the world at large, and loving it duly and wisely is to cultivate an intimate friendship and affection towards those who are immediately about us.[9]

Newman's strong affections are there to see in the ordinary intercourse of daily life, the exchange of news in his personal letters. The strongest expressions of love come in the letters that mourn the loss of his dear ones. His best-loved sister, Mary, died suddenly at nineteen. The two great friends of his youth, John Bowden and Hurrell Froude, died young of tuberculosis, the great scourge of the Victorian era. He also suffered many losses because of his conversion to Rome. All his siblings abandoned him except for his sister Jemima and even she kept him away from her house for many years, keeping contact with him by letters and rare visits to Birmingham. The letters sent from Littlemore in October 1845 are short and poignant:

Littlemore, Oct 8 1845

My Dear Jemima,

    I must tell you, what will pain you greatly, but I will make it as short as you would wish me to do.

    This night Father Dominic the Passionist, sleeps here. He does not know of my intentions, but I shall ask him to receive me into what I believe to be the One Fold of the Redeemer.

    This will not go, till all is over,

Ever Yours affectionately John H Newman[10]

He was perhaps even more distressed to send the news to John Keble and the other friends who had laboured with him in the founding of the Oxford Movement and he missed them over the years. Keble, Pusey and Newman met once in 1865 and a powerful and moving letter resulted, a description of a harrowing day where past and present, the remembrance of the closeness they had had and the distance now between them all combined to make for "as painful thoughts as I ever recollect." The great positive was that Keble was "as delightful as ever,"

---

[9] P.P.S. II, pp. 52–53.
[10] LD XI, p. 8.

and Newman had a little time alone with him to talk "in a tone of intimacy as if we had never been parted."[11]

Newman's life, however, was never barren of friends and it seems entirely appropriate that his choice in his Catholic life was to be a priest in the Oratory of St Philip Neri where its members are bound more by mutual affection than by a rigid Rule.

He had many friends who came over to Rome and he made many more. Some were priests or nuns and he was in touch with Roman cardinals, with Wiseman, Ullathorne and Manning but his correspondence after 1845 could not be described as predominantly ecclesiastical. Most of his friends were lay men and women. Some of the men were very much of the world of affairs: they were lawyers, journalists, parliamentarians, learned men who would be useful when Newman wanted staff for the Catholic University. They gave him hope that the Catholic Church in England would have, increasingly, an educated and active laity. The women inhabited a much more narrow sphere but many of Newman's female friends, doing all they were permitted to do, laboured steadily to improve the condition of the poor, to help in the parishes, to write. Mothers of families had the responsibilities of teaching their daughters and nursing the sick. All this is mirrored in the letters.

There were many families who had Newman as constant friend and advisor. One was the family of William Froude, the younger brother of Hurrell, so that it seemed that Newman's dear friend had left him this human legacy. His wife was a gentle and intelligent woman who became a Catholic and so did four of their five children while William, a naval architect, was a man of practical and scientific bent who had no use for religion. Letters to and from this little group show how Newman related to people of different ages and temperaments. He did not have time to visit them in Devon but letters kept their friendships in good repair. He exchanged letters with William, the religious man and the agnostic arguing peaceably, and with Catherine who did not accept Catholicism until she had examined its doctrines and its practices with care. She was never gushing but she was accustomed to say that Newman always contrived to say what suited her mind.

The three boys went to the Oratory School and letters came at the end of term to give an informal report on their behaviour and their progress or lack of progress in their studies. Newman did this for all the parents and knew every boy well. The second boy, Eddy, believed at the

---

[11] LD XXII, p. 52.

end of his schooldays that he had a vocation to the priesthood or to religious life (though he seemed suspiciously hazy about the difference between the two modes of life) and this was a delicate matter, for William's tolerance would be sorely tried if he sent him to a university and then found he had educated him for the Catholic priesthood. Newman made it clear that a genuine vocation must be followed but he behaved with great discretion and in fact Eddy followed his father's profession.

The elder daughter, called Eliza but known as Isy, wrote to Newman with zest and affection and was one of a band of girls who held him to be the best of priests and counsellors. The story of Mary Froude, the younger girl, is a sad one. She developed tuberculosis at sixteen. Her mother had to watch her decline and wished she could be helped and sustained by Catholic faith (Mary chose to remain an Anglican) but Newman told Catherine to leave the child to the God who loved her even more than her mother did. Mary Froude died in May 1864 and her father sent the news to Newman who replied promptly and tenderly, saying, "Dear child, she is gone to heaven and is safe."[12]

Newman was often sending such letters and promising Masses, as he did also for joyful events, for a couple about to marry, for a child that had just been born and he made notes to make sure he did not forget prayers he had promised to his friends in their times of sorrow and joy.

Many people received guidance from Newman, particularly converts to Rome and those who were contemplating conversion. He learned the art of spiritual direction in his Anglican days but he was busier with counselling when he became a Catholic priest. It is possible to see from the letters that he had certain principles that he set out for each enquirer, though he tailored his advice to suit each person, believing that no one could give advice without knowing the particular case. He would never hurry the enquirer along or force the issue. Difficulties should be faced and discussed before any decision was made and it was not enough to be urged by Catholic friends, to enjoy Catholic ritual, to feel dissatisfaction with Anglicanism. He put matters succinctly when writing to a Mr Smith in January 1869: "I am glad you see your way more clearly. You are not bound to become a Catholic till you feel it your duty to be one, and then you are

---

[12] LD XXI, p. 111.

bound."[13] He said over and over again that it is only by grace that a man or woman can be led through perplexity, led to see the hour and moment of decision and strengthened to choose aright.

Once a Catholic, the convert in England in the nineteenth century often had a hard time. He might be ostracised by his family and friends; however, if they were tolerant, the intransigence of Catholic rules forbade any praying with them. Newman reminded his converts that gain was greater than loss and bade them be happy with Catholic ways and devotions. He recommended an old prayer manual, 'The Garden of the Soul', and was insistent on Bible study which he thought was sadly neglected by French and Italian Catholics. By the same token, he told the converts there was no need to use the elaborate and flowery books of devotion emanating from the Continent. Newman was something of a John Bull.

All the letters asking for help and counsel, from the converts and others, weighted Newman's post and added to his considerable workload. They had to be taken very seriously. When he took his infrequent holidays, away from attending to pastoral concerns and writing books and from his other employments, another kind of talent had full rein, his ability to write humorous pieces. Sometimes humour came in a witty phrase, as in a letter sent back to the Oratory when he was on holiday in Deal in 1862. He had chosen an unsatisfactory hotel which served poor dinners and curious incidents took place there, for when he went into the coffee room two girls ran out as he came in, "running apparently from a young gentleman who was over his wine and walnuts."[14] He went on to Ramsgate where he found "wonderful wicket doors to Pugin's Church – about as high as the entrance to a kennel – simply wonderful – say three feet six high."[15] At other times the Oratorians at home had a humorous story filling up the letter. When Newman was visiting Cambridge with Father William Neville in 1861, they went to see Kings College chapel and a little man stared at them. The story continued:

> William, who acts as a sort of Guardian Angel or Homeric god, instantly enveloped me in darkness, rustling with his wings and flapping about with a vigour which for the time was very successful. But, alas, all through the day, wherever we were, this little man haunted us. He seemed to take no meals, to say no prayers, or elsewhere to know our times for these exercises with a preternatural

---

[13] LD XXIV, p. 204.
[14] LD XX, p. 302.
[15] LD XX, p. 315.

exactness. William was ever saying, whether we were here or there, in garden or in cloister – don't look that way – turn this way – there's the little man again … ."[16]

Some of Newman's funniest writing came to his Oratorian community from Ireland where he was certainly not on holiday but engaged in a hard struggle with the establishment of the Catholic University. He said that he was planning a new work which would be called 'The doleful disasters and curious catastrophes of a traveller in the wilds of the west'. He sketched out five chapters, each giving a racy account of some incident. The last chapter concerned a visit to a convent school in Waterford where the young ladies (dressed in blue and wearing medals of various colours) were to be given a speech. The speech was made but it was passed over by the nun in charge who went on asking for it. Newman's fifth chapter would recount all this in full:

> And how he would not, because he could not make a second speech; and how, to make it up, he asked for a holiday for the girls, and how the Mother schoolmistress flatly refused him, by reason (as he verily believes) because she would not recognise and accept his speech, and wanted another, and thought she had dressed up her girls for nothing – and how he never the less drank her raspberry's vinegar [sic], which much resembles a nun's anger, being a sweet acid and how he thought to himself, it being his birthday, that he was full old to be forgiven if he would not at a moment act the spiritual jack pudding to a girl's school.[17]

Of course not all letters were written in a mild or humorous tone and when Newman was uttering a rebuke he hit straight from the shoulder. When his community first came to Birmingham one member, John Morris, was convalescing at Oscott after mumps and received a letter which had much kindness in it but made it clear that Morris had acted selfishly when they were settling in at Maryvale. His faults were listed in detail and Newman made his point particularly clear with the observation: "You would be surprised to be made aware how frequent the word 'I' is in your mouth."[18]

One rebuke comes in what is probably Newman's most famous letter, his reply to a snobbish priest who asked him to preach in Rome. This was Monsignor George Talbot, remembered now for this stinging letter of refusal though he wished to be remembered for the position he had attained in the ecclesiastical world:

---

[16] LD XX, pp. 17–18.
[17] LD XVI, p. 53.
[18] LD XI, p. 158.

July 25, 1864

Dear Monsignor Talbot,

I have received your letter, inviting me to preach next Lent in your church in Rome, to 'an audience of Protestants more educated than could ever have been the case in England.' However, Birmingham people have souls; and I have neither taste nor talent for the sort of work, which you cut out for me: and I beg to decline your offer.

I am &c JHN[19]

There is one group of letters that Newman would have called "growls". Sometimes, like all letter writers, he was not out to inform or entertain or commiserate with his correspondent but wanting to unburden his mind; letters are reciprocal and friends are there to listen to complaints occasionally. Newman's friends for this purpose were usually Henry Wilberforce and Emily Bowles, both converts and known since Anglican days. In 1869 Wilberforce complained that his work was finished. Newman thought of his friends' dismal state and compared it with his own:

I have wished earnestly to do some good work … and have, to the best of my lights, taken what I thought God would have me do – but again and again, plan after plan, has crumbled under my hand and come to nought.[20]

He was thinking particularly of his scheme to set up an Oratory in Oxford, which had been blocked, and he may have thought too about his educational ventures, the Catholic University in Dublin and the Oratory School, both beset by troubles. He, and Wilberforce, would remember the frustrations of their Oxford Movement days. Then Newman turned to his writing, for he was working on his *Grammar of Assent* and wondered if its publication would be stopped. His orthodoxy had already been questioned. The letter goes on, complaining of the tight censorship practised in Rome:

Our theological philosophers are like the old nurses who wrap the unhappy infant in swaddling bands on boards – put a lot of blankets over him – and shut the windows that not a breath of fresh air may come to his skin – as if he were not healthy enough to bear wind and water in due measures. They move in a groove, and will not tolerate anyone who does not move in the same.[21]

---

[19] LD XXI, p. 167.
[20] LD XXIV, p. 316.
[21] LD XXIV, p. 316.

Growls were written too at the time of the first Vatican Council for, though he had no difficulty with papal infallibility, he thought a definition inopportune and he feared that the extremist party, who were vociferous for more centralisation and extended powers for the Pope, would upset many people, especially the converts and enquirers.

In his old age, the feeling of uselessness was a sorrow to Newman and he was depressed (and sometimes depressing) because of the frequent news of the deaths of his friends. Henry Wilberforce died and, at much the same time, a great friend, James Hope-Scott, but the most crushing blow was the death of Ambrose St John. When his sister Jemima died he wrote a touching letter which catches exactly the way that memory fastens on a particular characteristic of the person who has gone. He wrote to Anne Mozley:

> What I miss and shall miss in Jemima is this – she alone, with me, had a memory for dates – I knew quite well, as anniversaries came round, she was recollecting them, as well as I – e.g. my getting into Oriel – now I am the only one in the world who knows a hundred things most interesting to me. E.g. yesterday was the anniversary of Mary's death – my mind turned at once to Jemima but she was away.[22]

There is a deep loneliness expressed here but there was usually a positive note in the letters that mourned the death of someone very dear to him, as when writing of the death of Ambrose, he said: "What a faithful friend he has been to me for 32 years! yet there are others as faithful. What a wonderful mercy it is to me that God has given me so many faithful friends!"[23] There were good times too in those later years. Old friendships with Anglican friends had been renewed, for instance with William Copeland who had once been Newman's curate. He took to sending the Birmingham Oratory a turkey every Christmas and letters of thanks went back with a humorous flourish to them: one year Newman told him that the turkey was as big as a baby and that, "we shall make a good Catholic of it by means of a hot fire, before it comes to table."[24]

The great year of triumph was 1879 with Newman's elevation to the cardinalate. He rejoiced, not because of its splendours but because his loyalty had been recognised. He wrote to another Anglican friend, R. W. Church, with the news, telling him that "all the stories which

---

[22] LD XXIX, p. 226.
[23] LD XXVII, p. 311.
[24] LD XX, p. 564.

have gone about my being a half Catholic, a liberal Catholic, under a cloud, not to be trusted, are now at an end."[25] Church replied that many people in England felt that the honour was "just what it ought to be and was the proper crown and finish."[26] In many letters Newman thanked God for the affection shown him by the Pope and by his friends and sometimes used the homely expression "a turn up" for what had happened to him.

In the last ten years of his life, a time of diminishing health and strength, Cardinal Newman was not idle and the letter writing continued though it was difficult; he could not see well and his fingers were too stiff to handle a pen with ease. Eventually many letters were dictated.

The last letter was an act of reconciliation. His niece, Grace, the only child of his sister Harriett, had emigrated to Australia with her husband and was visiting England. She wanted to see her uncle but was shy of proposing it and sent a message by Jemima's daughter-in-law. The letter came back:

> The Oratory, Birmm Aug 2/90
>
> My dear Grace,
> Thank you for your wish to see me. I embrace it readily and I will see you whatever day next week suits you for that purpose.
> Yours affectionately, JHN
>
> P.S. I am sometimes engaged with the doctor.[27]

He had not seen Grace since she was a small child and she probably had no recollection of ever seeing him. She came on the afternoon of 9 August and they sat in a parlour and talked, hand in hand. Newman fell ill the next day and died on Monday 11 August.

---

[25] LD XXIX, p. 72.
[26] LD XXIX, p. 72.
[27] LD XXXI, p. 299.

Newman's writing desk in the library of the Birmingham Oratory. From the end of March to early June 1864, he wrote standing at this desk, sometimes in shifts of more than ten hours, to complete the manuscript of his Apologia.

Chapter 10

NEWMAN THE NOVELIST

by Michel Durand

O ne might think that the complexity of Newman's work – which is the fruit of his extraordinary intelligence, his vast erudition, his speculative powers and his spiritual rigour – is further increased by the astonishing variety of literary genres to which he turned his hand. In reality, these different genres complement and often throw light upon each other, enabling us to grasp more fully the thought and the spirituality of the author. If Newman's major writings indubitably remain his autobiography, his sermons, his lectures, and his apologetic, historical or philosophical essays, his other works, and in particular his two novels, must therefore not be neglected.

Up until the age of forty-six, he was wholly absorbed by his involvement in the Oxford Movement and his pastoral duties, and subsequently by his conversion to Catholicism, which prevented him from turning his hand to this particular genre, even though he was familiar with and fond of it. But in 1847, when the religious and moral motives of the Oxford converts were attacked and caricatured in an Anglican novel, he retorted using the same literary weapon, and the following year he published *Loss and Gain*, which describes a conversion to Catholicism in the academic environment of Oxford. After this first experience of novel-writing, he immediately began a second novel at the beginning of 1848.

If he opted for the form of the historical novel, it was above all because intellectually he lived in symbiosis with the Early Church, which provided the key to his conversion to Catholicism and remained his chief reference point in theological and spiritual matters. But he was less conversant with the history of the rise of Christianity in the seconf and third centuries than with that of its triumph and of the heresies which threatened it in the following two centuries. Moreover, he lacked time as well as a specific cause impelling him to write. He therefore abandoned the project and was even prepared to hand over his notes and drafts to friends who might wish to make use of them.

Then, suddenly, during the Summer of 1855, while he was busy at the Birmingham Oratory preparing for the new University year and seeing to the construction of his church in Dublin, he resumed work on the novel and completed it. The head of the Catholic Church in England, Cardinal Wiseman, had just provided him with the external impetus which he needed. Following the publication in 1854 of his own novel, *Fabiola, a Tale of the Catacombs*, Wiseman suggested that Newman write another novel describing the situation of the Church of the basilicas in the fourth and fifth centuries. Newman bowed to the wish of the Cardinal, though he did not deal with the desired period. The novel was finished in September 1855, and first appeared in the spring of 1856 under the title *Callista, a Sketch of the Third Century*. It would run to its eighth edition by 1890, the year of Newman's death; and on the occasion of the editions of 1876, 1881 and 1889, the author would make a sizeable number of corrections, add a second postscript to the Advertisement, give titles to the chapters, and change the sub-title, which would become 'a Tale of the Third Century'. It is therefore this final edition of 1889, and not that of 1856, which should be regarded as the definitive one.

The literary qualities of 'Callista'

In the first instance, Newman avoids many of the failings inherent in the 'early Christian novel' genre. He rejects most of the melodramatic or sensationalistic elements which then constituted the norm, just as he succeeds in integrating into the novel the fruits of his vast research, of which the reader in general remains quite unaware.

Guessing the point at which monotony is likely to set in, he skilfully interrupts his narrative by inserting into it passages of dialogue. True, these cannot be regarded with unqualified admiration, for their pious tone is occasionally stilted, whilst the structure of Newman's sentences, influenced by that of Latin, may appear somewhat archaic and rhetorical. But they are deftly constructed and at times create great dramatic intensity, especially when their subject is God or faith, and at other times moments of relief thanks to their humour.

The narrative style is as varied as it is enjoyable. It avoids monotony thanks to changes in tense, the accumulation of precise nouns and adjectives, and its rich and complex sentence structures which follow the wanderings of a character's thoughts; but it also succeeds in remaining clear and concise, even attaining, at moments of drama, great sobriety. Finally, it can be rich and luxuriant in descriptive passages. The novel has no lack of dramatic scenes or of colourful and vivid tableaux. Three of these have aroused particular interest: the vivid and pitiless description of the crowd baying for the blood of Christians; the mad wandering of Juba, possessed by the devil (a strange and fascinating episode whose violence and frenzy produced great surprise but whose force more often gave rise to admiration); and the invasion of the locusts, which is a veritable *tour de force* and has always been the most popular scene of the novel. Newman describes their implacable advance by the skilful use of elements of colour and sound, together with an ever-increasing number of military images, and above all by retaining a perfect mastery of the rhythm which, over several pages, creates an impressive crescendo effect:

> Thus they advanced, host after host, for a time wafted on the air, and gradually declining to the earth, while fresh broods were carried over the first, and neared the earth, after a longer flight, in their turn. For twelve miles did they extend from front to rear, and their whizzing and hissing could be heard for six miles on every side of them. The bright sun, though hidden by them, illumined their bodies, and was reflected from their quivering wings; and as they heavily fell earthward, they seemed like the innumerable flakes of a yellow-coloured snow. And like snow did they descend, a living carpet, or rather pall, upon fields, crops, gardens, copses, groves, orchards, vineyards, olive woods, orangeries, palm plantations, and the deep forests, sparing nothing within their reach, and where there was nothing to devour, lying helpless in drifts, or crawling forward obstinately, as they best might, with the hope of prey. [...] Heavily and thickly did the locusts fall: they were lavish of their lives; they choked the flame and the water, which destroyed them the while, and the vast living hostile armament still moved on. [...]

> Unrelaxed by success and by enjoyment, onward they go; a secret mysterious instinct keeps them together, as if they had a king over them. They move along the floor in so strange an order that they seem to be a tesselated pavement themselves, and to be the artificial embellishment of the place; so true are their lines, and so perfect is the pattern they describe. Onward they go, to the market, to the temple sacrifices, to the baker's stores, to the cook-shops, to the confectioner's, to the druggists; nothing comes amiss to them; wherever man has aught to eat or drink, there are they, reckless of death, strong of appetite, certain of conquest. (chap. 15)

175

Of course, all these qualities are offset by certain weaknesses or limits. Some are inherent in the genre of the didactic or religious novel. The thread of the narrative is often interrupted by biblical quotations, authorial disquisitions, or even veritable lessons in catechism. Moreover, given that the author tries less to recreate life in all its complexity and contradictions than to outline the problems which concern him personally, the psychology and human experience of the characters can be lacking in complexity. Callista seems at times to be a somewhat abstract spokesperson for the author, even if she remains on the whole an engaging character. On the other hand, Jucundus, the uncle of Agellius, is a truly colourful and vivid creation. He appears periodically throughout the novel, enlivening it by his unceasing and amusing chatter, his tyrannical but good-natured outbursts, and his complicated schemes which invariably come to nought.

Other limits belong to the genre of the historical novel. The geographical and historical descriptions scattered throughout the work prevent it from maintaining a sustained dramatic quality. The reader is also likely to be put off by the frequent use of quotations or Latin terms, even though many of them enable the author to stress the direct link between the Early Church and the nineteenth century Catholic Church.

It is therefore not surprising that, in spite of its remarkable qualities, *Callista* cannot be put on the same plane as the great Victorian novels. But if we are to judge its true value, we must consider it in the light of the author's aims in writing it. The most obvious of these is historical in nature. Newman was far less concerned with writing a novel than he was with creating an authentic reconstruction of Proconsular Africa in the third century.

The historical value of 'Callista'

If Newman originally gave his novel the subtitle 'a Sketch of the Third Century', it was because he wished to paint a general portrait of Christianity and paganism in a country of the Roman Empire, and he went to great lengths of scrupulousness in order to ensure an abundance of precise detail. When we read in the Advertisement that "it has required more reading than may appear at first sight," we suspect that the writing must have been preceded by a substantial amount of research, but nothing prepares us for our surprise when we discover the 'Prefatory Work for *Callista*' (unpublished but preserved at the Birmingham Oratory). It contains references, quotations, sketches and long passages taken in 1848 and 1855 from some 43 books and 24 articles! In his concern for exactness Newman even asked friends to check whether certain points of detail had not escaped his vigilance, despite the keen nature of the latter.

The 'Prefatory Work' contains extracts from at least 11 books and 6 articles which had provided him with precise information concerning the fauna, flora, crops, climate and archaeology of North Africa in general, and the region of Tunis and the Kef (the ancient Sicca Veneria) in particular. But it was the Christian world of the first centuries and its confrontation with paganism which interested him most. His principal source here, apart from Gibbon, is naturally made up of patristic texts, of which he had an exceptional knowledge. The work of Cyprian helped him particularly, as well as that of historians of the Early Church. But that did not satisfy him: the 'Prefatory Work' reveals that he consulted at least 21 studies devoted to the Roman or African churches.

He paints a precise portrait of the situation of Christian Africa, its leaders and its problems in the year 250, at the beginning of the persecution of Decius. Interested above all in the attitude of the pagans towards Christians, he points out that up until that time persecutions had rarely been the result of legislation but had consisted chiefly of sporadic outbursts on the part of mobs, brought about by personal rivalries or the search for those believed responsible for natural disasters. He then presents, in an excellent summary, the true relationship of Decius to Christianity: the Emperor's onslaught was not directed against Christian doctrine but against those who refused to sacrifice to the gods of Rome and placed their religious beliefs above the loyalty which was due to him.

The manner in which Christians reacted to his edict of persecution is briefly but no less accurately recalled. If there were of course many martyrs, there were even more apostates, whilst many Christians sought refuge in flight or in hiding rather than seeking martyrdom.

Three historical personages are introduced into the novel: Arnobius, Lactantius and Cyprian. While the first two, who have not yet been converted, figure only episodically, the Bishop of Carthage plays an important role: it is through him and his prayers that the state of the Church in the Roman Empire is depicted, his intervention brings about the healing of the body and the soul of Agellius, and he plays an active role in the conversion of Callista. In addition to a perfect knowledge of his life and writings, Newman had a particular fondness for Cyprian. These two Churchmen possessed a large number of features in common, in regard to both their characters and their difficult and late conversions.

Newman was much less well informed concerning the life of the pagans during the first centuries, as is witnessed once again by his 'Prefatory Work', which mentions only one work dealing with their religions and philosophies. Only Greek pagans are regarded by him with any sympathy. His admiration for the ideal and the influence of Greek civilization was already to be found expressed in several of his writings, and his artistic tastes and sensibility resonate to the elegance and beauty of ancient Greece. Several passages of the novel describe Callista's nostalgia for her native country, and it is clearly the attachment of the author which expresses itself here:

> Yes, the poisonous dews, the heavy heat, the hideous beasts, the green fever-gendering swamps. This vast thickly-wooded plain, like some mysterious labyrinth, oppresses and disquiets me vith its very richness. The luxuriant foliage, the tall, rank plants, the deep, close lanes, I do not see my way through them, and I pant for breath. I only breathe freely on this hill. O, how unlike Greece, with the clear, soft, delicate colouring of its mountains, and the pure azure or the purple of its waters! […]
>
> Where is the genius of our bright land? where its intelligence, playfulness, grace, and noble bearing? (chap. 10)

Apart from Greek civilization, which remains in the background of the novel, the pagan world is described with almost unmitigated hostility. The Epicureans are spokesmen less for a true Epicureanism, in the philosophical sense of the term, than for a mere harmless and conformist hedonism, while the satire upon neo-Platonism is so gross as to partly lose its point. Magic, which was indeed truly popular in Proconsular Africa, is represented by the character of the witch Gurta, whose hatred and ferocity Newman describes at great length.

It is above all the pagan mob which appears repulsive and terrifying. The people of Africa were undeniably always ready to riot, and likely to be more vulgar and bloody than those of Rome; but this way of portraying a crowd made up solely of brutes and fanatics bent on pillage and murder is also to be explained by the fear of riot and lawlessness which was then so widespread in England and so often expressed in the novels of the period. This fear was further enhanced in Newman's case by recent memories of the reaction against the restoration of the Catholic hierarchy in England, as well as by an instinctive revulsion in him owing to his character and tastes. It must also be recalled that his rather caricatural conception of the pagans, which would be rejected by historians today, was widely current in Victorian novels, in which their only function was to highlight the qualities and virtues of the persecuted Christians. We have to await works such as Walter Pater's *Marius the Epicurean* (1885) before the pagan world would begin to be portrayed with greater subtlety, and indeed sympathy.

If Newman's historical reconstruction remains on the whole brilliant and fascinating, it is nonetheless far from being a complete success. The explanation lies in the fact that, although Newman was a historian, he was first and foremost a man of the Church. His choice of Proconsular Africa in the 3rd century was determined less by his concern to paint a historical portrait than by his desire to express his ideas and spirituality in an authentic context of persecution and conversion. One has the impression, indeed, that with the passing of time he felt that his novel could not claim to present a purely impartial and harmonious picture of the Early Church and the pagan world. It was undoubtedly this which led him to change the subtitle from 'a Sketch of the Third Century' to 'a Tale of the Third Century'.

This manner of placing history in the service of religion is not unique to Newman. It corresponds to a general tendency of the age, which consisted in giving a religious, moral or social tone to art, literature and the writing of history. The historical novels of the time aim to instruct and to edify. Historical requirements being thus subordinated to the didactic function of the novel, it is the latter's religious message which in fact constitutes its chief source of interest. It was this above all which enabled Newman to show what he was truly capable of, and which can continue to move the reader today.

The autobiographical interest and the religious dimension of 'Callista'

On one level, the commitment displayed in the work makes it a document of interest to the historian of ideas of the Victorian era. It was, as a matter of fact, written in a period of religious confrontation, a few years only after the uproar created in England by the restoration of the Catholic hierarchy (labelled by its adversaries the "Papal aggression"). From the moment of the novel's publication, Anglican critics reproached Newman with identifying the Roman pagans of the third century with English Protestants of the nineteenth, and with having presented in his African novel a caricature of Victorian England. Having already been sensitised by his first novel and his lectures, they expected to be directly attacked or at least challenged in *Callista*, and they were all the more ready to find in it a parallel between the Ancient world and the nineteenth century because contemporary England is mentioned several times and because Newman here derides the national pride extolled by so many Victorian writers.

It is clear that this supposed parallel has no real foundation and that the novel does not constitute a deliberate or systematic attack upon Anglicans. On the other hand, its apologetic character is flagrant and quite intentional: Newman openly defends the dogmas and characteristics of the Catholic religion habitually denounced by Protestants. If he was writing above all for Catholics, he knew that he could not fail at the same time to reach Anglican readers, and the very subject of the novel lent itself splendidly to apologetics: the portrayal of religious life in the third century enabled the author to demonstrate that the dogmas and traditions of contemporary Catholicism are a direct and legitimate continuation of those of the Early Christian Church.

Thus the authority of the Church and the importance of the priesthood appear in the forefront of the narrative, which shows that the priest played a key role in the life of the Early Christians. If their faith has all but disappeared in Sicca Veneria, it is because there is no longer any priest to be found there. The arrival of Cyprian in the house of Agellius, at the point at which the latter is going through the crucial phase of his sentimental and religious crisis, thus takes on a particular meaning: thanks to the authority conferred on him by his priesthood, and his rank in the Church hierarchy, he is able to give the confused and disorientated young Christian the religious instruction and the spiritual direction which he is lacking.

For many years, Newman had been particularly attached to the Eucharist, in which the function of the Catholic priest attains its plenitude. He therefore particularly wished to present this sacrament, emphasizing its central role in the life of Christians. He also introduces penance into his narrative: Cyprian hears Agellius's confession after having explained to him the benefits of the sacrament of penance and having prepared him at some length for it. The liturgy, whose importance Newman had discovered in Rome after his conversion to Catholicism, also occupies an important place in *Callista*, in which he sets out to demonstrate that it has barely changed between the third and the nineteenth centuries and that the rites and prayers rejected by Protestants are in reality merely the legitimate continuation of the divine office of the Early Church.

Angels, the Virgin and the saints occupied an important place in his spiritual life. Several references in the novel to their power of intercession greatly displeased his first Protestant readers. The references to the Immaculate Conception irritated them even more. Keenly aware of this reaction and perfectly conscious of the difficulty created by the issue for the majority of his fellow-citizens, Newman therefore tried to explain it, most notably in 1866 in his 'Letter to Dr Pusey', which develops a systematic apology of the devotion to the Virgin and of the belief of the Early Christians in her Immaculate Conception, even if the latter did not yet constitute a dogma. In 1881, he felt the need to add a long Postscript to the Advertisement of the novel in order to defend himself against the accusation of having committed a polemical anachronism in referring to this devotion and this belief in a story set in the third century.

His great attachment to relics also appears in the novel, in which Agellius, before carrying away the body of the martyred Callista, carefully collects the sand soaked with her blood. Finally, Newman had always felt a keen interest in miracles. Up until the end of the novel they are introduced indirectly and in a relatively subtle manner, but in the last few pages they multiply and are portrayed with a fervour and a profusion of detail which upset Protestants and even surprised a number of Catholics, at the very time when Victorian science was calling into question many of the miracles hitherto accepted.

Although *Callista* thus constitutes an apology for Catholicism, the reaction of Victorian Protestants seems exaggerated and due in large part to the extreme polemical sensitivity of the age. In fact, this apologetic remains discreet, in the novel taken as a whole, and only bursts forth enthusiastically in its final chapters. Moreover, no one can totally reject the argument put forward by Newman in his Postscript of 1881: the novel was written by a Catholic priest, and if he had not made mention of the doctrines and forms of piety that his Church had always considered important, he would have been "simply untrue to [his] idea and apprehension of Primitive Christianity."

On a second level, it is necessary to emphasize the original and exciting way in which the themes of persecution and martyrdom are dealt with in the novel.

As in *Fabiola*, the martyrs are not poor, weak victims, but combatants who courageously accept the sacrifice demanded of them. All the same, Newman, unlike Wiseman, does not allow himself to be carried away by unbridled enthusiasm: he does not describe a systematic and continuous persecution, any more than he unduly exalts the joy of sacrifice. In 1852, in his sermon 'The Second Spring', he had expressed the wish that the Catholic Church might escape persecution, whilst expressing his determination to accept it stoically if it could not be avoided. This position is reaffirmed in *Callista*. The Bishop of Carthage himself sets an example by escaping from his pursuers in order to continue his pastoral mission. In the other towns of Proconsular Africa, most of the Christians flee and hide rather than surrender spontaneously to the Roman authorities.

The same sense of measure is displayed in the way in which the author describes the tortures inflicted upon the Christians. It is true that Newman speaks of the imprisonment, trial, condemnation, instruments of torture and execution which await them; but if the instruments of torture are mentioned, they are not used, whilst the execution of the heroine is not portrayed by means of a great array of vivid and horrific details:

> A few minutes sufficed to put the rack into working order. She was laid down upon its board in her poor bedimmed tunic, which once flashed so bright in the sun, – she who had been ever so delicate in her apparel. Her wrists and ankles were seized, extended, fastened to the moveable blocks at the extremities of the plank. She spoke her last word, 'For Thee, my Lord and Love, for Thee! ... Accept me, O my Love, upon this bed of pain! And come to me, O my Love, make haste and come!' The men turned round the wheels rapidly to and fro; the joints were drawn out of their sockets, and then snapped in again. She had fainted. They waited for her coming-to; they still waited; they got impatient.
>
> 'Dash some water on her,' said one. 'Spit in her face, and it will do,' said a second. 'Prick her with your spike,' said a third. 'Hold your wild talk,' said a fourth; 'she's gone to the shades.' They gathered round, and looked at her attentively. They could not bring her back. So it was: she had gone to her Lord and her Love.

(chap. 34)

At the same time, Newman deals with the question of martyrdom in a detailed and often carefully nuanced way. He does not simplify in the extreme the moral state of those tortured or their religious orthodoxy. Nor does he make martyrdom an action whose logic is plain for all to see, but he adds a certain number of carefully qualified reflections by pondering, for example, on the unfathomable mystery whereby such a demand for destruction could come from a good and perfect God. Finally, he describes the persecution soberly, not overlooking the disadvantages for the Church, explaining that it scattered the Christians of Carthage and Sicca, leading to a large number of apostasies, preventing bishops from taking care of their flock, and destroying the centres of catechism.

This austere and, in human terms, almost desperate aspect of *Callista* becomes more understandable when we reflect that since his conversion to Catholicism and especially since the episode of the "Papal aggression", Newman had had to face the hostility of numerous Protestants, the incomprehension of the leaders of his own Church, and a series of painful and unbroken trials. He never complained, aside from very occasional remarks made in confidence to a few correspondents; but he allowed this sense of persecution to express itself freely in his personal writings, and in *Callista* perhaps more than anywhere else. His novel therefore reflects his own state of mind in 1855 just as much as the historical reality of the first centuries.

This autobiographical character of the novel is even more evident and instructive when it comes to the theme of conversion, which constitutes the most important of all Newman's personal experiences described here. It had already been dramatized in *Loss and Gain, the Story of a Convert*. It will reoccur in the *Apologia pro Vita Sua*, which recounts his spiritual evolution, and again in the *Grammar of Assent*, in which he examines the true foundations of belief in God. But it is probably in *Callista* that this theme is dealt with in the most vivid and interesting manner. Here, in fact, he goes beyond the polemical aspect of his first novel by describing a conversion to Christianity, and no longer just to Catholicism. The distance and the screen provided by the literary genre of the novel as well as by the exotic setting of Proconsular Africa enable him to portray himself with even greater freedom and precision than in the *Apologia*. Finally, the use of characters whose ideas and reactions he comments upon leads him to reveal himself in a more concrete manner than in the *Grammar of Assent*.

It is the spiritual transformation of the two brothers Agellius and Juba, and even more that of Callista, which gave the novel its final structure and enabled Newman to distinguish clearly the different stages of what he considered to be an authentic conversion.

First of all, such a conversion comes about much more easily when it has already been prepared. It does not, in fact, create a new personality, but orientates the existing one towards a precise object, towards an ideal into which it is at last possible for it to be absorbed entirely. If Callista can undergo conversion, it is because Christianity corresponds to her deeper nature and answers an urgent inner call.

Secondly, applying the principle of development not only to the domain of doctrine but also to that of religious experience, Newman, in place of the idea of a sudden and radical change, or that of a succession of sudden discoveries and illuminations, particularly characteristic of the Evangelical school, substitutes the concept of a slow and arduous evolution, which occurs without dramatic shifts and therefore seems interminable. This slowness is further increased by the necessity of passing through two clearly distinct stages: first, abandoning one's scepticism or one's belief in a false religion, then adhering to the true religion. These two stages are separated by a long period of painful searching and uncertainty, since one has achieved awareness of error without yet being able to accept truth, a state which external observers have great difficulty in understanding.

For Newman, the conscience forms the true keystone of faith, a certitude which precedes all other ways of perceiving truth. Whatever the religious belief or scepticism of men, there exists in them a voice which it is impossible for them to silence totally and which leads them to feel satisfaction when they do good, or remorse when they commit evil. It is not a question of a mere natural morality, but of a true commandment given by a person, which is at once imperious and precise:

> 'Well,' she said, 'I feel that God within my heart. I feel myself in His presence. He says to me, "Do this: don't do that." You may tell me that this dictate is a mere law of my nature, as is to joy or to grieve. I cannot understand this. No, it is the echo of a person speaking to me. Nothing shall persuade me that it does not ultimately proceed from a person external to me. It carries with it its proof of its divine origin. My nature feels towards it as towards a person. When I obey it, I feel a satisfaction; when I disobey, a soreness – just like that which I feel in pleasing or offending some revered friend. So you see, Polemo, I believe in what is more than a mere "something". I believe in what is more real to me than sun, moon, stars, and the fair earth, and the voice of friends. You will say, Who is He? Has He ever told you anything about Himself? Alas! no! – the more's the pity! But I will not give up what I have, because I have not more. An echo implies a voice; a voice a speaker. That speaker I love and I fear.' (chap. 28)

Instead of resisting this voice, as Juba does, Callista surrenders herself unconditionally. The first stage of her conversion is thus complete. She finds herself in a state of total openness towards, and impatient expectation of, Revelation. Great assistance can then be given by the influence of others and above all by their moral example. The intervention of Cyprian plays a crucial role in the conversion of Callista, Agellius and Juba. But it is Holy Scripture, and it alone, which provides the Revelation, that is to say effective knowledge of the person who speaks to the conscience. It brings what Newman will call in his *Grammar of Assent* the "real apprehension" of the divine image. Since, by his nature, his life and his teaching, Christ corresponds perfectly to the demands and the appeal of conscience, the reading of the Gospel constitutes the decisive stage in the conversion of Callista.

This conversion being described in terms of struggle and confrontation, and every struggle being necessarily accompanied by fatigue and sacrifices, the ultimate gain of the discovery of God is perforce linked to painful losses. In 1833 and 1845, Newman himself underwent this experience, already described in his first novel, to which he gave the explicit title of *Loss and Gain*. The martyrdom of conversion is first and foremost moral. It can involve for those who accept to undergo it, the loss of social rank, of the esteem of friends, and even of family love. It is also physical. Here too, the author has recourse to personal recollections. First of all, the new conversion of Agellius takes place at a time of violent fever whose manifestations, as well as the remedies applied, are absolutely identical to those relating to Newman's own illness in Sicily. Moreover, when he describes the physical disorders which accompany the conversion of Callista, he recalls the exhaustion brought about in 1845 by his long inner struggle and arduous periods of study, as well as lack of sleep and adequate nutrition, these two activities often being interrupted by prayer and fasting. Such physical changes possess for Newman a very deep meaning: they represent the necessary condition for a true spiritual epiphany, for they signify the renunciation of earthly goods and glory which is indispensable in order to attain the ineffable happiness of the knowledge of God. The young Greek girl (whose name means "The Very Beautiful One") must willingly accept the destruction of her beauty.

Finally, Newman expresses in a concrete and vivid manner his conception of evil and of sin, together with the intensely personal nature of the relationship which unites the creature to God.

He held a very pessimistic view of man, and history expressed in his eyes the unending struggle between the forces of good and evil. We should not therefore be surprised to find the latter so very present in *Callista*. The Christians in the novel have a keen sense of their imperfection, they live with the burden of sin, and they struggle, in suffering, against temptation.

For Newman, one of the most serious sins was that of pride. This theme, and therefore also its opposite, that of submission, recur constantly in both his Protestant and Catholic sermons, as well as in his private diaries and meditations. They occupy a significant place also in his novel, in which the essential function of Juba is to represent the man called by God but refusing to surrender to him and to lose his independence. But sins cannot remain unpunished: true, God is love, but he is also a redoubtable Judge, and the inhabitants of Sicca are pitilessly punished for their sins. Absolute pride which can go so far as to refuse divine Omnipotence can thus receive a terrible punishment: demonic possession. The introduction into the novel of this phenomenon is not the result of a mere literary device but corresponds to an important trait of Newman's spirituality. For him, reality comprises the permanent presence of invisible forces, whereas tangible objects are transient and illusory. His whole life bears witness to a quest for truth beyond the world of appearances and sense-impressions, a quest summed up in the epitaph he chose: '*Ex umbris et imaginibus in veritatem*'. But the invisible universe is not just the ultimate goal which we may attain after death. Newman truly possessed the certitude of living with it, a fact which helps to explain his spiritual force and his extraordinary influence over those who came to him. The angels were for him real beings, while evil is not a simple abstraction, a vaguely defined general principle: it is the Devil, the implacable Enemy whose presence is real and concrete. Newman comes close here to the tone of St Paul for whom the actions of the Evil One are clearly visible in men's lives. Devils do indeed appear in his writings. They are present later in his poem *The Dream of Gerontius*, and they are already at work in *Callista*. Nor should one forget that the case of diabolical possession present in the novel is based on a true historical tradition. It seems very difficult, in fact, to paint a faithful portrait of the Early Church without introducing into it the problem of possession, for this was often considered by the Early Christians as the normal punishment for apostasy, and Cyprian himself quotes an example of it in his treatise *De Lapsis*. Newman was thus obliged both by his own most personal religious convictions and by his duty as a historian to grant a place in his novel to this phenomenon.

A link may exist, also, between the less serious sin represented by lukewarmness of faith and a less terrible punishment: illness. Even if Newman frequently accused himself of the sin of pride, he never succumbed to scepticism. When, in 1833, in the delirium of fever he affirmed repeatedly that he had not sinned against the Light, he meant thereby that, despite his pride, he had never gone so far as to deny his Creator. In the same way, Agellius, despite his weaknesses, never cuts himself off completely from God. This character serves in fact above all to express the sin of which the author once felt himself guilty, that is to say the refusal to respond fully to the call of God.

The natural pessimism of Newman finds a Catholic outcome in *Callista*: the God of vengeance who punishes sins by illness or diabolical possession can also be a forgiving Father to the repentant sinner. Despite his feeling of indignity and guilt, Agellius does not think that he will go to hell, so deeply persuaded is he of God's mercy. When Cyprian comforts him by reminding him of the existence of the sacrament of penance and by describing the benefits which it brings, the tone changes abruptly: the horror of sin gives way to the humility of penance and the joy of forgiveness. Those critics who affirmed categorically that they saw nothing in the novel but despair and guilt therefore read it in far too cursory a manner and failed to see the light with which Newman sought to illuminate it. The fact remains, though, that this light shines in a fleeting manner: Agellius's confession and his absolution by Cyprian are followed immediately by the terrifying episodes of the invasion of locusts, the demonic possession of Juba, the savage outburst of the mob and the inhuman treatment inflicted upon Callista. If the reading of the novel is extremely stimulating, it is far from being joyful. Although Newman's ultimate conclusion points to man's salvation and the redemption of sins, his character and his spirituality led him to emphasize heavily sin itself and its punishment.

Lastly, he shows that religion consists in a personal relationship between each and every being and his Creator. Every soul, every spiritual experience is a closed world which no one else can really enter. As a general rule the Christian characters concentrate their attention and minds not upon those with whom they speak, but upon the invisible world. They converse with themselves or with God. The phenomenon is displayed most strikingly in Cyprian, whose spirituality is the most fully developed: when he speaks to Callista of the salvation of her soul, he explains to her, in terms which find a direct echo in the *Apologia*, that he is not really addressing his remarks to her but that he is alone, face to face with his Lord, with whom he is interceding.

As we are reminded from the title page of the novel by its epigraph, quoting a poem by Aubrey De Vere, this intensely personal relationship with God leaves no place for the carnal love of any other creature and renders necessary the states of virginity and celibacy. Newman felt himself called from an early age to this state, and his attitude, expressed and explained many times over in his various writings, had given rise to an easily caricatured reputation as a rabid defender of celibacy. In his novel, human love is systematically pushed into the background. Agellius is the only character to experience a sentimental relationship which it would be difficult to describe as truly amorous.

Conclusion

No one today would think of classifying *Callista* among the great novels of the nineteenth century. However, its weaknesses and limitations, the multiple and often contradictory aims of the author, and indeed the changes in literary fashion and taste which have occurred since the time of its writing, do not prevent it being placed easily in the forefront of Catholic novels written between 1800 and 1880.

It stands in a class of its own in the genre of the 'early Christian novel', almost on the fringes, and its success has never matched that of *Fabiola*. This is due, paradoxically, to two of its principal qualities: its personal character, both meditative and intense, and its great sobriety. After 1856, many novelists tried to imitate Wiseman, or even to rival him, and contemporaries witnessed a profusion, in England, France and many other countries, of descriptions of the luxury and debauchery of the Imperial court, of horrifying underground cemeteries or of bloody executions in amphitheatres, but few authors followed in the more sober and austere path traced by Newman.

His novel still deserves to be read and reread, however, for its literary and historical qualities, but even more for its stimulating spirituality and for all the precious details with which it provides us concerning its author. If we take an interest in the religious experience recounted in the *Apologia pro Vita Sua*, it would be a shame and a loss to ignore the experience illustrated with such fervour and inspiration by *Callista*.

Chapter 11

NEWMAN THE POET

by Joseph Salvatore Pizza

Admittedly, the poetry of John Henry Newman has garnered little interest from scholars. After all, Newman's primary claim on our attention is as a theologian, as founder of the English Oratory, or, at the present moment, as a candidate for sainthood. Moreover, if we think of him in literary terms at all it is usually as the prose stylist who influenced such eminent imitators as Matthew Arnold and Walter Pater,[1] or as the novelist who penned *Loss and Gain* and *Callista*. At times, it may seem that Newman's achievements are so numerous that it would be convenient, if not necessary, to put aside a few until the principal ones have been debated and appraised. But this is to misunderstand the importance of poetry, and of poets, in Newman's life and thought. It should not be forgotten that, before there were any *Tracts for the Times*, John Keble's collection of poems, *The Christian Year*, achieved unparalleled popularity, managing to convert thousands of English households to many of the controversial opinions of the then nascent Tractarian party. Newman himself did not underrate the book's importance, calling it, "one of the classics of the language," and adding that, "[w]hen the general tone of religious literature was so nerveless and impotent, as it was at that time, Keble struck an original note and woke up in the hearts of thousands a new music, the music of a school, long unknown in England."[2] Unknown, perhaps, but not rootless; for there is reason to believe that the school of poetry which presaged the Oxford Movement was itself the fruit of a similar reconsideration of pre-Enlightenment culture, Romanticism. In fact,

---

[1] See David J. DeLaura, *Hebrew and Hellene in Victorian England: Newman, Arnold, and Pater* (Austin: University of Texas Press, 1969).

[2] John Henry Newman, *Apologia pro vita sua*, ed. Martin Svaglic (London: OUP 1967), p. 29, hereafter cited as *Apologia*.

in weighing the place of Coleridge, one of the prime exponents of English Romanticism, upon the Oxford Movement, it could be said that Newman describes the effect of the Romantics upon the Tractarians:

> [He was] a very original thinker, who, while he indulged a liberty of speculation which no Christian can tolerate . . . yet after all instilled a higher philosophy into inquiring minds, than they had hitherto been accustomed to accept. In this way he made trial of his age, and found it respond to him, and succeeded in interesting its genius in the cause of Catholic truth.[3]

Thus, by resisting the Utilitarian Industrialism of the early nineteenth-century, Coleridge offered a "higher philosophy" that contributed to the revived interest in the kind of "Catholic truth" that would be so ardently pursued by the Tractarians of the succeeding generation. This, of course, is not to claim that Tractarianism is merely a tributary of Romanticism; rather, it is simply to point out the essentially poetic character of the Oxford Movement and, in so doing, to show the importance of poetry in its formation. It may be surprising to consider Coleridge's Romanticism as helping to pave the way for Catholic truth, but Newman and his contemporaries readily acknowledged their influence. Indeed, in many ways the poetry of the Tractarians was an extension and refinement, in Christian terms, of the poetry of Coleridge and his companions.

And this view is borne out later in the century, in the writings of the second-generation of Tractarian converts to Roman Catholicism. In a letter in which he attempted to map the major movements of nineteenth-century poetry, Gerard Manley Hopkins made the prescient remark that, "[t]he Lake School expires in Keble and Faber and Cardinal Newman."[4] By the "Lake School" Hopkins of course meant Coleridge, Wordsworth, and Southey, and by positioning him in this way, Hopkins was in fact not only reiterating Newman's description of Coleridge, but he was also anticipating the judgments of more recent literary critics who have discovered in the Tractarian Movement an equally important school of poetry. Scholars like G B Tennyson and Margaret Johnson have argued that not only do the literary efforts of the Tractarians form a significant body of poetic

---

[3] *Apologia*, p. 94. For the original source, see John Henry Newman, 'Prospects of the Anglican Church,' collected in *Essays Critical and Historical*, vol. 1, (London: Longman, Green and Co, 1891).

[4] See Gerard Manley Hopkins, *The Correspondence of Gerard Manley Hopkins and Richard Watson Dixon*, ed. Claude Colleer Abbott (London: OUP, 1939), p. 99, cited hereafter as *Letters*.

theory, but they also reveal the extent to which the Oxford Movement was indebted to Romantic poets and novelists such as Coleridge, Wordsworth, and Scott.[5] Moreover, in linguistic and theological terms, John Coulson has shown that Newman's conception of the Church as essentially poetic in its development has its roots in Coleridge's literary and social criticism, and that it therefore witnesses a "common tradition" extending from Coleridge to Newman, F D Maurice, and, as Coulson's later work suggests, even T S Eliot.[6] And this is only to glimpse the scholarship dedicated to the relation of Newman to Coleridge, and of the Tractarians to the Romantics. Though much of this work takes the form of a debate as to how much and in what way the poetic and critical achievements of the Lake Poets may have inspired the Tractarians, it is perhaps not claiming too much to perceive with Hopkins a Romantic lineage for Tractarianism, in so far as the Romantics can be said to have restored a certain measure of reverence and awe to post-Enlightenment culture. Indeed, it could be said that just as Newman saw Pagan philosophy and literature as, in a sense, prefiguring Christian revelation, so the Lake Poets figured as harbingers of truth, if not truth in its fullness, for the Tractarians.

As a closer look shows, Hopkins's letter suggests nothing less. When he describes the "Lake School" as "the mean or standard of English style and diction, which culminated in Milton but was never very continuous or vigorously transmitted," Hopkins is in fact situating Newman among a tradition of poets extending back not only to Coleridge, but to Milton and his predecessors.[7] At this point, however, one may feel that Hopkins is claiming too much. After all, in his Dublin lecture on "Catholic Literature in the English Tongue," Newman had described Milton and Gibbon as, "great English authors, each breathing hatred to the Catholic Church in his own way, each a proud and rebellious creature of God, each gifted with incomparable gifts."[8] The final note of approbation here, if it is not reluctant, is at the very least grudging. And this is crucial. For, as a Catholic, Newman

---

[5] See the chapter titled, "Tractarian Poetics," in G B Tennyson, *Victorian Devotional Poetry: The Tractarian Mode* (Cambridge: Harvard UP, 1981), pp. 12-71. And also, Margaret Johnson, *Gerard Manley Hopkins and Tractarian Poetry* (Aldershot: Ashgate Publishing Ltd, 1997).

[6] On the affinities between Coleridge, Newman and F D Maurice, see John Coulson, *Newman and the Common Tradition: A Study in the Language of Church and Society* (Oxford: Clarendon Press, 1970). For his discussion of the possible relation between Newman and Eliot, see John Coulson, *Religion and Imagination, 'in Aid of a Grammar of Assent'* (Oxford: Clarendon Press, 1981).

[7] *Letters*, p. 98.

[8] John Henry Newman, "Catholic Literature in the English Tongue, 1854-1858," *The Idea of a University*, ed. Frank Turner (New Haven: Yale UP, 1996), p. 186.

could hardly celebrate the Lake Poets, with all their Miltonic pieties, to the extent that Tractarians like Keble and Isaac Williams could continue to do. Yet at the same time, as countless commentators have noted and Newman himself attested, there is a significant sense in which the progression from Tractarian to Roman Catholic was not so much a break as a development of the principles that Newman had always held. Thus, it is the sense of wrestling with a tradition from within that characterizes the ambivalence of Newman's description of Milton and Gibbon. And this sheds light back onto Hopkins's letter. For it suggests that the real insight of it is not so much that Keble, Faber, and Newman, as poets, descended from Coleridge and Wordsworth, but that in so doing they each in their own ways developed that school to its end. For Newman and Faber this meant recovering or resuscitating, with Tractarian tools, an English Catholic poetry that had all but expired with the Reformation. In this way, it is significant that Newman's major contribution to the process, *The Dream of Gerontius*, is itself a poem about a man's expiration, about endings; but then like all endings, and especially in Gerontius's case, it is also a poem about beginnings. In other words, just as the poem literally deals with the liminal period between life and death and ultimately finds peace in a distinctively Roman Catholic afterlife, so does it in literary terms realize the stylistic shift from Tractarian to Roman Catholic modes of expression, and, in so doing, witnesses that for the English Catholic there is poetic life after the Oxford Movement. More than anything else, it is this aspect of Newman's poetry that I would like to explore here. In order to do that though, since the vast majority of Newman's poetry was written as an Anglican, one must begin with an examination of the poetics of Tractarianism.

Newman as Tractarian poet

Both Tennyson and Johnson have shown that the two key elements of Tractarian poetry are specialized senses of "analogy" and "reserve."[9] By analogy what is usually meant is that natural phenomena are merely the veil behind which the truth of the divine noumena dwells. The terms are of course Kant's and ultimately Plato's, and the debt that Coleridge and Wordsworth may owe to the German and Platonic traditions has been much discussed, but Newman's sense of analogy came mainly from Bishop Butler and the economy of reserve he discovered in

---

[9] See the above cited chapters of their respective works.

the church of Alexandria. As Newman famously describes it in the *Apologia*, his most vivid encounter with the concept of analogy came through his reading of Bishop Butler while an undergraduate at Oxford:

> It was at about this date, I suppose, that I read Bishop Butler's *Analogy*; the study of which has been to so many, as it was to me, an era in their religious opinions ... for myself, if I may attempt to determine what I most gained from it, it lay in two points, which I shall have an opportunity of dwelling on in the sequel; they are the underlying principles of a great portion of my teaching. First, the very idea of an analogy between the separate works of God leads to the conclusion that the system which is of less importance is economically or sacramentally connected with the more momentous system, and of this conclusion the theory, to which I was inclined as a boy, viz. the unreality of material phenomena, is an ultimate resolution.[10]

In his pronouncement here of the unreality of the material world, Newman expresses not only the Romantic sense of nature as veiling the divine, but more importantly, through Bishop Butler, he has developed that understanding to realize the sacramental sense of God's presence in the created world. A closer look at Butler's *The Analogy of Religion* will help to make this clearer. There, Butler's argument is framed as a kind of apologetic or imaginative comeback at Lockean empiricism. Indeed, Newman may have prized it for just this reason. In considering it briefly, of course, much of the richness and complexity of the whole must be left out, and it is to be hoped that in the future scholars of Tractarian poetics may take a fuller account of such a key text to that movement. For now, it is perhaps enough to extract the main points of Butler's argument. To begin, before introducing his theory of analogy, Butler describes its companion, probability: "Probability is expressed in the word likely, i.e., like some truth, or event (verisimilitude) ... For when we determine a thing to be probably true, ... it is from the mind's remarking in it a likeness to some other event, which we have observed has come to pass."[11] Here Butler seems to understand probability as itself a form of simile, sometimes even analogy, depending on the terms. And this is important. For, in response to the empiricist stricture that all knowledge comes from the senses, Butler seems to agree, though with one key distinction: namely,

---

[10] *Apologia*, pp. 22–3.

[11] Bishop Joseph Butler, *The Analogy of Religion Natural and Revealed* (London: J. M. Dent & Sons LTD, 1906), p. xxiv, hereafter cited as *Analogy*.

that such data as the senses can gather are meaningless until we reflect on them analogically, comparing them to previous experiences and allowing ourselves to make probable decisions, identifications, and so on about them based on our past, similar experiences. A more complex development of this argument is at the heart of Newman's thinking and resurfaces in the *Grammar of Assent*, which itself takes Locke to task for similar reasons. As Newman was often to quote, "probability is the very guide of life."[12] Having distinguished his understanding of sense-data from Locke's, Butler is now free to formulate more plainly the version of analogy that so inspired Newman and his Tractarian companions:

> The analogy here proposed to be considered is of pretty large extent ... It will undeniably show, what too many want to have shown them, that the system of Religion, both natural and revealed, considered only as a system, and prior to the proof of it, is not a subject of ridicule, unless that of Nature be so too.[13]

Taken together with the quotation above, Butler's thesis claims that, because of the necessity of probability in interpreting sense-data, it is no more reasonable to scoff at religion, neither natural religion, which posits a vague moral governor, nor Christianity, with its claim to revelation, than it is to doubt atheism, since all are based upon the same, merely probable evidence. Of course, his argument develops from here to discussions of our ignorance in regard to what death actually is, to the necessity of a moral governor, and, based on these, to the further probability of Christian revelation, but this is all predicated upon his first analogy and the inherent probability of our knowledge. As will be seen, Butler effectively offered Newman a defense of religion on the very grounds of economy promulgated by the Church Fathers, a defense that would have a profound effect on both his controversial writing and his poetry.

"Reserve," the other important element in the Tractarian theory of poetry, is akin to their understanding of analogy. In the *Apologia*, Newman recalls that his conception of the "Economies," a term that in Newman's use might be considered an umbrella under which both analogy and reserve take their meaning, was rooted in the Fathers, particularly in the writings of Clement and Origen, and as such serves as an apt transition from one concept to the other:

> The broad philosophy of Clement and Origen carried me away; ...

---

[12] *Analogy*, p. xxv.
[13] *Ibid.*, p. xxxi.

some portions of their teaching, magnificent in themselves, came like music to my inward ear ... These were based on the mystical or sacramental principal, and spoke of the various Economies or Dispensations of the Eternal. I understood these passages to mean that the exterior world, physical and historical, was but the manifestation to our senses of realities greater than itself. Nature was but a parable.[14]

This sense of nature as veiling the divine reality in the way that the literal narrative of a parable veils the metaphorical or spiritual meaning it is intended to convey runs throughout Tractarian poetry in their representation of analogy. A result of this kind of analogical or sacramental understanding of nature is that God appears to be hidden. This is of course a biblically sanctioned view, apparent in passages like Isaiah's, "Verily thou art a hidden God," and countless others.[15] As Robin Selby has shown in his study of the concept of reserve, Clement understood God in just this way: "Since God is incomprehensible, revealed only through the Logos, Clement tells us that the Ruler of All is a Being difficult to grasp and apprehend."[16] As a result of this difficulty, Clement taught that, "[t]he prophets, Scripture, and Christ each bring the truth before us in a way suited to our faculties."[17] This individualized and gradual process of revelation was understood by Newman as the economy of reserve, and can be seen, for instance, in the ancient practice of removing the unconfirmed before the profession of the Credo during the Mass. Among the writings of Clement it can be seen most explicitly in his *Miscellanies*, or *Stromateis*. There he teaches that the mysteries of the faith should not be divulged to those who have not yet been prepared to partake of them:

> But since this tradition is not published alone for him who perceives the magnificence of the word; it is requisite, therefore, to hide in a mystery the wisdom spoken, which the Son of God taught. Now, therefore, Isaiah the prophet has his tongue purified

---

[14] *Apologia*, p. 36.

[15] As it was the only sanctioned English translation at the time of Newman's conversion, and is known to have been used by him and other English converts for devotional purposes, I have quoted from the following edition of the Douai-Rheims Bible: "The Prophecy of Isaias," *The Holy Bible, Translated from the Latin Vulgate and Diligently Compared with other Editions in Divers Languages* (London: Burns, Oates and Washbourne LTD, 1914), 14:15. All further biblical quotations are from this source.

[16] Robin Selby, *The Principle of Reserve in the Writings of John Henry Cardinal Newman* (London: OUP, 1975), p. 5, cited hereafter as *Reserve*.

[17] *Reserve*, p. 5.

> by fire, so that he may be able to tell the vision. And we must purify not the tongue alone, but also the ears, if we attempt to be partakers of the truth.[18]

Clement's teaching here is firmly based on Christ's command not to, "cast ye your pearls before swine: lest perhaps they trample them under their feet: and turning upon you, they tear you."[19] As Clement explains:

> It is difficult to exhibit the really pure and transparent words respecting the true light, to swinish and untrained hearers. For scarcely could anything which they could hear be more ludicrous than these to the multitude; nor any subjects on the other hand be more admirable or more inspiring to those of noble nature.[20]

Therefore, in the transmission of divine truths, a certain sense of reserve, or, as it would become termed in the sixteenth-century, a *disciplina arcani* is necessary on the part of those in possession of the tradition. Only by gradually revealing the divine mysteries to them can communicants be properly instructed in the faith. During times of controversy this was especially true, as Newman himself noted in his *Essay on the Development of Christian Doctrine*:

> The very fault found now with clergymen of the Anglican Church, who wish to conform their practices to her rubrics, and their doctrines to her divines of the seventeenth century, is, that, whether they mean it or no, whether legitimately or no, still, in matter of fact, they will be sanctioning and encouraging the religion of Rome, in which there are similar doctrines and practices, more definite and influential; so that, at any rate, it is inexpedient at the moment to attempt what is sure to be mistaken. That is, they are required to exercise a *disciplina arcani*; and a similar reserve was inevitable on the part of the Catholic Church, at a time when priests and altars and rites all around it were devoted to malignant and incurable superstitions.[21]

Here Newman is drawing a parallel between the controversy that surrounded the early Church and that of the Oxford Movement. In both cases a reserve is required, and, as a look at some of his Tractarian

---

[18] All quotations from Clement are from the following source: Clement of Alexandria, *The Miscellanies*, collected in *The Ante-Nicene Christian Library*, vol. IV, trans. William Wilson, eds. Alexander Roberts and James Donaldson (Edinburgh: T & T Clark, 1869), p. 388, cited hereafter as *Miscellanies*.

[19] Mt 7:6.

[20] *Miscellanies*, p. 388.

[21] John Henry Newman, *An Essay on the Development of Christian Doctrine* (London: Longmans, Green, and Co., 1891), p. 28.

poetry will show, this way of instructing, via analogy, guarded the poetry of the Oxford Movement in a similar way. In order to understand these complex notions of analogy and reserve in action, it is necessary to turn now to a brief consideration of Newman's Tractarian poetry.

As opposed to Keble's, Newman's Tractarian poetry was more polemical in nature and didactic in intention.[22] Instead of wafting God's presence out of a landscape, Newman is moved most often by the prophet's ire or the controversialist's retort. Poems like "Liberalism" perhaps express this best, with the unequivocal judgment of its opening, "Ye cannot halve the Gospel of God's grace; / Men of presumptuous heart!"[23] A slightly milder tone is found in "The Eucharist," a poem that replies to accusations that the Tractarians were teaching the "Romish" belief in the Real Presence. After considering both the strictly Protestant and the strictly Roman Catholic positions on the Eucharist, the poem ends on a distinctively Anglo-Catholic note:

> I will not say with these, that bread and wine
> Have vanished at the consecration prayer;
> Far less with those deny that aught divine
> And of immortal seed is hidden there.
> Hence, disputants! The din, which ye admire,
> Keeps but ill measure with the Church's choir.[24]

The speaker in this passage will assent neither to Transubstantiation, nor to purely symbolic representation, but rather makes his case somewhere in-between. And somewhere, as opposed to a particular statement of doctrine ('consubstantiation,' perhaps, would have been more exact), is precisely the kind of effect to which the Tractarians aimed in these matters. "Hence, disputants!" is effective because it resolves the argument into silence. This is exemplary of the Tractarian note of reserve, of refraining from any direct public speech regarding the divine mysteries. As opposed to argument, Newman instead offers the image of a church choir, that is, an image of simultaneity within difference. Rather than bald argument, Newman has here shifted into an analogy that neutralizes the "din" of both parties. The analogy is distinctively Tractarian because, in Newman's terms, it connects sacramentally the "lesser system" with the greater. In other words, the

---

[22] Tennyson makes this distinction the basis of his chapter on Newman, which is at present the most convincing discussion of Newman as a Tractarian poet. See "Newman and the Lyra Apostolica," in the above cited *Victorian Devotional Poetry*, pp. 114-37.

[23] John Henry Newman, "Liberalism," *Verses on Various Occasions*, (London: Longmans, Green, & Co., 1900), lines 1-2, hereafter cited as *Verses* with corresponding line numbers.

[24] *Verses*, ll. 7-12.

image of the church choir is a kind of "economy," representing on one level the likeness of the disputants despite their apparent differences, while on another, by portraying the various and distinct members of the Church in harmony, it suggests Saint Paul's apprehension of the Church as the mystical body of Christ.[25] Thus in this way the choir's song is symbolic of Christ's unifying presence among the members of His Church. "The Eucharist" is therefore a fitting introduction to Newman's early poetry, though his most famous Tractarian poem, "The Pillar of the Cloud," exemplifies these qualities best.

Alternately titled, "Lead Kindly Light," the poem's popularity was almost universal among Victorians and, to a certain extent, continues to this day. Indeed, the work was so revered that even Alfred Lord Tennyson's son Lionel, who was thought to be an atheist at the time, requested the poem read to him as he lay dying in 1886.[26] That the poem was later included in the *Oxford Book of English Mystical Verse* suggests the potentially arcane nature of its subject matter.[27] In fact, the enigmatic character of the poem may in part account for its wide appeal. This effect is apparent from the very beginning, as the title's allusion to a passage in Exodus shows:

> And the Lord went before them to shew the way by day in a pillar
> of a cloud, and by night in a pillar of fire: that he might be the guide
> of their journey at both times. There never failed the pillar of the
> cloud by day, nor the pillar of fire by night, before the people.[28]

Here, Moses has just led the Israelites out of Egypt, and God's guiding presence among them is figured as "the pillar of the cloud by day" and "the pillar of fire by night." The astronomical source of the figure need not weigh one down, since its significance in the poem is precisely that it introduces an image somewhat difficult to imagine – or vice versa. But just as the title deflects any precise description, so it also fixes the speaker as, analogically, like an Israelite, or perhaps even like Moses, fleeing Egypt. As with the other poems of the Tractarian anthology *Lyra Apostolica*, this one bears both its date and place of composition. "June 16, 1833" is of course the initial year of the Oxford Movement

---

[25] See for example I.Co 12:12-27.

[26] See John Henry Newman, "Supplement," *The Letters and Diaries of John Henry Newman*, ed. Charles Stephen Dessain, et al, vol. 31 (London: OUP, 1977), p. 151. Hereafter this title will be referred to in notes simply as *Letters and Diaries*, with volume number and page cited respectively with a colon.

[27] See *Oxford Book of English Mystical Verse*, eds. D. H. S. Nicholson and A. H. E. Lee (Oxford: Clarendon Press, 1917).

[28] Ex 13:21-22.

(almost exactly one month before Keble's famous Assize Sermon on "National Apostasy"), and so there is also a sense in which the speaker of the poem is John Henry Newman the Tractarian. The place works in the same way as the title: "At Sea," unlike "Palermo" or even "Off Sardinia" as many of the others are described, seems purposely vague, yet also fitting given the fact that the speaker's experience of feeling lost, both on the map and in spirit, is the subject matter of the poem. Admittedly, Newman is on one level simply fulfilling the conventions of lyric poetry, keeping the reader at arm's length as concerns the autobiographical details of the piece's composition so as to foreground the intensity of the experience he is attempting to convey. Yet the mode in which he does this is distinctively Tractarian in its employment of an analogy to convey God's presence (and it is really a double analogy, the first being Moses', the second Newman's) and discipline of reserve as regards the theological controversy that the date implies. Not surprisingly, the subject matter works in much the same way.

In the opening stanza the speaker begins in the imperative mood that characterizes much of the poem, entreating God in the famous refrain to "Lead Thou me on!"[29] This is significant because the agent of the action in the imperative can be omitted and simply implied. Implication, as "The Eucharist" exhibited, is one of the Tractarians favorite ways of representing God's analogical presence. Thus it is that the "Kindly Light" of "The Pillar of the Cloud," rather than the more direct "Lord" or "God," is appealed to throughout the poem. Of course the agent is never absent, never omitted from the phrasing, but the mood lends itself to the kind of indirect, symbolic, and analogical expression of God's presence that the Tractarians consistently aimed to represent. The stanza proceeds to circumscribe the speaker in a moving image of reserve:

> The night is dark, and I am far from home –
> Lead Thou me on!
> Keep Thou my feet; I do not ask to see
> The distant scene, – one step enough for me.[30]

In other words, rather than explanation or argumentation, the speaker here is content, like Clement's catechumen, to allow the mystery to be revealed to him one step at a time, to follow the light wherever it may lead. As Newman explained the passage to a young convert, the image is one of blind faith:

---

[29] Verses, l. 2.
[30] Verses, ll. 3-6.

> All religion is a call on us for Faith; ... Evil and the origin of evil is
> the fundamental trial of Faith. This is one of the pregnant meanings
> of "Lead Kindly Light." The moral is contained in the words "One
> step enough for me." Beyond that one step is the province simply
> of Faith.[31]

Thus, the feeling of abandonment suffered by the speaker in the
opening of the poem is tempered by his faith to follow, without
expecting the mystery of God's ways to be explained or justified to
him. The second stanza works as a kind of confession, repenting for
the speaker's willfulness and pride:

> I loved to choose and see my path; but now
> Lead Thou me on!
> I loved the garish day, and, spite of fears,
> Pride ruled my will: remember not past years.[32]

The speaker here admits in general terms to the willful pride of
his past, and the action in which it is expressed is significant for a
consideration of Tractarian poetry. Once again, a kind of reserve is
exercised. Just as in the previous stanza he agreed to follow blindly,
so here he chides himself for not doing so earlier, for wanting to
plan his life independent of God, and for wanting to do so without
any reverence or mystery, in the "garish," or excessively bright and
unrestrained light of day. In the final stanza the speaker is returned
to daylight, but now it is not with the empirical clarity of before, but
rather the graced mystery of one who has found faith:

> So long Thy power hath blest me, sure it still
> Will lead me on,
> O'er moor and fen, o'er crag and torrent, till
> The night is gone;
> And with the morn those angel faces smile
> Which I have loved long since, and lost awhile.[33]

Only now, after the lonely darkness of the sea at night, and his
repentance for trying to force his own way apart from God, is the
speaker able to submit himself to the mystical perception of God's
presence in his life. By its implicit presentation of the speaker's path
as exemplary, the poem displays Newman's conviction that poetry
should, like parables, teach. As he explained in a letter to Frederic
Rogers in 1832, the aim of his verse during this period was to be both
poetical and persuasive:

---

[31] *Letters and Diaries,* 31:227.

[32] *Verses,* ll. 9–12.

[33] *Verses,* ll. 13–18.

> Do not stirring times bring out poets? Do they not give opportunity for the rhetoric of poetry and the persuasion? And may we not at least produce the shadows of high things, if not the high things themselves?[34]

The "shadows of high things" are here particularly evocative of his method as a Tractarian, suggesting as they do the economy of analogy and reserve. Though this style would continue to be successful for Keble, Williams, and a generation of imitators, Newman would be led in a slightly different direction.

Newman as Roman Catholic poet

In *The Dream of Gerontius*, Newman's major poetic contribution as a Roman Catholic – and perhaps his greatest poetic achievement – the senses of analogy and reserve that guided his Anglican work would be either modified or abandoned altogether. After his conversion, Newman was drawn into controversy regarding his religious beliefs, so much so that he had to write a history of them in his celebrated response to Charles Kingsley, the *Apologia pro Vita Sua*. In this atmosphere, Newman could hardly avoid discussing the most sensitive and mysterious Roman Catholic doctrines publicly, if only to defend them. As a result, his sense of reserve developed from the measured silence of "Hence, disputants!" in "The Eucharist," to a practice of plain and direct speech. As Robin Selby has shown:

> Newman gave up "economical half-speakings" when he became a Catholic . . . When he was an Anglican, he was the leader of a Movement, the success of which demanded the use of all allowable methods, but when he became a Catholic, the necessity for this application of the principle of reserve came to an end.[35]

Thus, although certain applications of reserve would be helpful to Newman throughout his life, for the most part, in his poetry as in his speech, he would have little use for them as a Catholic. Considering the accusations of casuistry and Jesuitry that such reserve brought upon him as a Tractarian, Newman could hardly do other than abandon such tactics as a Catholic, if only to disarm his critics. Indeed, it might be more accurate to say that, on the occasions when he seems to be practicing reserve as a Catholic, Newman is simply exhibiting the shyness and reticence that characterized his personality throughout his life.

---

[34] *Letters and Diaries*, 3:121.

[35] *Reserve*, p. 32.

In contrast to his developing attitude toward reserve is Newman's use of analogy after his conversion. As his comments above show, Bishop Butler's version of analogy accounted for the "underlying principles" of a "great portion" of Newman's teaching. But although his comments in the *Apologia* suggest that he persisted in the belief that the lesser system was connected to the greater sacramentally, such a belief cannot be observed in *The Dream of Gerontius*. Indeed, by setting the majority of the poem in the moment just after death, Newman has no need for Tractarian analogy whatsoever. To put it simply, with no material world to interfere, there are no symbols to interpret. But neither does this mean that the poem is baldly literal. In the absence of Tractarian aims, economy is just as well understood as the ambiguous and figurative language that all poetry thrives on; and indeed, at the key moment of the poem when the soul's meeting with God is described, Newman is forced to resort to an ambiguous and consequently reserved – at least in a broad sense – figure of speech. Perhaps the best description of Newman's practice as a Roman Catholic poet would be that, like other Tractarian converts, he left behind whatever aspects of the Movement were no longer necessary and, in their place, he took up the expression of elements of Catholic life that were hitherto unexplored in English literature. Again, it must be stressed that a change of manner is not a change in principles. In many ways *The Dream of Gerontius* could not have been written – would not perhaps need to have been written – by anyone other than the poet of "Lead Kindly Light." Thus it is by following Tractarianism to its end, by pushing the scene quite literally out of this world, that Newman effectively broke the boundaries set by the Tractarian principles of analogy and reserve. In this way, he introduced new methods of rendering distinctively Roman Catholic experiences that would be taken up and developed by later Catholic poets like Gerard Manley Hopkins and Francis Thompson. *The Dream of Gerontius* therefore marks the end of one poetic tradition and the beginning of another, just as its subject matter describes one soul's passage from this world to the next.

Unlike the gnomic, tightly rhymed stanzas of his Tractarian lyrics, *The Dream of Gerontius* is a narrative pastiche of blank verse, hymn, and prayer. Reserve has now been pushed beyond its limit; as Fr Drew Morgan shows, the poem deals explicitly with some of the most arcane aspects of Catholic doctrine: "In the seven sections, or as Julius Gliebe calls them, seven *paragraphs*, Newman reviews for us the four last things (Death, Hell, Heaven, and Judgment) i.e., the Catholic theological tradition known as eschatology."[36] Moreover, analogy has been seemingly discarded, as Newman avoids the natural world almost completely for the spiritual. In fact, the loosely constructed narrative strand is the only structural principal that ties one section to the next. In place of these Tractarian modes of expression are a number of distinctively Roman Catholic devotional elements, and in surveying them one can see both the shift in Newman's style and the achievement of the poem. The first of these elements appears in the very beginning, when Gerontius cries out the demotic, "Jesu, Maria – ," representing a distinctive aspect of Tridentine Catholic devotion.[37] As Ian Ker has shown, prior to Vatican II, short, monosyllabic injunctions known as "'ejaculatory' prayer," such as 'My Jesus, mercy!' and 'Jesus, Mary!' were very common.[38] And this is not the only form of Catholic prayer in the opening section. Once Gerontius begins to lose sense of his body – and here Newman skillfully arranges for the alternately rhymed iambic pentameter that began the opening monologue to unravel into blank verse as Gerontius slips away – the Assistants enter and begin an incantatory style prayer that, in its parallelism and anaphora, resembles an abridged version of the Litany of Saints:

> Kyrie eleison, Christe eleison, Kyrie eleison.
> Holy Mary, pray for him.
> All holy Angels, pray for him.
> Holy Abraham, pray for him.
> St John Baptist, St Joseph, pray for him.
> St Peter, St Paul, St Andrew, St John,
> All Apostles, all Evangelists, pray for him.
> All holy Disciples of the Lord, pray for him.
> All holy Innocents, pray for him.
> All holy Martyrs, all holy Confessors,
> All holy Hermits, all holy Virgins,
> All ye Saints of God, pray for him.[39]

The Assistants and Priest will continue in this style throughout the first section, their prayers plodding along in a kind of incantatory plain-song to which Gerontius's hymns, prayers, and spiritual flights might be said to give the effect of counterpoint. In the final section

---

[36] Fr Drew Morgan, CO, "Awakening *The Dream of Gerontius,*" *Newman Studies Journal,* 2.2 (Fall 2005): 13.

[37] *Verses,* l. 1.

[38] Ian Ker, *The Catholic Revival in English Literature, 1845-1961* (Notre Dame: Notre Dame UP, 2003) 41, hereafter cited as *Catholic Revival.*

[39] *Verses,* ll. 29-41.

of the poem, the Angel of Agony will sing in a similar manner just before Gerontius goes to his judgment, but between then and now is Gerontius's long intercourse with his Guardian Angel.

In the beginning of the second section an Angel appears to escort Gerontius to his final judgment and to help him adjust to his new condition:

> My work is done,
> My task is o'er,
> And so I come,
> Taking it home,
> For the crown is won,
> Alleluia,
> For evermore.[40]

Having now fulfilled his duty to Gerontius in life, the Angel rejoices at bringing his soul to meet God. In opposition to this, when they come upon the Court of Judgment in section four, Demons appear to taunt Gerontius' soul, doing so in a dissonant and largely spondaic verse that seems to counter the mostly balanced, iambic harmony of the Angel's hymn:

> Low-born clods
> Of brute earth,
> They aspire
> To become gods,
> By a new birth.[41]

Recalling Newman's reluctant praise for Milton, an author he described as "breathing hatred to the Catholic Church," it is perhaps no coincidence that as a Catholic he has created Demons whose reasoning mimics both Satan's speech to his cohorts and his temptation of Eve in Milton's *Paradise Lost*. Moreover, the demons are especially gifted speakers, each of them breathing hatred toward Gerontius through their taunts. In the succeeding sections, as Gerontius approaches the throne of God, these Demons are succeeded by five Choirs of Angelicals who sing praises to the Lord, each beginning with the famous refrain, "Praise to the Holiest in the height, / And in the depth be praise."[42] Each of these choirs serves to prepare Gerontius for his judgment, the crux of which his Angel explains:

> [T]hese two pains, so counter and so keen,–
> The longing for Him, when thou seest Him not;

---

[40] *Verses,* ll. 236–42.
[41] *Verses,* ll. 401–5.
[42] *Verses,* ll. 596–97.

> The shame of self at thought of seeing Him,–
> Will be thy veriest, sharpest purgatory.[43]

Here, in fact, is the heart of the poem: a description of the pains of purgation in a work about Purgatory. There is a measure of economy in having the Angel describe the experience of meeting God in such ambivalent terms. Unlike in Newman's Tractarian poems, Gerontius will here see the Lord unmediated by any of the shadows of this world, though the experience will be almost indescribably, and perhaps fittingly, ambiguous. In this way Newman employs a hint of the Tractarian poetic mode, though rather than use it to mystify the uninitiated, he makes it here an expression of his belief in the distinctively Roman Catholic realm of Purgatory. In the final section of the poem the Angel departs, leaving Gerontius on his "bed of sorrow," though not forever, as he promises:

> Swiftly shall pass thy night of trial here,
> And I will come and wake thee on the morrow.[44]

As all of these passages show then, the principal effect of reading *The Dream of Gerontius* is the overwhelmingly Roman Catholic nature of its subject matter. That this did not keep Protestants from enjoying the poem is notable, but even more so is Newman's apparent determination not to write in a way that could be considered Anglican or even Anglo-Catholic. As Ian Ker has argued, after his conversion Newman strove to show that Catholicism and Protestantism were not merely branches of the same religion:

> An important part of Newman's apologetic for Catholicism lies in trying to show how different a religion in kind it is from Protestantism – that it is not as if Protestantism, seen from the Catholic perspective, is simply a truncated form of Catholicism, or as if Catholicism, from the Protestant point of view, is essentially Protestantism plus a great many more or less undesirable accretions or corruptions.[45]

And much of the initial reception of *The Dream of Gerontius* reflects just this. In a letter from R H Hutton, Gladstone's surprising praise for the poem is recounted:

> P.S. I was introduced in the autumn to Mr Gladstone and had a long chat with him chiefly about your Apologia and poems. He expressed as warm an admiration for both as even I could feel, and was especially full of admiration for the Dream of Gerontius, the

[43] *Verses*, ll. 734–37.
[44] *Verses*, ll. 899–900.
[45] *Catholic Revival*, 21.

slight notice of which by the press had filled him with amazement. Probably the subject is too theological, and too full of Catholic theology to attract the notice which its imaginative power deserved in so keenly Protestant a country.[46]

To have the support of such an eminent politician in "so keenly Protestant a country" for a poem perhaps "too full of Catholic theology" is praise indeed. Gladstone's own reply on receiving a copy of Newman's verse is equally remarkable:

> I have been greatly delighted with the Volume. That which I may call its chief ornament indeed, I mean the Dream of Gerontius, it is not new to me. I have read it several times, and more than once aloud to friends. Opinions will form themselves independent of competency, and I own that to me it seems the most remarkable production in its own very high walk since the unapproachable Paradiso of Dante, and less but not very much less wonderful Purgatorio.[47]

Although the comparison with Dante shows Gladstone to be quite "independent of competency," it also shows that, aside from his admiration for the poem, its primary effect led him to describe it as a distinctively Roman Catholic work. Notice that against the available English devotional poets – Donne, Herbert, Vaughan, Traherne, or even Keble and Williams – Gladstone has chosen Dante for comparison. This is in consonance with Hutton's view above, and is seconded by R W Church's review of *The Dream of Gerontius* in the *Guardian*.[48] In reply, Newman, with characteristic humility and humor, took the opportunity to put all Dante comparisons to rest:

> One thing made me blush, if an old man can blush – that about the bow of Dante. I will tell you the parallel which struck myself. Do you recollect the story of humdrum and bashful Tom Churton? how at some great Ashmolean gathering he gently breathed into something that looked like a wind instrument – and what followed?[49]

Thus, however much he may have appreciated their admiration, Newman couldn't help but laugh away such comparisons to Dante. What they recognize is both the overwhelmingly Roman Catholic nature of the poem and the lack of precedence for it in English literature. There was, admittedly, a large body of Recusant Catholic literature,

---

[46] *Letters and Diaries*, Footnotes, 23:385.

[47] *Letters and Diaries*, Footnotes, 24:7.

[48] See the *Guardian* of February 26, 1868, pp. 244–45. In the review, Church describes Newman as having dared to "bend the bow of Dante."

[49] *Letters and Diaries*, 24:42.

as well as a substantial amount of medieval Catholic literature in existence, but neither of these would begin to gain popular attention until the twentieth, and in the case of the former, the twenty-first-century.[50] For all of these reasons, *The Dream of Gerontius* appeared to its mid-Victorian audience as a uniquely Catholic work of English poetry, and it is no slight achievement on Newman's part to have successfully popularized such a form.

As even a brief survey of his work shows that Newman's poetical development was along much the same lines as his theological one. From the late 1820s to his conversion, Newman cultivated a kind of Anglo-Catholic style that, in its often gnomic, prophetical tone, and oblique use of allusion and autobiographical detail, displayed the senses of reserve and analogy that were important elements of the Tractarian poetic. In becoming a Roman Catholic, Newman did not so much break from this poetic tradition as he developed it to its end. By putting aside analogy and pushing the boundaries of Tractarian reserve in *The Dream of Gerontius*, Newman effected, in his own way, the end of that tradition and the beginning of a Victorian Catholic style of poetry. As Gerard Manley Hopkins would later write, "the Lake School expires with Keble and Faber and Cardinal Newman." To a certain extent, despite their obvious differences, it could be said that Hopkins's own achievement is indebted in part to the way in which Newman brought about the end of that school, and the beginning of another.

---

[50] Of course interest in Chaucer's work had revived by this point, but it would have been rare for someone of Newman's generation, whose study was mainly theological, to have known or read much of it. As for Anglo-Saxon and Middle-English works, they too were a specialized study and did not begin to attract widespread attention until the later part of the century.

The Oratory church in Birmingham in Newman's time.

Chapter 12

FATHER NEWMAN AT CONFESSION

by John Kirwan

O ne of the paradoxes of Cardinal Newman's career is his aversion to open confession despite being, as Henri Brémond calls him, "the most autobiographical of men."[1] When the *Apologia* was first publicly received, Newman was frequently faulted for his omission of the personal dimension of his conversion, holding onto the "secretum meum" despite his promise that his response to Kingsley must come in the form of his presentation of the whole man to extinguish the phantom that he had become to the public. His brother's complaint, "we want to know why he changed, not who taught him,"[2] typified early responses, and these were amplified later in Geoffrey Faber's observation, "Newman's confessions would have had a wider circle of readers today than his *Apologia*."[3] Faber's attempt to stretch Newman out "on his procrustean couch,"[4] eliciting the confession that Newman presumably was reluctant to give, characterized the work of many biographers, who, acting like confessors, attempted to plumb what came to be known as "the Newman mystery." These early journeys up the Nile of Newman's private life abruptly ceased when Meriol Trevor adamantly insisted that Newman "was not telling the story of his life, but of his religious opinions. It is not confessions."[5]

More recent albeit very different studies of the *Apologia* have recognized, though, that a very private dimension of Newman is coded

---

[1] Brémond, Henri. *The Mystery of Newman.* trans. H.C. Corrance. London: William and Norgate, 1907.

[2] Newman, Francis. *Contributions Chiefly to the Early History of the Late Cardinal Newman.* London, 1891, p.117.

[3] Faber, Geoffrey. *Oxford Apostles: A Character Study of the Oxford Movement.* London: Faber and Faber, 1993, p. 23.

[4] Lawler, Justus George. "Newman: Biography or Psychography." *Renascence* 14 (1961): 42–47.

[5] Trevor, Meriol. *The Pillar of the Cloud.* London: MacMillan, 1962, p. 6.

into the *Apologia*. Margery Durham argues, for example, that Newman evokes a spirit of intimacy through his persistent use of the language of family life to establish himself as the good Father Newman[6], while Oliver Buckton presumes a hidden identity that Newman struggles to represent before a hostile audience.[7] These, among other studies, recognize the power that the *Apologia* has to seduce readers beyond the history of religious opinions to deeper forces at work in the shaping of his identity. Of course, Newman's references to St Philip Neri at the outset of the *Apologia*, where he quotes St Philip's motto, "Secretum Meum Mihi," and at the end where he pays tribute to Philip's feast day, are reminders of St Philip's mild and tender approach as confessor. These cues, in addition to Newman's appendices regarding lying, equivocation and the principle of economy, suggest that Newman may be recommending the confessor's art in collecting the whole man from the *Apologia*.

Before the merits of this approach are explored, though, it is instructive to review Newman's understanding of confession, a subject that was highly controversial during his life as both Anglican and Roman Catholic. Confession became a popular tool of the Oxford Reformers as they grappled with how to appropriate the growth of Christian piety from the preceding era of Evangelical reformers like Wesley and Whitefield into the High Church. Sacramental confession had long been removed from the Church of England and was generally considered, as Samuel Wilberforce would call it, "one of the worst developments of Popery".[8] The general Evangelical aversion to the practice of confession is evident in one of Newman's earliest works, *St Bartholomew's Eve* that he coauthored in 1818 with his college friend John William Bowden. Characteristic of the anti-Catholic literature of its time, this verse romance with its villainous confessor illustrates many of the suspicions regarding the confessional practice, namely that it surrenders too much authority to the priest, it compromises the privacy of family intimacy while encouraging an unhealthy intimacy between confessing subject – usually women – and the priest, and it is a vehicle of political influence (a particularly sore subject during the era of Catholic Emancipation).

These objections notwithstanding, the Oxford Reformers found

---

[6] Durham, Margery S. 'The Spiritual Family in Newman's *Apologia*.' *Thought* 56 (1981): 417-432.

[7] Buckton, Oliver S. '"An Unnatural State": Gender, "Perversion", and Newman's *Apologia Pro Vita Sua*.' *Victorian Studies* 35 (1992): 359-383.

[8] Liddon, Henry Parry. *The Life of Edward Bouverie Pusey*. 4th ed. London, 1894, p. 234.

that the cure of souls in their parochial work, achieved traditionally through the pastoral visit, required an unrealistic amount of footwork. The population growth of the parishes resulting from the development of canals in the preceding century, increased the burden upon the parish priest to attend to his flock. In a letter to fellow Tractarian Edward Bouverie Pusey, John Keble makes the difficulty of his work clear: "We are in our parishes like people whose lantern has blown out, and who are feeling their way, and continually stepping in puddles and splotches of mud, which they think are dry stones." For this reason, Keble insists "we go on working in the dark, and in the dark it will be, until the rule of systematic Confession is revived in our Church."[9] Keble's letter colorfully elides the difficulty of the visit (he was renowned for the miles he covered in this effort) with the elusiveness of conscience, which was the sought-after game of the Reformers in an age of growing secularism.

One year following his reception of this letter, Pusey delivered a series of sermons during the week of consecration of St Saviour's in Leeds, the church that he built and retreated to when the storm descended upon the Reformers following the publication of Tract 90. During the consecration of the new church, Pusey delivered a series of sermons that articulated a moral theology emphasizing penitence and absolution, setting the stage for the central feature of his ministry to be realized in this pastoral stronghold, his practice of confession. These themes, establishing the theological groundwork of Pusey's ministry in 1845 when he had run afoul of episcopal authority, were in fact arrived at earlier by the Tractarians. Thus, Pusey's most famous tract, Tract 70 (itself a compilation of three preceding tracts), argued that while baptism was the instrument by which the grace of regeneration was conveyed to the soul, it nevertheless could not insure the sinner against the forfeiting of this grace through post-baptismal sin. The sermon, as Pusey described it, "fell on people's hearts like a thunderclap," leaving them suddenly without the comfort of salvation. "From the moment of my completing the tract on Baptism," Pusey noted reflecting on his career, "I felt that I should have written on Christian repentance, on confession and absolution."[10]

While Christian piety expanded outward in the preceding era through missionary travel, during the Oxford Movement, the

---

[9] Coleridge, J.T. *A Memoir of the Rev. John Keble.* Oxford. 1870, p. 302.
[10] Pusey, Edward Bouverie. Ed. *Advice for Those Who Exercise the Ministry of Reconciliation Through Confession and Absolution being the Abbe Gaume's Manual for Confessors.* Oxford, 1878, p. vi.

confessional practice acted centripetally, drawing the faithful toward the locus of the church where confession and absolution could be provided. The challenge was how to promote this practice given the cultural, ecclesiastical, and ultimately political resistance to it. The strategy of the Reformers was to attack or revise the Protestant concept of Justification, as did John Keble:

> Then the tradition which goes by the name Justification by Faith, and which in Reality means, that one who has sinned, and is sorry for it, is as if he had not sinned, blights and benumbs one in every limb, in trying to make people aware of their real state. ... And this is why I so deprecate the word and idea of Protestantism, because it seems inseparable to me from "Every man his own absolver," that is in other words the same as "Peace where there is no Peace, and mere shadows of Repentance."[11]

One would think that there was great opportunity for the Anglican Establishment to take advantage of this system of confession to enlarge its hold upon the populace. Yet the episcopate remained greatly opposed to the practice of confession, which is more than apparent in the attacks Pusey received from his bishop, Wilberforce, who proved to be one of the most vehement opponents of confession: "You seem to me to be habitually assuming the place and doing the work of a Roman Confessor, and not that of an English Clergyman."[12]

The resistance to the growing practice of confession was instanced, not only in Pusey's suspension from the pulpit for the two years prior to his retreat to St Saviour's, but further in the no-Popery lectures and literature of the 1850s, and culminating in the anti-ritualist campaigns of Archbishop Tait in the 70s at which time Anglican clergymen were threatened with removal for hearing confessions. In 1874 Tait's Public Worship Regulation Act outlawed specific ritualist abuses including sacramental confession, and in 1877, a manual entitled *The Priest in Absolution*, which was being privately circulated among clergymen as a guide to the confessional practice, was revealed to the House of Lords, creating a national scandal. These regulations, and the refusal of the Upper House of Convocation to allow license to 483 clergymen who had signed a petition to request permission to hear confessions, all suggest that despite institutional resistance, confession had become a vastly popular practice among clergymen and increasingly among their flock.

---

[11] Coleridge, J.T. *A Memoir of the Rev. John Keble*. Oxford, 1870, p. 302.

[12] *The Life of Edward Bouverie Pusey* 234.

What, then, was Newman's position regarding confession during this fervor, or perhaps it is better to ask where was he? Not coincidentally, in the same month that Pusey consecrated St Saviour's, Newman converted to Rome, undergoing an intense two day confession to Fr Barberi who received him into the Catholic Church. While Pusey's response to episcopal hostility was to fortify himself in a privately financed edifice and to promote a confessional practice that secured his influence through the role of parish priest, Newman sought out an institution where the sacramental nature of confession was supported by the authority of the church. Like his fellow reformers at Oxford, he found himself moving toward the practice of confession. In his autobiographical writings, he recounts the first confession that he conducted in 1838, an experience that he found "painful" and "distressing," but one that he believed he was prepared for by the Exhortation to Communion and the Visitation Service of the Church of England. Additionally, Newman notes that the episode evolved out of the need of the laity, a recurring defense of the Tractarians, and in this case with the additional irony of a conscience (that of the young man visiting him) being pricked by the reading of Anglican Divine Bishop Taylor:

> Then I told him that I felt Confession could not be separated from Absolution, referring to the Exhortation to the Communion — and while I thought it would be well for many of us at least in certain seasons of our lives, if we were in the practice of Confession, that I was thus far decided as to the use of Absolution, that it was a removal of the disabilities & bar which sin put in the way of our profiting by the Ordinances of the Church — that I did not see it was more than this, though I had not a clear view on the subject, that if it was more I trusted I should be guided to see it — but that any how the act was God's, & He could as readily use me as His instrument, though ignorant, as He could the inanimate element in Baptism.[13]

As the controversy surrounding confession heated up during Pusey's contributions to the tracts, Newman's position that would ultimately separate him from his lifelong friend became clearer. In Tract 71, following Pusey's advocacy of a penitential practice, Newman approaches the topic more cautiously, skeptical of the degree to which confession, as he saw it then, is part of a system that requires in the Roman Church absolute adherence to all Church teaching:

---

[13] Newman, John Henry. *Autobiographical Writings*. ed. Henry Tristam. London: Sheed and Ward, 1956, p. 214.

You must believe every one of them [point of faith]; if you have allowed yourself to doubt any one of them, you must repent of it, and confess it to a priest. If you knowingly omit any one such doubt you have entertained, and much more if you still cherish it, your confession is worse than useless; nay, such conduct is considered sacrilege, or the sin against the Holy Ghost.[14]

While Newman was to rethink the absolute nature of the act of confession as he articulates it here, envisioning the Church less as a spiritual tyrant and the act of confession more as a process than a perfected act, still this passage reveals his concern for how the practice could be validated by reference to the authority of the Church. In an 1842 letter to John Keble, Newman's interest in confession is clear, but the awareness of the conflict surrounding its use is acute: "Confession is the life of the Parochial charge – without it all is hollow – and yet I do not see my way to say that I should not do more harm than good by more than the most distant mention of it."[15]

When Newman retreated to his nascent monastic community at Littlemore, however, he established confession as a regular practice and, indeed, as a requirement for admission. Pusey saw this retreat from Oxford and Newman's eventual conversion to Rome as a product of Newman's overreaction to episcopal hostility to the tracts and more largely to Newman's enormous influence at Oxford: "One cannot trust oneself to think, whether his keen sensitiveness to ill was not fitted for these troubled times."[16] Newman, on the other hand, accused Pusey of sustaining a "vague theology," adopting Roman Catholic practices while dismissing the doctrines that necessitated an obedience to authority in the Church. Newman saw Pusey's continuation of the Movement as a growing cult of personality, operating outside episcopal authority. In 1864, when Pusey found himself embroiled in controversy over the confessional practice, having been publicly challenged by a group of converts to Rome (Allies, Maskell and Dodsworth) who sought to sever the thread keeping Pusey in the Anglican Communion, Newman lent his support privately to Maskell, noting, "The question seems to me who gave Pusey faculties – not who gave his penitents leave."[17] Naturally, Newman was hesitant to enter into the public debates over confession to avoid a conflict

---

[14] *AW* 10.
[15] Newman, John Henry. *Letters and Diaries of John Henry Newman*. ed. Ian Ker, Thomas Gornall. Oxford: Clarendon Press, 1978, Vol. ix, p. 175.
[16] LD xxvii 379.
[17] LD xiv·100.

with an old friend, but in curious ways they were drawn into rivalry over potential penitents as revealed in this letter Newman wrote to Catherine Ward who had sought advice from both men:

> To this then it must be imputed, if, (as your letter says) converts smile at confession in the Anglican Church; – they smile, not at those who religiously take part in the ordinances, but at those who out of their own heads invent rites or ceremonies, or again, who borrow the rites, while they disown the authority of the Catholic Church.[18]

Newman's insistence upon the principle of authority of the Church and his grave skepticism regarding individualized authority which he saw in Pusey's ministry and which he feared in himself, led him toward the Catholic Church where confession enjoyed a long history and where it was recognized as a sacrament.

Pusey's influence upon Newman's career, despite their differences, however, should not be underestimated. It was Pusey who answered so many of Newman's doubts about his fitness for the religious vocation at the outset of his career and Pusey who provided an inspirational model of piety and candor. Looking back at his journal entries on an early encounter, Newman observes in his memoir the evident impression Pusey had made upon him in 1824:

> Took a walk with Pusey; discoursed on Missionary subjects. I must bear every circumstance in continued remembrance. We went along the lower London road, crossed to Cowley, and coming back, just before we arrived at the Magdalen Bridge turnpike, he expressed to me ...

Here is a blank in the manuscript. The writer has not put into writing what this special confidence was, which so affected him. He continues,

> O, what words shall I use? My heart is full. How should I be humbled to the dust! What importance I think myself of! My deeds, my abilities, my writings! Whereas he is humility itself, and gentleness, and love and zeal, and self-devotion. Bless him with Thy fullest gifts, and grant me to imitate him.[19]

When Newman wrote the original journal entry for this episode in 1824, he used the phrase "he confessed to me," but changed this in the 1872 memoir cited above to "expressed to me." No doubt he wanted to avoid confusing a private exchange with an ecclesiastical function.

---

[18] LD xii 274.
[19] *AW* 76.

As he was preparing these journal extracts for publication, he may also have been sensitive to the charged nature the term "confess" assumed when associated with Pusey, the era's most renowned confessor. Still, the narrative continues to reveal that the contents of Pusey's expression, if not confessional, deeply moved Newman, so that he was led a few days later to remark, "Pusey is so good and conscientious, he quite frightens me, and I wish him not to see what I do."[20] While these lines survive in the journal extracts for 1824, they were omitted in Newman's *Autobiographical Memoir* (and they have similarly been omitted by the editors of the voluminous *Letters and Diaries*, where journal entries are provided with the evolving correspondence). Whatever, those missing words were for which we have only an alluring ellipsis, they must have powerfully impacted Newman, suggesting a manner of discourse that he was not ready to engage in himself. Newman instead finds himself recoiling from the prospect of being seen, as though a guilty penitent.

Newman's instinctive withdrawal from Pusey may be the first sign of the great divide that separated the two men, ultimately resulting in separate vineyards that they would work. Pusey in his promotion of confession tried to address the reservations that Newman would have about this practice by attempting to establish an authoritative legacy for it. Thus, he adopted and distributed confessional guides like *Hints for a First Confession* and *The Priest in Absolution* based upon Roman manuals. When the latter was censured, he published Abbé Gaume's *Manual for Confessors*, to which he provided a 150-page preface asserting the Anglican heritage of confession as practiced by the Divines and as called for by the teachings of the Prayer Book. Moreover, he helped establish the Holy Cross Society (S.S.C.) which hosted religious retreats for clergy among other activities where clergymen could develop their understanding of the emerging confessional practice. These were the lengths Pusey pursued to restore confession to the Church of England. Meanwhile, Newman converted to Rome.

Despite the gap that broadened between Newman and Pusey, one can't overlook the remarkable coincidence of Newman's pursuit in his Catholic life of an order that was distinguished for its use of confession. Unlike the Jesuits and other orders who take vows, the Oratorians seek to perpetuate the type of St Philip, an imitation of his way to spirituality. In his Oratorian papers, Newman observes of Philip, "He was the most unwearied of Confessors, the most gentle and

---

[20] *AW* 198.

wise of directors. And what he was, such were his followers in their measure."[21] The practice that Newmàn explored as an Anglican as early as 1838, and which he regularly promoted at Littlemore, undoubtedly influenced his decision to join the Oratorians. This became a vehicle for his own growth, and one suspects whether Newman's letter to Keble in 1843 during the years of anguish between Oxford and Rome was the product of his use of confession:

> The most kind tone of your letter has strongly urged me to tell you something which has at last been forced upon my full consciousness. There is something about myself, which is no longer a secret to me … Some thoughts are like dreams, and we wake from them, and think they will never return; and though they do return, we cannot be sure still that they are more than vague fancies … [22]

Whereas Pusey wrote at length about confession to defend its use in the midst of the hostilities among his bishops, Newman remains relatively reticent about the subject, perhaps because he had no need to enter the controversy, having settled the matter when he became Catholic. He was, however, drawn into the Achilli affair, a lawsuit resulting from his criticism of a rogue priest who had realized the worst abuses of the confessional and then joined the no-Popery circuit in an attempt to damage the public image of the Catholic Church. It was a tricky situation for Newman: in trying to squelch the slander of Achilli's claims, he had to produce victims as witnesses to Achilli's misconduct as a priest, each with their own lurid tale. It was the type of defense that backfired on many levels, and while Newman writes regretfully about it in his Oratorian papers, he takes a more light-hearted perspective in *The Present Position of Catholics* where he satirizes the public paranoia of Roman devotional life.

Newman's fullest treatment of confession is couched in his novel, *Callista*, which he began in 1848, a time when anti-confessional literature was in mass production and rife with sinister confessors like the villainous confessor of Frances Trollope's novel *Father Eustace: A Tale of the Jesuits* (1847), who masterminds "intrigues of power by routinely excelling in spiritual, sexual, and material seduction."[23] In *Callista* Newman returns to themes evident in *St Bartholomew's Eve*,

[21] Newman, John Henry. Oratory Paper No. 33. *Newman the Oratorian*. Ed. Placid Murray. Dublin: Gill and MacMillan, 1969, p. 187.

[22] Newman, John Henry. *Correspondence of John Henry Newman with John Keble and Others … 1839-1845*. London: Longmans, Green, 1917, p. 218.

[23] Bernstein, Susan David. *Confessional Subjects: Revelations of Gender and Power in Victorian Literature and Culture*. Chapel Hill: University of North Carolina, 1997.

written in his Evangelical youth, replacing the sinister confessor of that drama with a goodly one who resolves the same fundamental conflict. Where *St Bartholomew's Eve* ends in the tragic separation of lovers, *Callista* configures these lovers as estranged halves of a divided whole, exploring how to reconcile them. The novel's protagonist, a lapsing Christian named Agellius, complains, "My Spring is gone and I have no summer. Nay, I have had no Spring; it was only a day, not a season. It came and went; where am I now? Can Spring ever return?"[24] As the story evolves, it becomes evident that Callista is representative of the "gracious impulses of his childhood" that Agellius is trying to reclaim. The resolution of Agellius' plight calls for the process of confession, which the narrator explicitly notes, "Great gain had it been for Agellius, even in its natural effect, putting aside higher benefits, to have been able to recur to sacramental confession; but to confession he had never been." The climax of the story arrives when Agellius has a chance to approach Callista, symbolically illustrating a review of the past that in the confessional process must precede confession and absolution. The narrator describes their encounter as "a strange contrast, the complaint of nature unregenerate on the one hand, the self-reproach of nature regenerate and lapsing on the other."[25] Inevitably, Agellius' attempt to resolve his ills by marrying Callista are rebuffed. When she chides him for "aiming at me, not at your God,"[26] she is correcting a narcissistic tendency to embrace a past self encountered through memory. While the encounter with this vitality of the past, embodied in Callista, is instrumental and necessary for Agellius, in the end, he must accept the loss of this past self, focusing instead upon his pursuit of God and trusting in Him to revive that spring.

While Agellius' encounter with Callista prepares him for confession, where his active intellect is redirected to his pursuit of God, for her the encounter is more painful: "You have thrown me back upon my dreary dismal self, and the deep wounds of my memory."[27] What these deep wounds are remain unknown, though clues to them are found in the character Juba, whose wildly rebellious spirit, the narrator reveals, has developed out of an abusive upbringing. In the subplot involving Juba, Newman demonstrates an awareness of a false

---

[24] Newman, John Henry. *Callista: A Tale of the Third Century*. London. Longmans, Green, 1901, p. 155.
[25] *Callista* 133.
[26] *Callista* 131.
[27] *Callista* 132.

self that grows out of sin that must be encountered and corrected in the confessional process.

The conclusion of *Callista* summarizes Newman's understanding of the confessional process. The exorcised Juba dies in a posture of prayer over the tomb of the recently martyred Callista, followed by Agellius' celebration of mass over the tomb. The attempt to achieve wholeness through a reunion with a past self is not achievable in this novel, and Newman insightfully realizes any such effort is a delusional form of narcissism. Agellius must learn to accept his loss and to entrust God with the revitalization of the deep springs, represented by Callista. Even though his encounter with her brings upon him the realization of their necessary separation, Agellius is revitalized in his faith, the result of processing this loss and restoring his trust in God to achieve, if only in an afterlife, the wholeness he desires. If Newman's sermon 'The Second Spring,' that he wrote while working on Callista, immortalizes the rebirth of Catholicism in England, we might well look to Callista as his monument to the process of confession that resulted in his own second spring, a connection he invites in his dedication to Wilberforce where he suggests, "you will recognise the author in his work."

Newman writes further about confession in his Oratorian papers where he describes his experience as confessor. According to the tradition of the Oratory, the role of confessor was assumed by the spiritual director, whose work Newman describes thus:

> He is a silent influence exerted continually towards the cultivation of a real and inward love of member towards member, and a watchful and prompt observance and evasion of all the small hindrances which are likely to interrupt the equable course of the day.[28]

The role of confessor demanded great effort, and while Newman took his turn willingly in this role, he did so with the knowledge that the focus required would take him away from his writing. More than once he acknowledges a "repugnance" that he felt toward this role, but he realized that this feeling emerged out of the great gravity with which he approached the work so that he could ultimately validate his own reservations, "the very repugnance I feel to it may be a reason for it."[29]

While Newman had his own confessors, Fr Barberi and Ambrose St John, his frequent review of his journal writings, which he continually transcribed and ultimately compiled in his *Autobiographical Memoir*,

---

[28] *Newman the Oratorian* 215.
[29] Ibid., 378.

reflect a tendency to act as his own confessor.

In these writings, he uses the third person when referring to himself, as though an outside observer to his life, and thereby he is able to assume the dual role of confessor and confessing subject. The use of third person is present also in the title of the *Apologia*, where the use of *vita sua* rather than *vita mea* allows Newman to draw attention to the division between dual roles he occupies in the text as both interpreter of his life (the confessor) and as subject of the text (penitent). Where epic poets might provide invocations to the muse to launch their enterprises, Newman in the *Apologia* draws attention to the confessional process he is undertaking. At the beginning of Chapter I, Newman draws attention to the heroic nature of the confessor's role:

> It is both to head and heart an extreme trial, thus to analyze what has so long gone by, and to bring out the results of that examination. I have done various bold things in my life: this is the boldest: and, were I not sure I should after all succeed in my object, it would be madness to set about it.[30]

A confessor's examination of the life history was frequently referred to as a spiritual vivisection, a metaphorical concept that clearly underlies the beginning of Chapter III in which Newman, as though journeying through an underworld, confronts his own rebellious spirit mirrored in the ghost of the heretic Eutyches:

> And who can suddenly gird himself to a new and anxious undertaking, which he might be able indeed to perform well, were full and calm leisure allowed him to look through every thing that he had written, whether in published works or private letters? Yet again, who could afford to be leisurely and deliberate, while he practices on himself a cruel operation, the ripping up of old griefs, and the venturing again upon the "infandum dolorem" of years, in which the stars of this lower heaven were one by one going out.[31]

By dramatizing the grief occasioned by this "cruel operation" Newman presents the *Apologia* as a sincere confession. This is an essential strategy for the achievement of the *Apologia*'s goal, the redemption of Newman's credibility and authority which had been compromised by the reversal of his state of mind during his conversion, particularly his virulent anti-papism. Newman must convince the reader that he has sought out, found and addressed the sources of his error; he must be truly

---

[30] Newman, John Henry. *Apologia Pro Vita Sua*. ed. David J. DeLaura. New York: Norton, 1968, p. 81.

[31] *Apologia* 90.

penitential. To this end, he personifies the significant religious positions so that we see them in terms of human relationships where we are more likely to recognize a struggling penitent. Thus, the climax of the *Apologia* comes in the form of a flashback to the ghostly apparition of that "*delirus senex*," Eutyches, who embodies the rebellious spirit of liberalism that Newman must confront in himself and ultimately purge. Similarly, the authority of the Catholic Church, which Newman journeys to accept, is represented in the figure of the pope, infallibility becoming the central issue toward the end of the narrative. Margery Durham astutely notes that Newman uses the intimate language of family, encountering fathers that are false and true, as he journeys to become Father Newman, a "fruitful celibate." He can only claim the authority of Father Newman by demonstrating how he expunged the false liberalism that resulted in his anti-papal statements earlier in his Oxford career, and by yielding to the greater authority of the institution of the Church coming to accept the figure and authority of the pope. It is paradoxically only from this position of humility that Newman can rise to reassume his authority in the church. Newman the confessor must be understood as Newman the penitent.

Toward the end of the narrative Newman reminds his reader of the importance of a tolerant reception of confession. In quoting St Philip Neri's motto and recognizing his feast day at the end, Newman essentially invokes Philip's approachable nature and his mild and tender skill in receiving confessions. In his two-part sermon entitled 'The Mission of St Philip Neri,' Newman contrasts Philip's nature with the earlier reformer Savonarola, whose inflexible piety characterized the "muscular Christianity" that Kingsley embodied: "Savonarola is associated in our minds with the pulpit rather than the Confessional; his vehemence converted many, but frightened or irritated more."[32] In contrast, toward the end of the *Apologia* Newman recommends a milder reception of a confession typical of the school of St Philip, and one imagines it is this tolerant spirit that Newman promotes among readers of his *Apologia*.

There is a way of winning men from greater sins by winking for the time at the less, or at the mere improprieties or faults; and this is the key to the difficulty which Catholic books of moral theology so often cause the Protestant. They are intended for the confessor, and

---

[32] Newman, John Henry. 'The Mission of St Philip Neri.' *Sermons Preached on Various Occasions.* London: Longmans, Green, 1913, p. 199.

Protestants view them as intended for the preacher.[33]

When Newman wrote the *Apologia*, he felt the urgent need to present the "true key to the whole self" though he was keenly aware that his audience was hostile to him. His strategic positioning of himself as confessor and confessing subject in the *Apologia*, allows him to create a persuasive narrative leading toward the redemption of his credibility and authority. Moreover, the confessional strategy allows Newman through the personification of positions he confronts, to infuse his narrative with a psychological depth that is rhetorically compelling at the same time that it is suggestive of profounder levels of growth that he experienced while journeying to Rome. Newman's exhaustive two-day confession on the eve of his entry into the Church illustrates what we see in the *Apologia*; he came to the Church as a penitent. As the *Apologia* illustrates well, the humble surrender of his will to the larger authority of the Church, in the end qualified him for the many ministries he would pursue, not the least of which was his role as confessor.

---

[33] *Apologia* 212.

Chapter 13

NEWMAN'S SPIRITUALITY
IN RELATION TO
HIS CONVERSION EXPERIENCES

by Robert Christie

One of the most famous conversion stories of the modern age is that of John Henry Newman, who converted from the Anglican to the Roman Church in 1845 after a long and harrowing process. Newman's spirituality had a critical impact on his conversion experiences, and this chapter reviews the relationship of those two experiences in the life of Newman.

In an 1832 sermon, John Henry Newman described conversion thus:

> When men change their religious opinions really and truly, it is not merely their opinions that they change, but their hearts; and this evidently is not done in a moment – it is a slow work: nevertheless, though gradual, the change is often not uniform, but proceeds, so to say, by fits and starts, being influenced by external events, and other circumstances."[1]

In his book *Spirituality and History*, Philip Sheldrake describes spirituality as:

> a conscious relationship with God, in Jesus Christ, through the indwelling of the Spirit and in the context of the community of believers ... A central feature is that spirituality derives its identity from the Christian belief that as human beings we are capable of entering into a relationship with God who is both transcendent and, at the same time, indwelling in the heart of all created things ...

---

[1] John Henry Newman, "Sudden Conversions," 25 Jan. 1832. *Parochial and Plain Sermons*, Vol. VIII (San Francisco: Ignatius Press, 1997), pp. 1695-96.

> (It) establishes a life-giving relationship with God, in Christ, within a believing community. In other words, contemporary Christian spirituality is explicitly Trinitarian, Christological, and ecclesial.[2]

There are two important distinctions in Sheldrake's description. Christian spirituality is intellectual and theological in that it is Trinitarian, Christological, and ecclesial. It is also interpersonal and affective in that it involves a major dynamic process of interrelationship which grounds the theological aspect. This dynamic process includes three related actors: God, the individual, and other individuals, or the community. Sheldrake notes the importance of this three-dimensional interpersonalism, since spirituality is lived out "not in isolation, but in a community of believers." From another source, we find an alternate definition of spirituality as the exercise of faith,[3] which is essentially an interpersonal relationship, grounded in the exchange of affection involving the innate drive to love and be loved.

Taking the two notes of relationship and community as the ground of spirituality, I suggest that an analysis of Newman's conversion experiences reveals that, at every stage, the process involved his affectionate relationship with a significant other person who served as the catalyst for his ongoing conversions. These relationships were key to both his religious as well as his intellectual development. In theological terms, these relationships were the vehicles for the grace of divine action, or the presence of God, in his conversions. I will note and review nine significant stages of Newman's affective relationships in four categories: family, mentors, friends, and his parishioners. These experiences indicate that Newman's spirituality was cued by his interpersonal relationships, which in turn grounded his intellectual development and ultimately his 1845 conversion.

Stage One – Affections and Religious Belief:

Newman's Early Embrace of Anglican Christianity Through the Affections of Parents and Family Life

Newman's family life was the first source of his relationship with God. The *Apologia*, his famous account of his conversion journeys, provides several helpful details regarding his early life. We learn from the opening page that the Newman home emphasized Bible reading and the Church catechism for religious instruction.

---

[2] Philip Sheldrake, *Spirituality and History*. (Maryknoll: Orbis Books, 1998), pp. 60-1.
[3] Karl Rahner, ed., *The Concise Sacramentum Mundi*. (New York: Crossroad, 1991), p. 1634.

The environment established by his parents was a hallmark of these early years. One of their objectives was to direct their children toward God as the source of their love, mediated through the Church of England. However, their conception of God was largely the result of private scripture reading and interpretation, a factor which played a primary role in Newman's development. In his formative years, he accepted the God of the Church of England as he accepted and trusted his loving parents. It was the loving devotion of his parents that engendered his faith in them, causing him to embrace what they embraced. Their relationship, especially that of father and son, had an ongoing influence on young Newman's development, as we shall see, and one biographer writes of "a very happy family circle."[4]

However, the *Apologia* omits all mention of a pivotal problem which occurred at a crucial stage in Newman's development in 1816 at the age of fifteen – the failure of his father's bank. From the *Letters and Diaries*, the multi-volume collection of his lifelong correspondence and private journals, we read of an emotionally wounded young Newman during this period, of his anger when rumors spread regarding the reputation of his father despite the senior Newman's claim that "our banking-house has to-day paid everyone in full."[5] Many years later, in 1874, when recounting the history of the problems of his father during those early days, Newman wrote: "He returned to London, and after a few years his anxieties brought him to an end. For his sake who loved and wearied himself for us all with such unrequited affection, I wish all this forgotten."[6] We find that Newman's early home life experiences were severely impacted by this event. Newman's deep love for his father caused him to suffer significant pain at this point in his life, with immediate major consequences for his conversion journey.

Stage Two – Affectivity and Evangelicalism:
Family Crisis and the Influence of Rev Walter Mayers

Just months after the failure of his father's bank, Newman had his first major conversion experience, mediated by another interpersonal relationship. The personal crisis of 1816 introduced a new factor, the first significant extra-familial influence on Newman's young life. He

[4] R.D. Middleton, *Newman at Oxford*. (New York: Oxford University Press, 1950), p. 4.
[5] John Henry Newman, *The Letters and Diaries of John Henry Newman*. Vol. I, ed. Ian Ker and Thomas Gornall. (Oxford: Clarendon Press, 1978), p.18.
[6] Newman, *Letters and Diaries*, p. 28.

wrote that Rev Walter Mayers, one of the classics masters at Newman's Ealing school, "was throughout this period his spiritual guide."[7] In the *Apologia* Newman makes just one, though powerful, mention of Mayers during this crisis: "The Rev Walter Mayers ... was the human means of this beginning of divine faith in me."[8] Here we find Newman's important distinction between the personal and intellectual influence of Mayers, relating many years later that "Above and beyond the conversations and sermons of the excellent man, long dead, the Rev Walter Mayers, of Pembroke College, Oxford, [was] the effect of the books which he put into my hands, all of the school of Calvin."[9]

It may seem at first that Mayers had a major intellectual influence on Newman, but if we examine the statement carefully, we find that it was Mayers's *person* which affected Newman's faith. His ensuing intellectual development, by means of the books recommended by Mayers, followed from, and was dependent upon, the impression made by Mayers the person. It was only after Newman accepted Mayers as a credible witness to truth that Newman embraced his recommendations. Newman's *Letters and Diaries* reveal not only the theological depth of influence, but more important, the loving concern Mayers expressed for Newman, which deeply affected him. This led Newman to embrace temporarily Mayers's Calvinist Evangelicalism, which placed emphasis on private religious feelings and their outward display, rather than rational analysis, as evidence of the presence of the Spirit. As he had accepted the Church of England through the loving experience of his parents, so he accepted Evangelicalism through the loving experience of Mayers. For this highly sensitive teenager, where the heart journeyed, the head followed, with his affections grounding his intellect. Newman's description of his conversion in 1816 is that of a spiritual awareness and relationship with God, mediated through his relationship with Mayers. However, both during and after this period, Mr Newman continued to be a major spiritual force in his son's life.

Stage Three – The Enduring Influence of Mr Newman

While home from Oxford for the holidays in early 1822, Newman received a severe and lengthy warning from his father for what the

---

[7] Middleton, p. 10.

[8] John Henry Newman, *Apologia pro Vita Sua*, ed. Ian Ker. (London: Penguin Books, 1994), p. 25.

[9] Newman. *Apologia*, p. 25.

elder Newman perceived as a dangerous state of mind due to young John Henry's increasing evangelical extremism. Newman recorded this admonition at length in his journal:

> Take care [because] you poured out [Scripture] texts in such quantities. Have a guard. You are encouraging a nervousness and morbid sensibility, and irritability, which may be very serious [and] it is a disease of the mind.[10]

Newman then recorded his reaction: "O God, make me and keep me humble and teachable, modest and cautious." At this point Newman was in the seventh year, and at the apex, of a religious conversion heavily influenced by evangelicalism. These events involving his father are significant in understanding that process. Newman responded positively to his father's admonition because of their affectionate relationship, a bond which fostered not only trust and faith but intellectual growth as well.

Just five days after his father's severe admonition, Newman recorded a momentous note in his journal which underscores the powerful influence of their relationship.

> My Father said this morning I ought to make up my mind what I was to be. So I chose; and determined on the Church. Thank God, this is what I have prayed for.[11]

This occurred so soon after the admonition, and Newman's response was so immediate, that it underscores the elder Newman's powerful influence on his son. Additional evidence of Mr Newman's effect on his son occurred two and a half years later, when we read the account of John Henry's reaction to his father's death. Perhaps the most poignant record of the impact of this event on Newman is found more than twenty years after the fact, through the voice of the hero in Newman's novel of conversion, *Loss and Gain*, in this thinly veiled autobiographical narrative:

> When Charles got to his room he saw a letter from home lying on his table; and, to his alarm, it had a deep, black edge. He tore it open. Alas, it announced the sudden death of his dear father! ... He felt now *where* his heart and his life lay. His birth, his parentage, his education, his home, were great realities; to these his being was united; out of these he grew ... He had great tangible duties to his father's memory, to his mother and sisters, to his position ... He could not do better than imitate the life and death of his beloved

---

[10] John Henry Newman, *Autobiographical Writings,* ed. Henry Tristram (New York: Sheed and Ward, 1956), 179–80.

[11] Newman, *Autobiographical Writings*, p.180.

father … A leaf had been turned over in his life … Charles had left Oxford a clever informed youth; he returned a man.[12]

His father's death caused yet another family relationship to have a great impact on Newman's development. As Maisie Ward wrote, after the senior Newman's death, "His children became John's responsibility."[13] Prompted by his mother's worries and his sense of duty to his father, Newman began counseling his younger brother Charles through a series of letters on religious issues. From all accounts a lifelong tormented, and tormenting, soul, Charles constantly challenged his older brother's religious beliefs. The correspondence was the means by which Newman learned through Charles one of the major principles expressed in his later work and in his own spiritual conversion journey: that predisposition or 'temper' is the basis of unbelief. With a note of irony, one is tempted to speculate on why Newman chose the name of his difficult brother as the hero of his conversion novel. But returning to the early 1820s, at this time Newman was deeply enmeshed at Oxford, the setting for the next stage of interpersonal influence.

Stage Four – Newman's Relationships with Richard Whately and Edward Hawkins:

Affectivity and the Transition from Evangelicalism to Liberalism

In April, 1822, Newman was elected a Fellow of Oriel, an event which he called the turning point of his life. Once again Newman was introduced to influences which were both interpersonal and intellectual, the latter characteristically conditioned again by the former. These intellectual influences, however, were of a much different nature. Whereas evangelicalism stressed emotion and feeling as a 'truth-check' of one's religious state, the intellectuals of Oxford interpreted these excesses as evidence of just the opposite: an anti-intellectual, anti-rational emotional state, far off course from the rationalist method by which they identified truth. Here Newman imbibed the heady wine of liberal rationalism, and his relationships with two leading Oxford figures, Richard Whately and Edward Hawkins, would each in their own ways contribute to Newman's personal, and then intellectual and theological, development during this period.

First and most important, his personal experiences with them,

---

[12] John Henry Newman, *Loss and Gain*. (London: Longmans, Green, and Co., 1911), pp. 157-9.
[13] Maisie Ward, *Young Mr Newman*. (New York: Sheed and Ward, 1948) p. 168.

as with Mayers, affected both his heart and his religious sensibilities. Only after Newman entered into intimate and loving friendships with Whately and Hawkins did their intellectual influence begin to flower.

Regarding Hawkins, Newman wrote, "I can say with a full heart that I love him, and have never ceased to love him," and "He was the first who taught me to weigh my words, and to be cautious in my statements."[14]

The operative words in Newman's description are "taught me." Again we see the personal bond describing the influence of Hawkins. In this account from his autobiographical *Apologia*, Newman placed his description of the personal affect of Hawkins prior to his description of the intellectual influence on him, using literary structure to emphasize the priority of the affective relationship. Through Hawkins, Newman "was led to give up my remaining Calvinism, and to receive the doctrine of Baptismal Regeneration."[15] Yet this was not all Hawkins imparted to Newman. "There is one other principle, which I gained from Dr Hawkins, more directly bearing upon Catholicism, than any that I have mentioned; and that is the doctrine of Tradition." Along with this he advanced the proposition that "the sacred text [Scripture] was never intended to teach doctrine, but only to prove it, and that, if we must learn doctrine, we must have recourse to the formularies of the Church; for instance, to the Catechism and to the Creeds."[16] Recalling Sheldrake's note of the Church's role in fostering spirituality, this was one of Hawkins's major intellectual influences on Newman.

The intellectual beginnings of an interest in Antiquity, the Fathers, and the seeds of the development of doctrine can be traced to Newman's relationship with Hawkins, whose critique of Newman's very first sermon dissuaded Newman from the evangelical hard-line he had adopted at the outset of his parish ministry in 1824. This intellectual influence would soon complement Newman's actual experiences with his parishioners, eventually causing Newman to refocus his theological and moral positions. But once again, as with Mayers, the essential note is that Newman was opened to Hawkins's theological insights by their loving interpersonal relationship.

Of Whately, the *Apologia* is equally revealing. "I owe him a great

---

[14] *Apologia*, p. 29.
[15] Ibid.
[16] Ibid., p. 30.

deal. He was a man of generous and warm heart," and "(W)hile I was still awkward and timid in 1822, he took me by the hand, and acted toward me the part of a gentle and encouraging instructor. He, emphatically, opened my mind, and taught me to think and to use my reason [and] I became very intimate with him in 1825."[17] The deep impression of Whately's fatherly guidance is quite obvious.

Again we find their intimate interpersonal relationship described at length in the *Apologia*, as with Hawkins, and likewise prior to the account of theological influence. By so doing, Newman continued to underscore the fact, by means of literary structure, that for him the heart conditioned the head. Newman recounts that Whately was

> first, to teach me the existence of the Church, as a substantive body or corporation; next to fix in me those anti-Erastian views of Church polity, which were one of the most prominent features of the Tractarian movement.[18]

Here again, as with Hawkins, we find the Church a prominent element of Whately's influence. In respect to intellectual development, the important note regarding Newman's relationship with both men is that they were primary sources of liberal influence. From another source we learn that "Whately's line of thought [was] definitely liberal in tendency."[19]

Thus, we find the recurring pattern: Newman's interpersonal relationships laid the foundation for the intellectual effects which followed. At this time, however, another series of interpersonal experiences had a profound effect on Newman, constituting the next major stage of his spiritual and then intellectual development.

Stage Five – Newman's Curacy:
The Influence of His Parishioners' Spiritual Experiences

Newman's parish curacy at St Clement's lasted from mid–1824 through the spring of 1826, overlapping both his father's death and his correspondence with Charles. Newman's diary accounts are of great value regarding the conversion experiences of his parishioners, especially influencing his thought regarding conversion. As with the Charles correspondence, these records are overlooked in Newman studies, and thus offer another original insight into his development at

---

[17] *Apologia*, p. 31.
[18] *Apologia*, p. 32. Erastianism is the heresy that the State controls the Church, taking its name from Thomas Erastus (1524–1583).
[19] Middleton, *Newman at Oxford*, p. 42.

the time. Theory and practice clashed in this environment, particularly Newman's concept of conversion versus the reality of the conversion experience, resulting in a significant intellectual change, altering his beliefs and theology.

In the spring of 1824, Newman noted in his journal a decision which would profoundly affect the rest of his life:

> To day I have come to a most important determination St Clement's Church is to be rebuilt ... The curacy has been offered to me, and, after several days consideration, I have accepted it ... Mr Mayers advises me to take it; so does Tyler, Hawkins, Jelf, Pusey, Ottley.[20]

Of note is the reference to the role which the advice of his mentors and friends played in his decision. Regarding his experiences with his parishioners, Newman recounts no less than ten specific personal cases, documenting his reflections on those who were seriously ill and dying or in need of serious spiritual counseling. These case reflections, so revealing as to the effect on Newman's intellectual and moral development, are a turning-point in his life, leading him away from evangelicalism by calling into doubt and then rejecting his evangelical notion of conversion.

From this evidence it is clear that Newman was in the midst of a great personal transition, the causes of which were undoubtedly his personal experiences in the parish and, second, the intellectual influences upon him. We have already seen the major influence of Hawkins and Whately, and their intellectual influence was grounded in their interpersonal relationship. But two other personal influences bore on Newman during his Oxford days of the 1820s, namely Charles Lloyd, one of his Oxford teachers, and Edward Pusey, a close Oxford friend, relationships which constitute our sixth stage.

Stage Six – The Influence of Charles Lloyd and Edward Pusey

Not surprisingly, we find the very same principle at work in these relationships. Newman was highly affected by the characters of both Lloyd and Pusey, and this led to their significant intellectual influence on him. As with Whately and Hawkins, their interpersonal relationships laid the groundwork for their intellectual influence.

As for Lloyd, when he died suddenly in 1829 at the age of 45, Newman wrote to his sister Harriett that:

> His death has shocked me much ... I had the greatest esteem,

---

[20] Newman, *Autobiographical Writings*, pp. 198-9.

respect, and love for him, as a most warm hearted, frank, vigorous minded, and generous man. His kindness for me I cannot soon forget. He brought me forward, made me known, spoke well of me, and gave me confidence in myself ... I wish he had ever been aware how much I felt his kindness.[21]

Again, the affective experiences opened the door to the intellectual effects of Lloyd, who as Regius Professor of Divinity at Oxford "employed his mind upon the grounds of Christian faith rather than on the faith itself ... (H)e made light of the internal evidence for revealed religion, in comparison of its external proofs."[22]

At the height of Newman's transition away from evangelicalism, Lloyd affected Newman's position on baptismal regeneration, and he approved of Newman's plan to read the Fathers, providing motivational support, if nothing more, to an instinct which would have profound theological repercussions.

Newman's heart, opened by Lloyd's heart, in turn opened Newman to Lloyd's intellectual influence.

As for Pusey, Newman wrote of him, "He is a searching man, and seems to delight in talking on religious subjects."[23] Newman described Pusey thus:

> (H)is devotional spirit, his love of the Scriptures, his firmness and zeal, all testify the operation of the Holy Ghost ... What am I that I should be so blest in my near associates?[24]

And again:

> He is humility itself and gentleness and love, and zeal, and self devotion. Bless him with Thy fullest gifts, and grant me to imitate him[25] ... Pusey is so good and conscientious, he quite frightens me, and I wish him not to see what I do.[26]

These noble, virtuous qualities so struck Newman that he found his friend worthy of imitation, and himself shamefully lacking. Through the moral example of Pusey, Newman was opened to his intellectual influence on such issues as imputed righteousness and baptismal regeneration. Combined with the influence of Lloyd, and these in conjunction with his parish experiences, Newman wrote of making a

---

[21] Newman, *Letters and Diaries*, Vol. II, ed. Ian Ker and Thomas Gornall. (Oxford: Clarendon Press, 1978), p. 146.

[22] Newman, *Autobiographical Writings*, p. 71.

[23] Ibid., p. 190.

[24] Ibid., p. 191.

[25] Ibid., pp. 197–8.

[26] Ibid., p. 198.

shift away from evangelicalism in January, 1825.

However, Newman's move away from evangelicalism was in the equally extremist direction of liberalism. Newman writes in the *Apologia* that at this time he "was beginning to prefer intellectual excellence to moral; I was drifting in the direction of the Liberalism of the day. I was rudely awakened from my dream at the end of 1827 by two great blows - illness and bereavement."[27] Bereavement is the sole word indicating the devastating blow Newman suffered upon the sudden death of his dear sister Mary in early 1828. The connection made by Newman at this juncture in the *Apologia* is evidence that his relationship with his dear sister Mary, a matter of the heart, was the spiritual medicine which checked the influence of liberalism. This marks another example that interpersonal relationship conditioned Newman's intellect, evidence of the significant effect of spirituality on Newman's religious journey.

Stage Seven – The Sudden Death of Newman's Beloved Sister Mary

On January 4, 1828, while at dinner and sitting next to her oldest brother John Henry, Newman's youngest sister Mary became ill and retired abruptly. By the next evening she was dead.[28]

Mary was an extraordinarily special person to Newman. Her innocence and joyful spirit gave her an other-worldly, almost sacramental quality which once caused him to comment in his journal: "It must have been in October, 1826 that, as I looked at her, beautiful as she was, I seemed to say to myself, not so much 'Will you live?' as 'How strange that you are still alive!'"[29]

The ensuing year chronicles some twenty letters exchanged between Newman, his mother, and his sisters sharing the grief of Mary's loss, and he expressed his deepest feelings in his poetry of the time. Meriol Trevor provides a relevant interpretation of the influence of Mary's death on Newman:

> But how could Mary's death ... affect this intellectual drift? The loss of Mary revived all Newman's sense of the overpowering reality of the unseen world ... (S)uch a spirit and imagination could never fit itself into the world of common-sense morality and intellectual

---

[27] *Apologia*, p. 33.
[28] Ward, *Young Mr Newman*, pp. 149-151.
[29] Newman, *Autobiographical Writings*, p. 213.

abstraction inhabited by Whately and his friends of the liberal school. Mary's going out of this world strengthened Newman's sense of exile in it, which success had been undermining, [and her death] did for him what falling in love does for some people – opened his heart to a more sensitive sympathy with others.[30]

This deeply spiritual experience of Mary's death redirected Newman once again, rescuing him from the excesses of liberalism. Subsequently, Newman dedicated himself to his duties as a tutor at Oxford for the next three years until another interpersonal experience with Hawkins caused a major change.

During the period from 1828 until early 1831, Newman clashed with his former mentor and now Oriel Provost Edward Hawkins over the role of the Oriel tutor, a position which Newman held with his good friend Hurrell Froude. Over the years the dispute grew increasingly bitter on Newman's part, resulting in his resignation in mid-1831, but not before he insulted Hawkins repeatedly in word and deed. The conflict centered on Newman's extreme willfulness in refusing to submit to Hawkins's authority, an important personal trait that would become increasingly more prominent in his conversion experiences. Newman then turned his attention to his first book, *The Arians of the Fourth Century*, which he completed in mid-1832, and then he accepted an offer to accompany Hurrell Froude and his father on a Mediterranean trip, undertaken primarily for the health of the younger Froude, who was chronically ill. This friendship marks our eighth stage, accompanied by the enduring influence of Edward Hawkins.

Stage Eight – Hurrell Froude, and Edward Hawkins Revisited

The group departed England in December, 1832. Deeply influenced by his friend Froude's theological acumen and gregarious personality, Newman imbibed Froude's Roman Catholic sentiments, and during the first part of the journey they visited Rome and met twice with Dr Wiseman, a Roman clergyman who was Rector of the English College in Rome. Their purpose was to explore the common grounds between the Roman Church, of which Newman was particularly critical, and the Church of England, with an eye toward some kind of reconciliation. The discussions broke down over the issue of submission of individual will to higher authority – Newman's long-

---

[30] Trevor, *The Pillar of the Cloud*, p. 75.

standing personal problem.

However, while in Rome Newman had a moving experience regarding the Roman Church when he attended a Solemn High Mass at which the Pope was present. Newman was struck with awe at the liturgy, which had a lasting impression on his imagination.[31]

After the Roman visit, Newman parted company with the Froudes and journeyed to Sicily alone. During his trip he had a second moving experience regarding Roman liturgy. Early one morning he accidentally wandered into a Roman Catholic church during mass and was deeply moved by the devout behavior of the local peasants, which left yet another impression on his imagination about the nature of the Roman Church.[32] But during the trip he became critically ill, to the point that he believed that death was imminent. The following year Newman reflected upon his Sicilian crisis. He wrote in his journal that his illness was a divine punishment for his willful, insulting behavior toward Hawkins.[33] He also entered a response to his insight: "And then I thought I would try to obey God's will as far as I could[34] ... I must put myself in His path, His way, that I must do my part."[35]

As a result of his Sicilian experience, Newman began an affective conversion of his willfulness which, in less than two months, culminated in both a moral and intellectual commitment to a vision of a reformed Church of England as the home for his faith.[36]

But a reformed Church of England would be only a halfway house for Newman, although he would reside there from 1833 until the early 1840s, when he began to doubt the accuracy of his conclusions about

---

[31] "On 25 March, Newman went to high Mass ... The pope and his 'court' were present." Ian Ker, *John Henry Newman: A Biography*, p. 68, p. 268. Newman's attendance at this liturgy appears to conflict with the account of his Roman visit in the *Apologia*, p. 48.

[32] *Apologia*, p. 65. Here Newman specifically mentions the conflict between reason and affection.

[33] Newman, *Autobiographical Writings*, pp. 121, 124, 126.

[34] Ibid., p. 118.

[35] Ibid., p. 127.

[36] Jean Smith's comprehensive analysis of Newman's Sicilian expeditions synthesizes the influence of suffering, the affection of strangers, and the possible ecclesiastical effects of the experiences: "Now, after a double crisis, spiritual and physical, of near-death and rebirth ... we cannot tell what deeper resonances the spirit of the place set up within him below the level of consciousness; perhaps it surfaces in that keener awareness of the Church (for years to come, of course, the Church of England) as 'Mother', which recurs in his verses and sermons from now onwards. Here and now, what he had experienced ... was hospitality, the mercy of Catholics, the kindness of a good house, whence he was sent on with commendations to friends, to Palermo, and the final stage of his journey home." 'Newman and Sicily', ed. Rosemary Smith *The Downside Review* (July 1989): 176.

both the Anglican and Roman Churches. Once again we find that a personal relationship was responsible for transforming his intellectual judgments and, ultimately, his will. His friendship with the Irish clergyman Charles Russell, the ninth and final stage of interpersonal influence on Newman, would be the catalyst for Newman's spiritual development and ultimate conversion to Rome.

Stage Nine – Charles Russell:
Conversion of the Heart Begets Conversion of the Head and Then the Will

Perhaps most important of all in relation to Newman's intellectual conversion was the affectionate nature of his relationship with the Irish Roman Catholic cleric, Dr Charles Russell. Newman stated in the *Apologia* that "he had, perhaps, more to do with my conversion than anyone else."[37] We will now examine what caused Newman to make such a statement. "Not to take into account the effect of Dr Russell's personal influence upon him would be a fatal omission ... Dr Russell, for ever afterwards his 'dear friend,' and he alone, won, and retained until the end, not only his esteem, but his affection,"[38] writes Henry Tristram. And Russell had written Newman that "I can scarcely account, even to myself, for the strangely powerful impulse by which I am drawn towards yourself, personally a stranger in all except your admirable writings."[39] It is of note that Newman dedicated the 1874 edition of his novel *Loss and Gain* to none other than Russell, and "it is a temptation to think that in *Loss and Gain* he was the prototype of the priest whom the hero Charles Reding met in the train on his way to London after his last farewell to Oxford."[40] Russell exposed Newman to the truth about Roman Catholic doctrine and devotional practices, which Newman had long misunderstood. It was the effect of this personal relationship which slowly turned Newman toward Rome. Once again, affection fostered his intellectual change.

Perhaps the best insight into the effects of Russell on Newman's conversion is provided by Tristram. Other than his article on the subject and Newman's brief but impressive reference to Russell in the *Apologia*, this relationship has been largely overlooked. In 1842,

---

[37] Newman, *Apologia*, p. 178.

[38] Henry Tristram, 'Dr Russell and Newman's Conversion', *The Irish Ecclesiastical Record*, lxvi (Sept., 1945), pp. 189-200.

[39] Newman, *Correspondence of John Henry Newman with John Keble and Others, 1839-45.* (London: Longmans, Green, and Co., 1917), p. 119.

[40] Tristram, 'Dr Russell and Newman's Conversion', pp. 189-200.

Russell sent Newman a volume of the sermons of St Alphonsus Liguori "as a specimen of our popular teaching; and perhaps there never was a writer who spoke more strongly upon the prerogatives of our Blessed Lady than St Alphonsus."[41] Newman wrote back expressing his affection for Russell's gift of the sermons, and for the gift-giver himself:"I shall be much obliged for your intended present, both for its own sake, and as given me by a person, who has written to me in so kind a spirit."[42]

In 1841 and 1842, Russell and Newman exchanged at least eleven letters, all dealing with topics about Rome which deeply troubled Newman. Russell painstakingly explained, corrected, and proved to Newman, through the devotional materials he supplied, that Newman's assumptions were essentially unfounded. As a consequence, we see the first important effect of Russell when Newman took, according to Tristram, "a significant step, perhaps as a result of his influence, by publishing anonymously, although the identity of the writer was never in doubt, in February, 1843, a *Retractation of Anti-Catholic Statements* notably dated just two days after his last letter to Russell."[43] Newman attributed his change to two factors: his uncritical faith in the Anglican divines and "an impetuous temper."[44] But while his retractations withdrew negative comments, they did not effect a positive resolution of the esslesiastical issue.

Just eight weeks after he authored his *Retractation,* Newman preached his Fifteenth University Sermon, and he began a serious re-examination of his position on the churches. His diary indicates that during this period, between December 1842 and May 1843, his intellectual conversion had in fact been accomplished in the sense that he now *knew* the truth of the Church issue. But this sermon culminated a period of further research by Newman on Catholic devotional materials obtained from Russell. Tristram concluded that the sermon revealed "the direction in which his mind was moving, obviously in consequence of Dr Russell's representations."[45]

Newman concludes the sermon by subordinating reason "to the obedience of Faith," and "in dutiful submission to His (God's) will."[46] It is this note of submission which provides the transition to the

---

[41] Tristram, 'Dr Russell and Newman's Conversion', p. 195.
[42] Ibid., p. 196.
[43] Ibid.
[44] *Apologia*, p. 184.
[45] Tristram, 'Dr Russell and Newman's Conversion,' p. 197.
[46] Ibid.

final stage of Newman's conversion. It appears clear that this sermon marks Newman's intellectual break with the Church of England. But it would take almost two more years for him to resolve the personal issues of willfulness and submission.

We now move on to the consequences and developments of Newman's intellectual conversion of early 1843. Three stages occur prior to his 1845 conversion. First, the influence of Dr Russell continued to provide both the affective ground and the intellectual momentum by exposing Newman further to Roman devotions. Second, as an apparent result of this, Newman's discovery and practice of the *Spiritual Exercises of St Ignatius* had a profound impact.[47] Thirdly, Newman's final major document of this period, *An Essay on the Development of Christian Doctrine*, provided the intellectual assurance Newman required to validate his beliefs and feelings in order to make an act of faith in, and submission and conversion to, the Roman Church.

Let us look at the influence of these three factors, Russell, the *Spiritual Exercises*, and the discovery of the principle of development, for further evidence of the spiritual ground of Newman's 1845 conversion.

The Influence of Dr Charles Russell, Continued

In his *Apologia* Newman described the affective influence of Russell: "He was always gentle, mild, unobtrusive, uncontroversial. He let me alone."[48] In early 1844, Russell sent him another volume of St Alphonsus's sermons and Catechetical Instructions, along with a "packet of little books" representative of common Italian devotions, which convinced Newman, contrary to his thinking, that such devotions were in fact not offensive.[49] Thus, Russell's influence was both affective and intellectual. But a third effect, a combination of these two elements, was perhaps Russell's major contribution to Newman's development and ultimate conversion. That was the exposure of Newman, most likely through his relationship with Russell, to the *Spiritual Exercises of St Ignatius* and the resultant deeply spiritual transformation of his 'willful temper.' Newman's use of the *Exercises*, which is recorded in his diary, in the *Apologia*, and in his final major work of the period, his *Essay on Development*, linked together

---

[47] *Apologia*, p. 180.
[48] Ibid., p. 179.
[49] Tristram, 'Dr Russell and Newman's Conversion', p. 198.

the elements of spirituality, affectivity, intellectual certainty, faith, and will, all of which were critical elements in Newman's final conversion to Rome. Let us now examine the influence of the *Exercises* on that conversion.

The Spiritual Exercises of St Ignatius and Newman's Unconditional Conversion

As noted, it appears that Newman was exposed to the *Exercises* either as a direct result of the devotional materials received from Russell, or at least as an indirect result of his being motivated to research Catholic devotional practices in general. This contention is supported by the connection between the sermons of St Alphonsus with their Marian devotional content and the *Exercises*. In the *Apologia* Newman discusses them together as if from the same source, although this is not specifically stated, but neither is any other source referenced.[50] Two very significant facts emerge from this account. First, through the devotional literature and then especially the *Exercises*, Newman was led to understand the true nature of Catholic belief in the primacy of an affective relationship with God. Second, and most importantly, Newman's struggle to control his will, the battle between self-will and God's will, is borne out by his diary entries during two specific Ignatian retreats he made in 1843. A review of these entries, along with the insights of several commentaries on the *Exercises*, is the source of evidence for this stage of Newman's conversion.[51]

In sum, these retreat diaries disclose Newman's confronting his willfulness, self-love, disobedience, self-centered intellectualism, and attachment to worldly fame, seeking the grace to surrender his will in obedience to God. The Catholic theologian Karl Rahner, commenting on the *Exercises*, notes the degree of submission required: "We should surrender ourselves to this Lord unconditionally,"[52] and commenting on the degrees of humility, he states that one "is completely subject to the unconditional disposition of God." It is this challenge of unconditional commitment which characterized Newman's final two years, and the importance which he placed on the *Exercises* during his

---

[50] *Apologia*, p. 180.
[51] For details of Newman's retreat notes, see the *Apologia*, p. 180, and *Autobiographical Writings*, pp. 223-233.
[52] Karl Rahner, *Spiritual Exercises*, trans. by Kenneth Baker. (New York: Herder and Herder, 1965), p. 188.

final stage of conversion confirms that he was indeed involved in this struggle of submission of his will.

The most significant other theme is ecclesial, his concern over the state of the English Church. It seems fair to say that these diary entries represent a microcosm of the forces and themes of this intense two-year period.

As his will began to change through the *Exercises*, he noted that "I had nothing more to learn; What still remained for my conversion, was, not further change of opinion, but to change opinion itself into the clearness and firmness of intellectual conviction."[53] Newman here described his final movement as the challenge of faith, "the necessity of passing beyond private judgment and of submitting one's will and intellect to a divinely accredited organ or oracle of religious truth."[54] In sum, the *Exercises* converted his will to an unconditional submission to God's will, expressed in a decisive act of faith. For Newman, this would be his unconditional conversion to the Roman Church which he knew to be the true heir to the Apostolic community.

To return to the link between Russell and Newman's acquaintance with the *Exercises*, Newman mentioned the *Exercises* in a letter as early as February 1843, and between then and June of that year, three more letters contain references to the *Exercises* and another to the Jesuits.[55] Given that Russell had sent Newman devotional material as early as October 1842, and the fact that Newman had virtually no other acquaintance with Catholics or Catholic devotional literature, Russell's connection seems quite likely.

As further evidence of this connection, one source on Liguori notes that his work entitled *Peace for Scrupulous Souls* "appeared in nearly all the collections of his spiritual writings."[56] Liguori states therein: "Scrupulous souls should quite simply obey the instructions of their director of conscience. The teaching ... of Ignatius discloses that one must obey in everything that is evidently not sinful."[57] Again this source notes that "no aspect of spiritual life is more central to the spirituality of St Alphonsus than prayer ... Alphonsus is among

---

[53] *Apologia*, p. 183.

[54] Avery Dulles, 'Newman: The Anatomy of a Conversion', *Newman and Conversion*, ed. Ian Ker, (Edinburgh: T & T Clark, 1997), p. 34.

[55] Daniel Patrick Huang, 'The *Spiritual Exercises* and the Conversion of John Henry Newman', *America*, 29 July 1995, pp. 25-7.

[56] Frederick M. Jones, ed., *Alphonsus di Liguori: Selected Writings*. (Mahwah: Paulist Press, 1999), p. 209.

[57] Ibid., p. 213.

the countless figures whose spirituality was formed by contact with the *Spiritual Exercises* of St Ignatius ... and the joyful and optimistic spirituality of St Philip Neri."[58] It is of significant note that after Newman's conversion to Rome, Newman eventually joined the Oratorians, the religious order founded by none other than St Philip Neri, again validating this connection between Newman's relationship with Russell and Newman's exposure to the spirituality of Alphonsus and Philip Neri.

From the 'Spiritual Exercises' to the 'Essay on Development' and Conversion to Rome

Moving on to the connection between the *Spiritual Exercises* and the *Essay on Development*, an aesthetic element – the beauty of the whole – emerged from Newman's experience of the *Exercises* when he perceived that the Catholic devotions were a part of a much more elaborate scheme. He wrote: "The harmony of the whole, however, is of course what it was. It is unfair then to take one Roman idea, that of the Blessed Virgin, out of what may be called its context."[59] This produced a pivotal intellectual insight:

> I saw that the principle of development ... was in itself a remarkable philosophical phenomenon, giving a character to the whole course of Christian thought ... It served as a sort of test, which the Anglican could not exhibit, that modern Rome was in truth ancient Antioch, Alexandria, and Constantinople.[60]

This insight led Newman to explore the nature of an 'idea' in the mind, the basis of the *Essay on Development*, which provided him with the intellectual certitude to convert his willful heart. This, however, was built upon the spiritual foundation of the *Exercises* which ultimately determined his final unconditional conversion.

In summary and conclusion, the elements of spirituality emphasized by Sheldrake, namely relationship with God, in Christ, through the Spirit, within the context of the believing community of the Church, were all promoted in one way or another by these nine stages in Newman's conversion process. Each stage was characterized by intense, affectionate, interpersonal relationships with deeply spiritual and intellectual consequences. Newman's unconditional conversion

---

[58] Frederick M. Jones, ed., *Alphonsus di Liguori: Selected Writings*, p. 265.
[59] *Apologia*, pp. 180–1.
[60] Ibid., pp. 181–182.

to the Roman communion in 1845 was ultimately a conversion of his will, through a change of heart mediated by significant others, culminating in an unconditional submission to the Transcendent Other.

Perhaps nothing emphasizes the importance of the connections between affectionate relationships and spirituality more than the motto Newman selected some thirty-four years later in 1879 when he was elevated to the cardinalate: 'Cor ad Cor Loquitur' – 'heart speaks to heart.' This succinct statement of Newman's life validates that the greatest truth and knowledge is indeed experienced when heart touches heart, a Newmanesque description of the experiential nature of spirituality.

Chapter 14

NEWMAN DOCTOR OF CONSCIENCE: DOCTOR OF THE CHURCH?

by Drew Morgan

Father Gregory Winterton, past Provost of Newman's Birmingham Oratory and founder of the *International Friends of Newman*, stated at the closing of the centenary celebration of Newman's birth,

> The influence of our Founder, the Venerable John Henry Cardinal Newman (1801-1890), is now worldwide. We are completely confident that in God's good time he will be beatified, canonized, and made a Doctor of the Church, to give the Church's authority to his already great and increasing spiritual influence.[1]

Fr Winterton is but one of an increasing number of visionaries[2] anticipating the day when the Church will actively engage the process of conferring upon Newman the title, *Doctor Ecclesiae* – Doctor of the Church.

While Fr Winterton is one of the most recent advocates of Newman's ecclesial doctorate, he is certainly not the first. Fr Vincent Blehl reminds us that the first strong demand for Newman's

---

[1] Peter Jennings, 'Newman Centenary Celebrations – Birmingham 1990', *Benedict XVI and Cardinal Newman* (Oxford: Family Publications, 2005), 105.

[2] Cardinal Alfons Maria Stickler, SDB stated in a homily preached at the Birmingham Oratory (St Philip's Day, 26 May 1990) "We can see in this *great* theologian a clear reflection of St Philip's *charism*, and one which continues to bear excellent fruits, through Newman's influence as a *Doctor of the Church* in the modern age, as the master of a true ecumenism, as a reformer of faith and morals that will bring about the real evangelization of Europe." Jennings, 120. (Italics are mine throughout this paper, unless otherwise indicated.) Father Paul Chavasse, present Provost of the Birmingham Oratory and Postulator General of Oratorian (and Newman's) Causes, has equal confidence in Newman's doctorate. "Is it any wonder, therefore, that the present pope (John Paul II) ... sees in Newman a *sure guide* for our era and wishes to ratify his significance through the traditional means of beatification, canonization, and – as one is assured – declare him to be a *Doctor of the Church?*" *Newman Studies Journal* 1:1 (2004): 31.

canonization included a call for the conferral of the doctorate. In November 1941, through an open letter to the editors and readers of the Jesuit magazine, *America*, the theologian Fr Charles J Callan, OP wrote,

> I am expressing the thoughts and sentiments of thousands upon thousands of Catholics and non-Catholics, at home and abroad, among the clergy and among the laity, of both English speaking and foreign countries, when I say that I hope John Henry Cardinal Newman will be raised to the veneration of our altars and be declared a Doctor of the Church.[3]

Fr Callan was indeed speaking for the thousands upon thousands of his day, as well as for the many more thousands since, who recognize Newman's holiness and advocate his canonization. But how many of us know what it means to be a Doctor of the Church?[4] Or, what authority does a Doctor's teaching possess? Let alone, what is the process of discernment that the Church utilizes to include someone in that select school of saints? This paper will examine Newman in light of these questions and in the context of what may be described as the Church's evolving understanding of the role of Doctor of the Church.

In the first section, this paper will briefly examine the nature of the office of Doctor of the Church by reviewing the history of the title and thereby defining the development of the process of discerning its conferral. The discussion will draw upon the Church's recent experience of conferring the doctorate on St Thérèse of Lisieux and the resulting reflection and literature.[5]

The second section will ask whether Newman fulfills the descriptive *Norms and Criteria*[6] established for the discernment process. Advancing the proposition that Newman is now theologically essential and indispensable for teaching Catholic doctrine today requires an extensive investigation, as was required for St Thérèse of Lisieux's doctorate. However, there is already a growing recognition

---

[3] Vincent F. Blehl, SJ, 'History of the Cause', *Positio Super Virtutibus – Cause of Canonization of the Servant of God John Henry Newman* (Rome: Congregation for the Causes of the Saints, 1989), xvii.

[4] See Appendix I for a listing of the thirty-three Doctors, their titles and their dates. Also available at http://www.doctorsofthecatholicchurch.com/

[5] Steven Payne, OCD, *St Thérèse of Lisieux: Doctor of the Universal Church* (New York: St Paul/Alba House, 2002).

[6] Ibid., 109-122. Payne does not provide a translation of this letter that he tells us has never been published. He does provide the six *Norms and Criteria* in the original Italian in his footnotes 57-64. See also pages 79-80. See unofficial English translation in Appendix II.

that Newman's thought and influence has resulted in one of the major watershed moments in the history of Catholic thought. As with Augustine and Aquinas, theology before them and after them was markedly different. This is precisely due to their impact not just upon the thought of their own day, but on the way that theological discourse subsequently would be done in the future. For Newman this is evidenced by his contribution to theological method, i.e., his theory of the development of Christian doctrine and his doctrine on conscience. If the required investigation into Newman's doctorate culminates with the formal conferral of the title, Doctor of the Church, it will be due in no small part to the factors that have led so many already to hold him to be the Doctor of Conscience.

Another recent event, the selection of Cardinal Joseph Ratzinger as the Roman Pontiff, Pope Benedict XVI, providentially supplies useful background information to support our present and future investigations. It is in Peter Jennings' recent volume, *Benedict XVI and Cardinal Newman* that we find evidence from the writings and addresses of Cardinal Ratzinger and Pope John Paul II that indicate an affirmative, positive response to Newman's fulfillment of the *Norms and Criteria*. Finally, the third section will conclude the investigation and provide some further reflections that may assist us in expanding our understanding of the meaning, character, and function of the Church's teaching on *Doctores Ecclesiae*?

The Role of the Doctor of the Church as Illustrated by its History

At the 1997 ceremonies conferring the Church's doctorate upon St Thérèse of Lisieux, Pope John Paul II explained the Church's intention regarding this practice.

> Indeed, when the Magisterium proclaims someone a Doctor of the Church, it intends to point out to all the faithful, particularly to those who perform in the Church the fundamental service of preaching or who undertake the delicate task of theological teaching and research, that the doctrine professed by a certain person can be a reference point, not only because it conforms to revealed truth but also because it sheds new light on the mysteries of the faith, a deeper understanding of Christ's mystery.[7]

While the conferral of the doctorate does not guarantee infallibility

---

[7] John Paul II, 'St Thérèse of Lisieux Proclaimed a Doctor of the Church: Homily', *Origins* 27 (1997): 3. See Payne, 3 and 159.

to the new doctor's teaching – Thomas Aquinas' objections to the doctrine of the Immaculate Conception is a case in point[8] – the doctorate does, according to John Paul II, invest the theologian with the "fullness of apostolic authority."[9] Steven Payne points out,

> To proclaim someone a 'Doctor of the Church' is in some sense to recognize that they are already a 'doctor' *in* the Church, that is to say, someone whose doctrine, by its depth, excellence, originality, and fidelity to the Gospel has exerted a profound influence on the life and teaching of the Church. But it is also to give his or her teaching new weight, to invest it with 'the fullness of apostolic authority,' and to recommend it to the Church of the present and future as a reliable guide for the interpretation of God's word and will.[10]

These statements are filled with vocabulary, words and phrases that collectively have formed a more systematic grammar and are used as a nomenclature for the apostolic authority of the Doctors of the Church. "Reference point", "sheds new light", "deeper understanding", "originality", "profound influence", and "reliable guide" are all expressions that emerged out of a fascinating history that developed through ages of ecclesial reflection on the process of making Doctors. A brief history of the title reveals not only the development or evolution of the discernment process, but the meaning, character, and function of the office as well.

The phrase "Doctor of the Church" is nowhere to be found in the Scriptures. The office of Teacher is found in both Old and New Testaments. The teaching of the Torah is attributed to God, and only subsequently to the rabbis.[11] In the Vulgate translation of Deuteronomy 29:10 and 31:28, the *doctores* are numbered with the princes and ancients of Israel.[12] Their function is simply to be the teachers of the Law. In the New Testament, the same designation is

---

[8] McGinn notes that the doctors often disagree with each other on doctrinal issues. See McGinn, 178. Regarding Aquinas' teaching on the Immaculate Conception, the explanation is offered in http://www.the-pope.com/stThomas.html: "St Thomas at first pronounced in favor of the doctrine in his treatise on the *Sentences* (in I. Sent. c. 44, q. I ad 3), yet in his *Summa Theologica* he concluded against it. Much discussion has arisen as to whether St Thomas did or did not deny that the Blessed Virgin was immaculate at the instant of her animation, and learned books have been written to vindicate him from having actually drawn the negative conclusion."

[9] John Paul II, *Divini Amoris Scientia*, No. 12. See Payne, 2.

[10] Payne, 27.

[11] Ibid., 5. See also McGinn, Bernard, *The Doctors of the Church: Thirty-Three Men and Women Who Shaped Christianity* (New York: Crossroads, 1999), 1-3.

[12] See http://www.newadvent.org/cathen/05075a.htm. The NRSV translates, "princes, ancients and doctors" as "leaders, elders and officials."

predicated of Jesus; in fact, Teacher is one of the most frequently used titles given to him in the gospel tradition.[13] Luke-Acts suggests the Christological and ecclesiological elements of the term doctor. In Luke 2:46, Jesus is found at age twelve in the midst of the doctors, and in Acts 13:1, there are found in the Church of Antioch prophets and doctors. In the Epistles, Paul refers to himself as the Doctor to the Gentiles[14] and writes to the Corinthians and Ephesians that God has appointed in the Church "first apostles, second prophets, third doctors (teachers)."[15] In the post-Apostolic Church, the teachers in the catechetical schools were known as *doctores audientium* (doctors of the hearers), and the title Doctor was soon applied to the most eminent teachers and preachers of the early Church community. And yet, it is because of the Pauline use of *doctores* (in Vulgate translation) that the Church in the West could find biblical precedent for the title *doctor ecclesiae*.[16]

By the eighth century, four names emerge as pre-eminent in the Western tradition: Gregory the Great, Ambrose, Augustine, and Jerome. Iconographically, these doctors would be represented holding a book (perhaps the Gospels) and are frequently portrayed surrounding the seated Mother of God, who is holding the Christ Child – the image of St Mary as the Seat of Wisdom.[17] The symbolism of four doctors should not be quickly overlooked. It corresponds to the four Gospel writers. This comparison is all the more surprising when one recognizes that Pope Boniface VII in 1298 designated that the Doctors should have their feasts celebrated with the same dignity as that of the Apostles and Evangelists. The Proper for the Doctors' Masses was borrowed from the *Theologus* par excellence, St John the Evangelist. Equally, the Magnificat antiphon for their double vespers

---

[13] Payne, 7. According to Payne, the words "teacher" and "teaching" appear over 150 times in the Gospels and 41 of these times are predicated of Jesus. Aquinas refers to Jesus as the primary Doctor of the Church. See McGinn, 9. St Thérèse refers to Jesus as "Doctor of Doctors." See Payne, 9.

[14] 1 Timothy 2:7.

[15] 1 Corinthians 12:28 and Ephesians 4:11-12.

[16] Payne, 8-9. The terms "Doctor" and "Doctor of the Church" began to appear with increasing frequency alongside the title "Father of the Church" to designate the great teachers, preachers, bishops of the early Church. John Fink, *The Doctors of the Church, volume I* (New York: St. Paul/ Alba House, 2000), *xi-xii* identifies the three categories as Apostolic Fathers, the Fathers of the Church and the Doctors of the Church.

[17] Thérèse is more often holding the "text" of the crucifix and the roses – the sign of her intercession from heaven. St Anthony of Padua is also more often represented with the "text" of the Christ Child. In a reported vision, a passer-by saw Anthony "reading from the Gospels," but when the person looked again, he was holding the Child Jesus.

was *O Doctor Optime*.[18] Their hymns, prayers and writings have been included in the various liturgies of the Church, not only on their own feast days, but throughout the liturgical calendar, specifically in the Eucharistic collect and in the liturgy of the hours.

In the East, the Trinitarian number was consigned to the three Holy Hierarchs, Basil, Gregory Nazianzen, and John Chrysostom.[19] Under the pontificate of Pius V (1566-1572), Athanasius was added to their number to form symmetry between East and West. In 1569, Pius V declared his fellow Dominican, Thomas Aquinas, a Doctor of the Church. Twenty years later, Sixtus V added his Franciscan confrère, Bonaventure, to the college of Doctors.[20] This expansion began to underscore the importance of the later great theologians and teachers, but also the value of the great religious families or "spiritual schools" that emerge in the development of the Church's liturgical and theological life. Sixtus V is also remembered for entrusting the examination of candidates for the doctorate to the Congregation of Rites.[21] This congregation would provide a pivotal leader who would refine the discernment process for selecting a Doctor of the Church. He would be the head of the Congregation of Rites and the Promoter of the Faith for thirty-two years: Cardinal Prospero Lorenzo Lambertini, the future Pope Benedict XIV.

Benedict XIV defined the classical statement on pre-requisites for recognition as a Doctor of the Church. He established three criteria.

> In order to constitute one a Doctor of the Church ... three things are necessary: namely, eminent doctrine (outstanding learning), marked sanctity of life (outstanding holiness), and the declaration of the Church, for example by her visible Head (the Pope), or by a legitimately assembled General Council.[22]

---

[18] McGinn, 10-11. Christopher Rengers gives us the full text of the Magnificat antiphon for the doctors' vespers: "O Blessed Doctor, light of holy Church and lover of God's law, pray to the Son of God for us." Christopher Rengers, *The 33 Doctors of the Church*. (Rockford, IL: Tan, 2000), *xi*.

[19] The three Holy Hierarchs appear together as frequently in Eastern iconography as do the four in Western art.

[20] For a very satisfying review of St Thomas' and the medieval scholastics' teaching on the authority of Doctors, see McGinn, 13.

[21] Payne, 14. The Congregation of Rites held this responsibility for 400 years until the Congregation was divided after the Second Vatican Council.

[22] Lambertini, 511. Translated by Br Joshua Kibler, CO. Regarding the actual manner by which one is declared a doctor, Payne tells us that any number of means has been used. "The process by which these candidates were identified and officially recognized was not uniform. Some (e.g., Thomas Aquinas, Robert Bellarmine) were declared "Doctors" by Solemn Apostolic Constitutions, while others (e.g., the two Cyprians and John Damascene) were included by

Of these three, only eminent doctrine has proven to be difficult to define. Over the centuries, the vocabulary, mentioned above, has been used to describe the eminent teaching of each new doctor. Descriptive titles emerged for each of the doctors. For instance, Aquinas is the Angelic Doctor and the Common Doctor; Anselm is the Marian Doctor; Thérèse is the Doctor of Evangelization.[23] These titles indicate the reason for the conferral of the doctorate at that time in the history of the Church and seem, at first, to indicate the presence of a hidden fourth criterion. However, they are, in actuality, prophetic utterances of the teaching office of the Pope during the proclamation and conferral of the degree. The prophecy is, in fact, twofold: in the Doctor's own age, using the charisms entrusted to him or her for the defense or renewal of the Church, and in the age of the doctorate, the prophetic teaching being charismatically drawn forward again by Pope or Council to address the present day needs of the Church for that charism. However true this may be, it does not constitute a fourth criterion, but a dimension of the descriptive nature of the first criterion – eminent learning. The discernment process of the candidate, and the conferral of the descriptive title, both help to clarify what exactly is meant by and constitutes each Doctor's particular eminence. Newman, as mentioned above, is already prophetically recognized *in his own* and *in our age* with the title, Doctor of Conscience. It seems inconceivable that one would attempt to teach within a Catholic context on the topic of conscience without recognizing the contribution made by Newman on this core theological concept. In this regard, Newman is already recognized as an indispensable Doctor and therefore his teaching is now essential for the Church today.

With each new candidate, greater clarity and more descriptive vocabulary emerged. Even with the earliest papal use of the title, Doctor of the Church, description of the teaching seems to be the manner of identifying a Doctor. This indicates a more or less functional definition. Doctors "revealed the mysteries of the Scripture, untied knots [i.e., dissolved perplexities], clarified difficulties, and explained

---

a single decree of the Congregation of Rites assigning them the liturgical office of "Doctors." Peter Canisius was declared a "Doctor of the Church" in the very decree of his canonization." Payne, 15.

[23] Fink, *xiv.* These titles (see Appendix I) were customary in the medieval universities to designate the more celebrated doctors with a surname to express their characteristic excellence and dignity. Francis Mayron, OFM (1325) was known as *Doctor Abstractionum* and *Doctor Illuminatus*, Dun Scotus, OFM (1308) as *Doctor Subtilis* and William Durandus (1296) as *Doctor Speculator*.

what was uncertain."[24] With each new candidate new examples emerged. During the examination of Alphonsus Liguori's candidacy, several points of clarification on eminent doctrine were set down. They include phrases such as illustrious service, explaining the deposit of revelation, and offering moral directives. The doctors provided "some great effect ... throughout the Church by their ingenuity, holiness and doctrine." An interesting metaphor was applied; the doctors may be compared one to another and "measured just as major and minor stars are judged in the sky." And yet, all of them "shed light on the universal Church in their own way."[25] During the process for Francis de Sales, eminence was associated with the doctrine being something truly original and it was stated, "A central prerogative of doctors is that they be considered columns and foundations ... that they serve as a new source of doctrine."[26] These various descriptive statements could easily be applied to the life, work, and influence of John Henry Newman.

In the modern period, the inclusion of Teresa of Avila and Catharine of Siena by Paul VI in 1970 renewed the sense that Doctors were the spiritual and mystical masters of the Church, and not an exclusive clique for academically trained male saints.[27] However, it was also Paul VI, who in 1972 suspended further declarations until there could be more thorough study of the requirement of eminent doctrine.[28] This would affect the subsequent appeal to have Newman declared a Doctor of the Church, which was set forth by the English Bishops in 1974 at their annual meeting.[29] Soon after Vatican II and, then, during the Pontificate of John Paul II, two more significant developments occurred: first, the Congregation of Rites was divided in 1969 into the Congregation for Divine Worship and the Congregation for the Cause of Saints. The latter would now oversee the causes of proposed Doctors. In 1988, John Paul II further refined the process,

---

[24] Payne, 11-12.

[25] Ibid. These comments are included in a March 11, 1871 document from the Congregation of Rites in its discussion on the doctorate of Alphonsus Liguori.

[26] Ibid., 21.

[27] Ibid., 17 and 221. Payne notes that this great step by Paul VI opened the door for a new range of potential women Doctors, e.g., Hildegard of Bingen and Veronica Giuliani. Others today may include St Teresa Benedicta of the Cross (Edith Stein), Blessed Elizabeth of the Trinity, St Faustina Kowalski, and even men, e.g., St Louis de Montfort, St Ignatius Loyola, St Francis of Assisi, and the *great* John Paul II. See also McGinn, 179-182.

[28] Ibid., 17.

[29] Blehl, *Positio, xviii.* "At the annual meeting of the English bishops, 20-25 April 1974, it was decided to petition Rome that Newman be made Doctor of the Church."

requiring the Congregation for the Causes of Saints to obtain a vote on the eminent doctrine of potential candidates from the CDF – the Congregation for the Doctrine of the Faith.[30]

Many new dimensions of the doctoral vocabulary for eminence have come to light in modern times,[31] but none are as concrete and specific as the six propositions contained in the CDF document entitled, *Procedural Norms and Doctrinal Criteria for the Judgment Concerning the Eminence of Doctrine of Saints Proposed as Doctors of the Church.*[32] By examining these six *Norms and Criteria* in the light of recent statements by Church leaders, we can consider the appropriateness and opportunity for the conferral of the doctorate on Newman as a charismatic sign for our times.[33]

Does Newman Fulfill the Descriptive Norms and Criteria?

The six *Norms and Criteria* for discerning the eminent doctrine of a candidate for *Doctor Ecclesiae* are: Does the candidate in his or her teaching (1) manifest a particular charism of wisdom, (2) excel in quality of writings, with height and profundity, mature sapiential synthesis, and a positive influence, (3) reveal him or her as an authentic master and witness of Catholic doctrine *and* Christian life, (4) draw from "the pure source of the Word of God, Tradition, and the Magisterium of the Church," (5) enjoy a large and "wide diffusion, positive reception and beneficial influence on the people of God – confirmed by magisterial usage," and (6) exhibit qualities that are durable and relevant and, thereby, are a secure message of lasting value? These six *Norms and Criteria* repeat the descriptive vocabulary mentioned above. And yet, there is an over-lapping element to them; they are for discernment purposes, rather than for a simple numerical calculation or analysis. The occasion for their formulation by the CDF was the candidacy of St Thérèse of Lisieux; however, they are to be applied beyond her particular case.[34]

How then does Newman stand in relationship to these six descriptive *Norms and Criteria*? Perhaps the most reliable approach

---

[30] Payne, 16. See in particular Payne's footnote 41 on his page 16 for John Paul II's directives.

[31] Ibid., 21–25. Here Payne reviews the leading ideas presented at a very important and fruitful plenary session of the Congregation for the Causes of Saints in regard to the requirement of "eminent doctrine."

[32] As mentioned above, an unofficial translation of this unpublished Italian document is available in Appendix II.

[33] Payne, 23.

[34] Ibid., 80.

in answering this question is to follow the direction given by those whose words weigh most decisively in the final decision – Pope Benedict XVI and his predecessor, Pope John Paul II. Of course, the *Positio* that must accompany the petition to name Newman a doctor will be extensive – Thérèse's numbered nearly 1,000 pages.[35] Even so, by recognizing the necessary doctoral vocabulary in the statements of Benedict XVI and John Paul II, one may find evidence that Newman, in his life and writings, has fulfilled the descriptive *Norms and Criteria* of the CDF for eminent doctrine.

1. *Charism of Wisdom.*

Does there exist in Newman, manifested in his teaching, a particular charism of wisdom, conferred by the Holy Spirit, that has edified the people of God? Benedict XVI, as then Cardinal Joseph Ratzinger, recognized the presence and importance of this charism in Newman. At the opening of the 1990 Academic Newman Symposium in Rome, Ratzinger addressed Pope John Paul II with words of greeting. The Cardinal reminded the Holy Father of his own words spoken during the Papal visit to England in 1982. There, John Paul II said:

> I cannot come to the Midlands without remembering that *great* man of God, that pilgrim for truth Cardinal John Henry Newman. His quest for God and for the fullness of truth – a sign of the Holy Spirit at work within him – brought him to a prayerfulness and a wisdom which still inspires us today…[36]

In his response, John Paul II reiterated his conviction of Newman's charism found in the title pilgrim of truth. He recognized that his gifts continue to be a source of inspiration for scholars and thoughtful readers of Newman. "Your symposium and other such celebrations during the centenary year offer the occasion for a deeper appreciation of Newman's *charism*."[37]

While the pontiffs are correct, the range of Newman's charism of wisdom is recorded more extensively in the *Positio* for his canonization. The charismatic qualities of Newman's life in the Spirit are described in this manner:

> What attracted people and continues to attract them to Newman is not simply his intellectual brilliance, his insights, his attractive

---

[35] Payne, 87.

[36] Joseph Ratzinger, *Cardinal Joseph Ratzinger's Words of Greeting to Pope John Paul II at Academic Newman Symposium*, Rome, 27 April 1990, quoting John Paul II, 'Homily at Coventry', *L'Osservatore Romano*, 31 May 1982. See Jennings, 27.

[37] John Paul II, *Address to Academic Newman Symposium*. Rome, 27 April 1990. See Jennings, 29.

personality, his goodness, his kindness and sympathy toward others, his humble estimation of his own gifts and his perception of his own limitations, or his complete dedication either as an Anglican or a Catholic, to the Church.... Ultimately, it is the mystery of Newman that keeps people coming back again and again to him, seeing him in new lights and shades. There can be no doubt that he is one of the great figures in the history of the Church, and many believe, one of its greatest saints.[38]

2. Mature Sapiential Synthesis.

Does Newman provide in his writing a teaching that "excels by its quality, with a height and profundity of doctrine, with a mature sapiential synthesis achieved, and an effective positive influence exercised?" John Paul II identifies this second of the Norms and Criteria again at the Roman symposium, "Newman's writings project an eminently clear picture of his unwavering love of the Church as the continuing outpouring of God's love for man in every phase of history."[39] He concluded his remarks with a prayer that the hearts of all participants be filled with the sentiments he noted in Newman's writings:

> [As] we commemorate this eminent churchman ... I invoke the light of the Holy Spirit so that through your efforts the teaching of this great English Cardinal may be better known and appreciated.[40]

In Ratzinger's address to the Newman Symposium, he recalls autobiographically the influence of Newman's profound and mature synthesis upon his own theological formation:

> [If I may speak] a little about my own way to Newman, in which indeed something is reflected of the presence of this great English theologian in the intellectual and spiritual struggle of our time.[41]

---

[38] Blehl, 411.

[39] John Paul II, Address to Newman Symposium. See Jennings, 30-31. Fr Paul Chavasse also uses this doctoral vocabulary of "eminence" in his Cause for the Canonization of John Henry Cardinal Newman, in Jennings, 85 and in NSJ 1:1 (2004) 37. The first written record of Newman's "eminence" is surprisingly early. In the Apostolic Brief establishing the Congregation of the Oratory in England (November 1847), Pius IX presents his intention to establish in England a society of members who are "outstanding in learning and holiness ... Among those now authorized to constitute that society is John Henry Newman, who in the estimation of all, is pre-eminent on account of his learning and virtue in the University of Oxford ..." Placid Murray, ed., Newman the Oratorian. (Herefordshire, England: Fowler Wright Books, 1980) 422-423.

[40] Jennings, 31. I point out here that both John Paul II and Cardinal Ratzinger referred to Newman as "great" at the beginning and end of their remarks. Only a few of the saints, and fewer still of the Doctors, have received this additional marker of excellence. Beyond a mere adjective, it indicates their essential influence on the life of the Church.

[41] Joseph Ratzinger, Newman belongs to the Great Teachers of the Church: Introductory Words for the Third Day of the Newman Symposium in Rome. See Jennings, 33.

Ratzinger continues his remarks by making special reference to the influence of *The Grammar of Assent* upon his theological and philosophical formation, as well as "Newman's teaching on the development of doctrine, which I regard, along with his doctrine of conscience as his decisive contribution to the renewal of theology."[42] Here Ratzinger clearly identifies the particularly eminent insight that Newman brought, not only to Ratzinger, but also to the formation of contemporary theology. Referring to the principle of development, Ratzinger notes,

> With this he had placed the key in our hand to build historical thought into theology, or, much more, he taught us to think historically in theology and so to recognize the identity of faith in all developments.[43]

This statement again underscores the essential and indispensable contribution that Newman has made to the theological method of the Church today. Unlocking the future developments of the Church's movement toward historicity in theological investigation was a major contribution that changed the way the Church would engage theological development from Newman's time into the future. This contribution certainly seems to provide evidence for the second of the *Norms and Criteria*. It is evidence of Newman's quality and excellence in writing, his height and profundity of teaching, which provided an impact of positive influence upon Ratzinger and the whole Church.

Beyond the development of doctrine, Newman's other areas of profound influence are found throughout his works. The virtual baptism of British philosophical empiricism by Newman's minister, "conscience," brought to new birth a Catholic religious epistemology in *The Grammar of Assent*. The deep psychological and spiritual analysis of the conversion process is explored in the *Apologia* and the fictional novels. The mystical revelation of Newman's *Dream of Gerontius* renews a sense of the immortality of the soul and the Church's doctrine of Purgatory in particular, and eschatology in general. The spiritual and pastoral influence of the *Parochial and Plain Sermons* was famous in his day and is celebrated in our own. The clarity and breadth of insight into the difficulties between faith and reason is worked out in the *University Sermons*. The Christological ecclesiology of the *Preface to the 3rd Edition* of *Via Media*, the renewal of interest in the laity and its

---

[42] Ibid., 34–35.
[43] Ibid.,

ecclesial authority in *On Consulting the Faithful*, and the revivification of patristic studies that informed the *Arians* and so many of his works have all had a beneficial influence on the Church since their first publications. The latter allowed Newman to be acknowledged as the leading 19th century authority on Athanasius, as well as recognized for his insights on the Alexandrian school. These are many, but still only a few, of the elements of the Newman corpus that confirm that his writings and teachings demonstrate a mature sapiential synthesis.

3. *Authentic Spiritual Master and Christian Witness.*

In a clear example of Newman's fulfillment of the third of the Norms and Criteria, Ratzinger compares Newman to Augustine. In his closing remarks at the Newman Symposium, he characterizes Newman as an authentic master and witness of Catholic doctrine and the Christian life with his statement:

> And faith is always 'development,' and precisely in this manner it is the maturation of the soul to truth, to God, who is more intimate to us than we are to ourselves. In the idea of 'development' Newman had written his own experience of a never finished conversion and interpreted for us, not only the way of Christian doctrine, but that of the Christian life. The characteristic of the great doctor of the Church [Augustine], it seems to me, is that he teaches not only through his thought and speech, but rather by his life, because within him thought and life are interpenetrated and defined. If this is so, then Newman belongs to the great teachers of the Church, because at the same time he touches our hearts and enlightens our thinking.[44]

This third norm and criterion looks beyond the writings and into the lived theology of the candidate. We are fortunate that Newman, like Thérèse, wrote an autobiography. However, it is the *Letters and Diaries*[45] that inform us of the true man. It is there that we really find him in the long suffering, the confusion, the frustration and the abandonment to Divine Providence, the trust in prayer, the perseverance in charity, the dedication to his mission in God. If this, his life poured out in love of God and neighbor, is not enough to convince us that he was an authentic master of Christian faith and life, then perhaps we should recall again the opening remarks of Cardinal Ratzinger to Pope John Paul II:

> Holy Father, over the years of your pontificate you have repeatedly

---

[44] Ratzinger, *Newman Symposium*. See Jennings, 35.
[45] John Henry Newman, *The Letters and Diaries of John Henry Newman;* hereafter cited as LD.

evoked the name of John Henry Newman as a spiritual father and inspiring master on the way to holiness and as a secure guide in the search for eternal truth.[46]

4. *Ecclesial Sources.*

The fourth of the *Norms and Criteria* states that the candidate's doctrine must flow from the "pure source of the Word of God, Tradition, and the Magisterium of the Church." That Newman's writings are brim-filled with references to Scripture, the Fathers, and the Councils cannot be contested. Even so, it has been noted that the Scriptures are beyond a doubt the single most significant source for Newman's insights and the very font of the themes he presents in his eight volume series, *The Parochial and Plain Sermons.* As Eric Griffiths remarks, "Newman himself is 'impregnated' with the scriptures."[47] Louis Bouyer confirms this insight: "Newman's knowledge of the Bible is equaled only by his knowledge of the human heart."[48] Again, Griffiths observes that, "Newman almost never quotes anything but the Bible in his Anglican sermons ... in this he is distinct from Keble, and especially from Pusey, whose sermons are tissues of Patristic references."[49] John Paul II recalled during the centenary celebration of Newman's cardinalate that drawing from these sources was the very reason why he was a spiritual teacher and guide in the way to holiness[50] for so many inside and outside the Catholic Church.

> The philosophical and theological thought and spirituality of Cardinal Newman, so deeply rooted in and enriched by sacred Scripture and the teaching of the Fathers still retain their particular originality and value. As a leading figure of the Oxford Movement, and later as a promoter of authentic renewal in the Catholic Church, Newman is seen to have a special ecumenical vocation not only for his own country, but also for the whole Church.[51]

---

[46] Ratzinger, *Newman Symposium, Words of Greeting.* See Jennings, 8 and 27.

[47] Eric Griffiths, 'Newman: The Foolishness of Preaching', in *Newman: After A Hundred Years*, Ian Ker and Alan Hill, eds. (Oxford: Clarendon Press, 1990), 74.

[48] Louis Bouyer, 'Great Preachers – XII. John Henry Newman', *Theology V* (March 1952), 89.

[49] Griffiths, 74. It is interesting to note that Newman's teaching on the indwelling of the Holy Spirit seems to come more naturally from his Pauline and Johanine reference than from the patristic emphasis on this teaching. The words, "*theosis*" and "divinization" do not appear anywhere in the eight volumes. His teaching on indwelling is therefore primarily Scriptural, not patristic.

[50] John Paul II, 'Letter to George Patrick Dwyer, Archbishop of Birmingham', *Centenary of Newman's Cardinalate, 1979.* See Jennings, 95.

[51] Ibid., 95.

5. *Wide Diffusion and Beneficial Influence.*

Here John Paul II directs us to the fifth of the *Norms and Criteria*, that the writings of the candidate enjoy a large or wide diffusion, positive reception and particular beneficial influence on the whole people of God and that this is confirmed by magisterial use of the writings. John Paul continued his remarks by stating that Newman's broad theological vision anticipated the renewal-minded orientation of the Second Vatican Council and the post-Conciliar Church.[52] Hence, we are reminded of the often-heard idea that Newman was an invisible or absent Father of the Second Vatican Council, it even being described as "Newman's Council."[53] No less than twenty times Newman is referenced in the *schema* and interventions at the Council.[54] There was even an attempt to have Paul VI beatify Newman at the Council for his influence on that magisterial event.[55] Another magisterial use of Newman's work is found in the inclusion of his poetry and hymns in the liturgy of the Church. The Divine Office suggests the use of Newman's works for prayerful reflection, including *Lead Kindly Light* and *Praise to the Holiest*. On the Solemnity of the Holy Trinity the selected hymn is Newman's *Firmly I Believe*. Furthermore, the appearance of Newman's name and teaching in the new *Catechism of the Catholic Church*,[56] as well as in many papal encyclicals and addresses, clearly points to Newman's fulfillment of the fifth norm and criterion.

Not to be forgotten here is the influence of Newman on the extensive system of secular college campuses throughout the United States. As St Thérèse has pilgrims in her cathedrals and basilicas, Newman has hosted a multitude in the Newman clubs and Newman centers. His foundation of the English Oratories is certainly a major lasting beneficial influence. Today, many Oratories look to them as guardians of Newman's legacy. Similarly, the members of The Spiritual Family The Work consider Newman their spiritual inspiration and through their mission, a wide diffusion of his influence is increasing.

---

[52] Ibid., 96.

[53] Paul Chavasse, 'John Henry Newman: A Saint for Our Times', (*NSJ* 1:1, 2004) 35.

[54] Chavasse, 35. Blehl's *Positio* for Newman's canonization contains a record of the interventions and statements on pages 438-448.

[55] Ibid., 35.

[56] Bernard McGinn compares both the number of references to Newman and other doctors and scholars in the Council documents (20), and the number of such references in the new *Catechism of the Catholic Church* (4). He notes that in such documents "no modern author has been quoted more than John Henry Cardinal Newman." McGinn, 182 and 189.

There is only growing interest in the national and international conferences, symposia, societies, associations, institutes, journals, books, articles and web sites dedicated to John Henry Newman. The *Newman Studies Journal* is distributed to countries throughout the world. The newmanreader.org website receives on average 1,300 'hits' per day – over a half million per year from users all over the world. This, we hope, will increase with the development of the *Newman Knowledge Kiosk* and its digital library containing the entire Newman corpus. Furthermore, Fr Vincent Blehl recalls that the positive reception of Newman's spiritual influence was widely acknowledged during his lifetime, at the time of his death, and even more so today.

> One Protestant writer called him a 'Roman Cardinal in title, but the light and guide of multitudes of grateful hearts outside his own communion and beyond the limit of these small islands.' That influence has never ceased and is so widespread that to us who pray and hope for his canonization ... it constitutes a special sign of divine approbation.[57]

John Paul II turns again to affirm the presence of a wide diffusion and beneficial influence of Newman's teaching. In his opening remarks to the Newman Symposium, he states, "I welcome all of you and thank you for drawing attention through your celebration to the great English Cardinal's special place in the history of the Church ..." He laments that he can mention in his brief remarks "only a few of the many lessons which Newman holds out for the Church and the world of culture. ..."[58] This again indicates the fulfillment of diffusion, reception and influence, but perhaps we could finally recall again the *Positio* for Newman's canonization.

> The editorial in the *London Times* at his death proclaimed, 'He will be canonized in the thoughts of pious people of many creeds in England.' This should be amended to read 'in the thoughts of thousands of people of many creeds all over the entire world.'[59]

6. *Durable and Relevant*.

Perhaps of all the *Norms and Criteria* of the CDF, Newman fulfills the sixth more than any other. The candidate's writings and teaching must demonstrate that they are durable and relevant, and thereby

---

[57] Vincent Blehl, *Newman and Birmingham: A Centenary Sermon Preached in the Church of the Birmingham Oratory, 21 February 1990*. See Jennings, 114-115. Blehl records many other such testimonies to Newman's "spiritual influence" in the *Positio*, pages 430-436.
[58] John Paul II, *Address to Newman Symposium*. See Jennings, 29.
[59] Blehl, *Positio*, 411.

be a secure message of lasting value.[60] Fr John Ford has anticipated the need to illustrate this norm and criterion in his emphasis on the continued popularity of Newman's writings. He notes, "One index of literary longevity is the continued availability of an author's writings."[61] Newman's works are widely available and continue to be published in special and critical editions.[62]

On two separate occasions, John Paul II has noted Newman's fulfillment of this norm and criterion.

> The great Cardinal's whole life and his copious writings seem to touch the minds and hearts of many people today with a freshness and relevance that has scarcely faded with the passing century.[63]

And again,

> The passage of a hundred years since his death has done nothing to diminish the importance of this extraordinary figure, many of whose ideas enjoy a particular relevance in our own day.[64]

Lawrence Cross affirms this analysis in his article, "John Henry Newman: Father of the Church?" Cross states, "Like many of his gifted contemporaries, Newman has been enormously influential, but his influence, while not yet exhausted, has even yet to reach its peak."[65]

Pope John Paul II notes several areas where this influence continues through what he calls Newman's timely message. These areas include the personal conquest of the truth, the importance of conscience for the acquisition of truth, the vital principle of Revealed Religion within the context of doctrine and morals, and conversion through the study of the Fathers, the common patrimony of all Christians.[66] John Paul II stresses that, "down to the present day, Newman remains for many a point of reference in a troubled world where he continues

---

[60] Payne notes that this is a modern requirement that some of the existing Doctors do not fulfill. He singles out that declaring Lawrence of Brindisi a Doctor in 1959 did not noticeably enhance interest in his doctrine either by professional theologians or by the faithful. Payne, 145.

[61] John Ford, 'John Henry Newman: A Spiritual Guide for the 21st Century,' (*NSJ* 1:1, 2004), 62-75, and 'John Henry Newman as Contextual Theologian', (*NSJ* 2:2, 2005), 60-76.

[62] Following Father Ford's approach, a visit to amazon.com on May 22, 2006 produced 944 new and used works by or about Newman. *Gracewing Publishing* currently has 12 volumes available for the *Birmingham Oratory Millennium Edition* of Newman's works and 10 volumes of Newman-related works.

[63] John Paul II, *Letter to Maurice Couve de Murville, Archbishop of Birmingham.* See Jennings, 107.

[64] John Paul II, *Address to Newman Academic Symposium, Rome, 27 April 1990.* See Jennings, 29.

[65] Lawrence Cross, 'John Henry Newman: A Father of the Church?' (*NSJ* 3:1, 2006), 11. Cross has a helpful section (pages 9-11) in this article that addresses Newman's preparatory or remote influence on Vatican II that indicates fulfillment of the fifth of the *Norms and Criteria.*

[66] John Paul II, *Letter to Murville.* See Jennings, 108.

to inspire, to uplift and to enlighten."[67]

While all this seems to leave little doubt that Newman and his message enjoy relevancy and durability, it is worth our attention to note that John Paul II confirms in the following final statement, not only the sixth, but most of the other five *Norms and Criteria* required of Newman by the CDF for his acceptance as an eminent doctor.

> With letters of spiritual direction and counsel he [Newman] helped countless others along the path of truth he himself had found and which filled him with so much joy. Newman's influence in this sense has increased over the past hundred years and is no longer limited to England. All over the world people claim that this master of the spirit by his works, by his example, by his intercession, has been an instrument of divine providence in their lives…. Still another area of Newman's spiritual itinerary stands out as particularly relevant in the wake of the Second Vatican Council. Because of it we feel Newman to be our true spiritual contemporary. This mystery of the Church always remained the great love of John Henry Newman's life. And in this there is a further profound lesson for the present.[68]

Taken collectively, these statements by John Paul II, Cardinal Ratzinger, Newman scholars and theological experts lead us to believe that, at least in their written statements, there is a consistent use of the vocabulary that is distinctive when referring to Doctors of the Church. One may ask about intentionality: Did the present and former pontiff really *intend* to use the descriptive language associated with the college of Doctors when referring to Newman? Were they simply "saying nice things" about our long-suffering and academically revered Cardinal? Even if they intended their words to be a eulogistic panegyric, were they aware that they were pronouncing the very vocabulary and speaking of Newman with the grammar descriptive of the Doctors of the Church? "Great"-ness, "charism of wisdom from the Spirit," "eminent," "spiritual father and inspiring master," "not only in the way of Christian doctrine, but that of Christian life," "secure guide," "deeply rooted in the Scriptures and the teaching of the Fathers," a mission "for the whole Church," "widespread influence that is increasing," "relevance in our own day," "all over the world." The use of this vocabulary predicated of Newman by John Paul II and Benedict XVI is either a most shocking coincidence, or, it teaches us that they believe that Newman fulfills the six *Norms and Criteria* established by the CDF and that they have described for us Newman's

---

[67] Ibid., 108.
[68] John Paul II, *Address to Newman Academic Symposium*. See Jennings, 30–31.

eminent doctrine. The use of this nomenclature has led Peter Jennings to ask the most pertinent question, "Will it be Benedict XVI, the first Pope of the twenty-first century, who will canonize John Henry Newman, and declare him a Doctor of the Church?"[69]

Conclusion and Reflections

As mentioned above, the *Positio* for Thérèse's candidacy numbered nearly a thousand pages. This chapter presenting Newman's doctoral cause, while not an official *Positio*, may seem to its reader as being nearly as lengthy! To summarize briefly, this presentation has provided two comparisons for consideration: first, a review of the history of the role of Doctor of the Church and how the discernment process contributed to the development of the Church's understanding of the title, using the recent evaluation of St Thérèse and the conferral of the doctorate upon her as our template; secondly, a careful and systematic evaluation of Newman's fulfillment of the Congregation for the Doctrine of the Faith's *Norms and Criteria* was offered based upon the commentaries of Pope John Paul II and his successor, Pope Benedict XVI regarding Newman's eminent doctrine. It now seems appropriate to offer a conclusion, with an attempt to open further reflection on the possibility of Newman's inclusion in the exclusive college of the *Doctores Ecclesiae*.

Advocating Newman's ecclesial doctorate will not be without its challenges. Though we have no evidence of obstacles regarding Newman's holiness or his eminent learning, the challenge lies not in Newman himself. Rather, we find the difficulty in an overly restrictive view of the role of this office, a role that could more fruitfully be expressed through a more expansive inclusion of many more Doctors of the Church. For example, concern was voiced during the deliberations for St Thérèse's candidacy that the addition of more doctors would diminish the exclusivity and prestige of the title. This perspective did not take into consideration Paul VI's desire to declare many women doctors.[70] If the issue is one of numbers, could one take a similar stance regarding the number of saints canonized by John Paul II? Did the increase of 482 additional saints during his

---

[69] Jennings, 10.

[70] Payne, 17. Some theologian opposed Thérèse's candidacy for fear that another exalted title for her would be "gilding the lily." This is ironic, given Thérèse's self-description as "the little flower." See Payne, 85.

pontificate diminish the desire to imitate those already canonized?[71] Did it lessen our attraction to the full Communion of Saints?

Perhaps the issue should not be addressed as a matter of numerical exclusivity, but as Newman would view it, as a matter of ecclesiology. The discussion concerns the manifestation of an ecclesial charism – a charism expressed within the Communion of Saints – a charism possessed and witnessed by Doctors of the *Church*. The number of Doctors should simply depend upon the manifestation of the Spirit through this charism and how it has been lived out in the Church. If a saint fulfills the descriptive criteria, why would the Church not want to celebrate that gift, let alone be formed and perfected by it? The manifestation of the charism by the cooperation of the saint with the Holy Spirit leads the Church to a new theological situation. This new ecclesial *Sitz in Leben* is finally and formally acknowledged when the essential and indispensable character of the Doctor is recognized by the Roman Pontiff or the legitimately convened Council and the doctorate is conferred. Newman's doctorate will be a sign that the Church has knowingly entered a new era of ecclesial existence – one that actively discerns legitimate developments and assents to the authority of well formed Catholic consciences.

The *Norms and Criteria* have allowed us to discern the extraordinary charismatic contributions of so many throughout the Christian centuries. Like our universe, the future of *Doctores Ecclesiae* seems set for expansion, rather than contraction. As referenced above, in the 19th century a similar metaphor was used to compare the various Doctors whose contributions may be viewed as "major and minor stars."[72] Building on this cosmic illustration, the Doctors and their represented schools form theological and spiritual constellations. The primacy of the original four and eight Doctors radiates the glory of the Church's eastern and western sky; the three women Doctors, rising later on the horizon, emit their own type of spiritual splendor; the great spiritual families form their own unique *scholae* or constellations and their founders, many not yet recognized as Doctors, have created entire galaxies as they have drawn souls to themselves with the gravity of their spiritual mass: Benedict and Scholastica, Francis and Clare, Dominic, Ignatius Loyola and many more.[73] The brilliance of these

---

[71] John Paul II celebrated 147 beatification ceremonies during which he proclaimed 1,338 Blesseds and 51 canonization celebrations for a total of 482 Saints. On January 22, 1991 John Paul declared John Henry Newman "Venerable".

[72] Payne, 20.

[73] McGinn, 175–182.

spiritual galaxies in no way diminishes the radiance of each individual star, whether it be the "little" twinkle of Thérèse, the supernova of Aquinas, or the birth of a new star – John Henry Newman.

Bernard McGinn goes on to show us how Newman's unique contribution corroborates our extended metaphor. Newman connects the great celestial points of light from the early Church to the Church of his and our own day.

> The diversity of Newman's contributions to Christian teaching is remarkable, reminding us of some of the great patristic doctors whom he studied and loved so well. ... In the way in which his life and thought link the first doctors of the Church with the issues of the modern age John Henry Newman witnesses to the doctoral charism as no other figure of recent history.[74]

The holy life and eminent teaching of John Henry Newman allow him to shine as brightly as his thirty-three peers, each illuminating the darkness, becoming our sure guides. As we chart our course on the journey through the night and its encircling gloom, let us pray with Newman to the Source of all Wisdom, "Lead, Kindly Light!" This is indeed a prayer befitting the spirit of every Doctor of the Church.

---

[74] Ibid., 182.

APPENDIX I

The Four Latin Doctors

1. St Ambrose, 340-397 (Pastoral Doctor)
2. St Jerome, 345-420 (Doctor of Biblical Science)
3. St Augustine, 354-430 (Doctor of Grace)
4. St Gregory the Great, 540-604 (Doctor of Hymnology)

The Four Eastern Doctors

5. St Athanasius, 295-373 (Doctor of Orthodoxy)
6. St Basil the Great, 330-379 (Doctor of Monasticism)
7. St Gregory Nazianzus, 330-390 (Doctor of Theologians)
8. St John Chrysostom, 345-407 (Doctor of Preachers)

Doctors of the Patristic Church

9. St Ephraem, 306-373 (Doctor of Deacons and Poets)
10. St Hilary, 315-368 (Doctor of Christ's Divinity)
11. St Cyril of Jerusalem, 315-387 (Doctor of Faith and against Heresy)
12. St Cyril of Alexandria, 376-444 (Doctor of the Incarnation)
13. St Leo the Great, 390-461 (Doctor of Doctrine)
14. St Peter Chrysologus, 400-450 (Doctor of Homilies)
15. St Isidore, 560-636 (Doctor of Education)
16. St Bede, the Venerable, 673-735 (Doctor of English History)
17. St John Damascene, 676-749 (The Icon or Image Doctor)

Medieval Church Doctors

18. St Peter Damian, 1007-1072 (Doctor of Reform and Renewal)
19. St Anselm, 1033-1109 (Doctor of Scholasticism)
20. St Bernard of Clairvaux, 1090-1153 (Devotional and Eloquent Doctor)
21. St Anthony of Padua, 1195-1231 (Evangelical Doctor)
22. St Albert the Great, 1200-1280 (Doctor of Science)
23. St Bonaventure, 1217-1274 (Seraphic Doctor)
24. St Thomas Aquinas, 1225-1274 (Angelic Doctor)
25. St Catharine of Siena, 1347-1379 (Doctor of Unity)

Counter-Reformation Church Doctors

26. St Teresa of Avila 1515-1582 (Doctor of Prayer)
27. St Peter Canisius, 1521-1597 (Doctor of Catechetical Studies)

28. St John of the Cross, 1542-1591 (Mystical Doctor)
29. St Robert Bellarmine, 1542-1621 (Doctor of Church-State Relations)
30. St Lawrence of Brindisi, 1559-1622 (Doctor of Conversions and Missions)
31. St Francis de Sales, 1567-1622 (Doctor of Authors and the Press)

Modern Era Church Doctors

32. St Alphonsus Liguori, 1696-1787 (Morality and Marian Doctor)
33. St Thérèse of Lisieux, 1873-1897 (Doctor of Confidence and Missionaries)

Unofficial English Translation of the CDF's *Norms and Criteria*
Dr Clare Godt, Professor Emerita, Italian Department, University
of Pittsburgh

Procedural Norms and Doctrinal Criteria for the Judgment Concerning the 'Eminence of Doctrine' of Saints Proposed as 'Doctors of the Church'

First Criterion: "The judgment regarding the eminence of doctrine takes the form of an *ecclesial discernment regarding the existence of a particular charism of wisdom* for the good of the Church, conferred by the Holy Spirit upon the Saints proposed as candidates for the title of Doctor, confirmed and borne out by the salutary influence which their writings and their doctrine have exercised in the People of God (cf. *Lumen Gentium* n. 12)."

Second Criterion: "To this end, one must demonstrate that the teaching of the Saints who are candidates for the title of Doctor not only conforms fully with Christian faith and life, *but excels ('eminet') in the quality of the writings, for the height and depth of the doctrine, for the nature and learned synthesis attained, for the positive and effective influence exercised*, such that they may be recognized as qualified witnesses of the living tradition of the Church (cf. *Dei Verbum*, n. 8)."

Third Criterion: "It is necessary therefore that future Doctors of the Church are authentic *teachers and witnesses of Catholic doctrine and of the Christian life*, and that their writings bring a particular light to bear upon the confession and the defense of the Catholic faith, in the preaching of the Gospel, in the understanding of the cult[1] and of the spiritual life, or in a specific field of Catholic doctrine."

Fourth Criterion: "This will be the more evident if one can demonstrate that their doctrine is drawn *from the pure fountains of the Word of God, of Tradition, and of the Magisterium of the Church, and constitutes an*

---

[1] The proper meaning of *culto* in Italian is "worship."

incisive and learned deepening of these. This deepening[2] is the fruit of the Holy Spirit. Such fruit advances the understanding of the realities and of the words transmitted to us, whether through the preaching of revealed truth, through theological reflection, through study and contemplation, or through the agency of a profound experience of these same supernatural realities (cf. *Dei Verbum* n. 8)."

Fifth Criterion: "Furthermore it should be demonstrated that the writings of the candidates for the title of Doctor of the Church have had *wide diffusion, positive reception, and particular beneficial influence among the People of God.* This should be confirmed if possible by the use that the Magisterium of the Church has made of their doctrine, and also by the particular attention given to their writings by Catholic theologians[3] in the study and the exposition[4] of the mysteries of the faith and of the Christian life. This influence must have the *quality of universality*[5] in such a way that it is of interest to the whole Church."

Sixth Criterion: "The examination of the doctrine of the candidate must lead to the conclusion that the doctrine is 'eminent' in as much as it possesses *a sure and durable message,* is capable of contributing to the confirmation and deepening of the deposit of the faith, and brings to light even new perspectives on doctrine and life. In this way *the special effect and relevance of the eminent doctrine* of the candidate for Doctor will be made clearer, and the candidate will be seen as a person in who is recognized a particular doctrinal charism, gift of the Holy Spirit. The Spirit guides the Church toward the entirety of truth, and to this end provides her in every age with hierarchical and charismatic gifts (*Lumen Gentium* n. 4)."

Note: all italics are in the original text.

---

[2] The new sentence and repetition are my addition, to make a manageable English sentence.

[3] The original says "Catholic theology."

[4] The original word is *illustrazione,* which can be translated as "exposition" as well as "illustration."

[5] The word is *carattere,* "character" or "characteristic," but "quality" seems to convey the sense better or perhaps just sounds better.

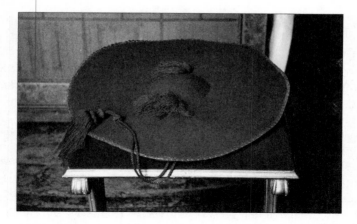

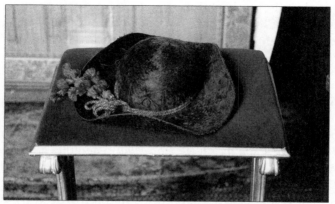

From top to bottom, Newman's galero, saturno and biretta
kept in his room at the Birmingham Oratory.

FR KEITH BEAUMONT CO was born in 1944 in Melbourne, Australia. He has a PhD in French literature and a Master's degree in theology. He was received into the Catholic Church in 1986 and ordained priest of the French Oratory in 1996. He is currently a student chaplain and engaged in teaching and writing on Newman and the history of spirituality. He is also the president of the *Association Française des Amis de Newman*.

DR ANGELO BOTTONE is an associate lecturer at the School of Arts of the Dublin Business School. He holds a PhD in philosophy from University College Dublin. He has published a book on Newman and Wittgenstein (CUEN, Naples, 1998) and several articles on John Henry Newman, Paul Ricoeur, Ludwig Wittgenstein, Multiculturalism, and the Philosophy of Religion. He also translated Newman's *The Idea of a University* into Italian (Studium, Rome, 2005).

FR PAUL CHAVASSE CO was born in 1954. He studied for the priesthood in Rome and was ordained in 1978. In 1980 he entered the Congregation of the Oratory in Birmingham, and has been its Superior since 1992. In 2000 he was elected Postulator-General of the Oratorian Confederation. A member of the College of Postulators attached to the Congregation for the Causes of Saints in Rome, he is actively involved in promoting the Cause for the Canonisation of Cardinal Newman.

DR ROBERT C CHRISTIE holds a doctorate in systematic theology from Fordham University, writing his thesis on the conversion experiences of John Henry Newman. He is a member of the Board of Directors of the Venerable John Henry Newman Association (USA) and editor of the Association's quarterly newsletter. He also serves on the Board of Trustees of the National Institute for Newman Studies, located in Pittsburgh, Pennsylvania.

SR MARY-BIRGIT DECHANT FSO belongs to the Spiritual Family The Work. She has an MA in Theology from the University of Vienna (Austria). She has been involved in the Newman mission of The Work both in Rome and at Littlemore, Oxford for many years.

DR MICHEL DURAND is the vice-president of the *Association Française des Amis de Newman*. and Professor Emeritus of Victorian Civilisation and Literature at Lumière University, Lyon. He wrote his thesis on *Les romans victoriens des premiers siècles chrétiens : Kingsley, Wiseman et Newman* and has written numerous articles about Newman. He has also translated *The Arians* (with Paul Veyriras) and *Callista* into French.

SR BRIGITTE MARIA HOEGEMANN FSO is a member of the Spiritual Family The Work. She spent 18 years at the College, Littlemore. She holds a PhD in Philosophy and has taught and lectured at Braunschweig University and at the Pontifical University Urbaniana in Rome.

CARDINAL JEAN HONORÉ is Archbishop Emeritus of Tours in France. He was made a cardinal by Pope John Paul II in recognition of his work on the Catechism of the Catholic Church. He completed his PhD on Newman and has written several books since about Newman.

DR JOHN KIRWAN teaches composition and literature at MiraCosta College in Oceanside, California. Born in San Francisco, he received degrees in English Literature from Washington University in St Louis and the University of California, Riverside where he wrote his dissertation on Newman under Professor Ruth apRoberts.

FR DREW MORGAN CO is the Provost of the Pittsburgh Oratory and Director of the National Institute for Newman Studies. Father Morgan received a PhD in Roman Catholic Systematic Theology from Duquesne University and has taught courses on the Doctors of the Church and on Newman at St Vincent's Seminary, Latrobe, Pennsylvania.

DR PETER NOCKLES is curator of the Methodist Church Archives and Research Centre, in the Department of Special Collections, John Rylands University Library, University of Manchester, and a Research Fellow in Religions & Theology, at the University. He is also a Visiting Fellow at Oriel College, Oxford, and a contributor to a planned new history of Oriel College to be published in 2010. He is the author of *The Oxford Movement in Context* (1994, paperback 1997) and has contributed to the nineteenth-century volume (6) of the *History of the University of Oxford* (1997). He is the author of numerous articles and research papers, and has given lectures and seminars widely in Britain, Europe, and the United States. He is currently the co-editor of a new OUP *Handbook of the Oxford Movement*.

JOSEPH SALVATORE PIZZA is a doctoral student in English Literature at University College, Oxford. His research interests include both Victorian and Modernist Literatures, with a particular focus on authors of the English Catholic Literary Revival. Having been a resident scholar at the National Institute for Newman Studies in the United States in 2005, his most recent work has explored the poetry of Gerard Manley Hopkins and David Jones.

FR DANIEL SEWARD CO is a priest of the Oxford Oratory. He studied philosophy and theology at Trinity College Oxford, Newman's old college, and gained an MA in spirituality from the Angelicum in Rome. He was ordained in 2001, and in addition to parish work he is a school chaplain.

DR PAUL SHRIMPTON is a graduate of Balliol College, Oxford and has taught for over twenty years at Magdalen College School, Oxford. He is the author of *A Catholic Eton? Newman and the Oratory School* (Gracewing, 2005) and a number of papers on Newman as an educator.

DR JOYCE SUGG is a convert from Anglicanism. She read English at Oxford, taught in schools and then trained teachers at Newman College, Birmingham, working also in catechetics. She has published four books and has given talks in schools, parishes and at Newman conferences in the UK and overseas. Now she has retired to Salisbury, Wiltshire and writes poetry.

COR AD COR LOQUITUR